What Others Say about this Book

«*In Search of Truth and Freedom* is the highly personal account of a bold and courageous quest for answers to life's ultimate questions. Dietmar Rothe concludes that we find ourselves in an "omniverse," sharing our lives with higher beings, all of us emanating from a Spirit of Creation. Rothe's omniverse, which draws much from the great wisdom traditions of the world, can accommodate many phenomena that have no place in the sterile material universe of modern science — such as telekinesis, telepathy, spiritual healing, reincarnation, astral travel, extraterrestrial intelligences, and UFOs. After all is said and done, however, we have to live our lives, and Rothe provides valuable tools for recognizing in ourselves what things are helping us in our spiritual progress and what things are holding us back. I can't agree with all that Rothe says. For example, he holds that the Spirit of Creation cannot be a person,[*] whereas I don't find that an impossibility. But on the whole, much in his book resonates well with me. As the old scientific certainties begin to dissolve, many thoughtful persons are looking for a new set of cosmological and philosophical concepts to guide our lives as we enter a new millennium. Dietmar Rothe is one of them, and he deserves an attentive hearing.»
Michael A. Cremo
Coauthor, Forbidden Archeology: The Hidden History of the Human Race

«It's an amazing work. I wept and laughed. This is a comprehensive writing about existence in the larger sense and the equally important issue of humanity's purpose within it; no small undertaking, indeed. So much is clearly presented in such a relatively short book. I received much value from Dietmar's book, and in so many ways, too.»
Robert Maynard Lantis, Laser Engineer

------

[*] The omnipotent Spirit of Creation can and does manifest itself in any and all material forms, including as a human person. When Creation brought forth the omniverse [including space and time] out of itself, however, its essence was pure spirit without form. *The Author*

IN SEARCH OF TRUTH AND FREEDOM
A Path from Ignorance to Awareness

DIETMAR ROTHE

First Edition

A V I L A

B O O K S

In Search of Truth and Freedom
A Path from Ignorance to Awareness

by DIETMAR ROTHE

Published by:

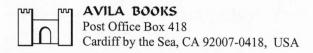

AVILA BOOKS
Post Office Box 418
Cardiff by the Sea, CA 92007-0418, USA

First Printing in 2000
Printed in USA by Bang Printing, P.O.Box 587, Brainerd, Minnesota

Library of Congress Catalog Card Number: 99-76710

Publisher's Cataloging-in-Publication
(Provided by Quality Books, Inc.)

Rothe, Dietmar.
    In search of truth and freedom : a path from
ignorance to awareness / Dietmar Rothe. — 1st ed.
    p. cm.
    Includes bibliographical references and index.
    LCCN: 99-76710
    ISBN: 0-9677453-2-2

    1. Philosophy and science. 2. Metaphysics.
3. Psychology and religion. 4. Conduct of life.
I. Title.

B67.R68 2000   110
                    QBI99-1907

LIST OF CONTENTS

About the Author

Throughout his life, Dietmar Rothe has enjoyed nature and has been fascinated by the mysteries of the physical world and by the secrets of life and the spiritual realm. Besides being well read in the subjects of philosophy, metaphysics, psychology and religion, he is also a respected professional in the physical sciences and is well qualified to critique established scientific theories. His views about physical reality often diverge greatly from accepted theories.

He was born in a remote corner of Germany in 1934. After surviving World War II, he attended the Hölty Schule in Wunstorf, West Germany, and then completed his formal scientific education in Canada, graduating with honors and a B.Eng. in Engineering Physics from McMaster University in 1961. He then pursued postgraduate research at the Institute for Aerospace Studies in Toronto and obtained an M.A.Sc. degree in Applied Science and a Ph.D. degree in Aerospace Engineering Science from the University of Toronto in 1962 and 1966, respectively.

For the next three decades, Dr. Rothe gained scientific knowledge and hands-on experience in the high-technology research field, while contributing to many branches of the physical sciences; ranging from laser physics, optics and spectroscopy, plasma physics and gasdynamics, to pulsed power technology, electrical engineering, mechanical engineering and product design. As program manager and division manager he has directed more than a dozen R&D programs, both for industry and for defense.

Dr. Rothe holds several patents in laser technology and is author of over 35 papers published in peer-reviewed scientific journals, such as Physics of Fluids, Journal of Quantitative Spectroscopy and Radiative Transfer, Physical Review, Applied Physics Letters and others. He has presented his research results at various scientific conferences.

He is a Member of Sigma Xi, Optical Society of America, The Planetary Society, Astronomical Society of the Pacific, Sierra Club, Association of Professional Engineers of Ontario.

On his softer side, Dietmar Rothe enjoys painting and creating poetry. Some of his poems have appeared in anthologies of the National Library of Poetry.

CHAPTER SUMMARIES

Mission Objectives
   Short poem asserting the author's commitment to life.

Chapter 1   Introduction
   Author's views of truth and freedom in relation to the US
   Constitution. Outline of the author's personal quest for truth and
   of the historical movements which influenced his philosophy.

Chapter 2   A Personal Quest
   Short autobiography, emphasizing events which shaped author's
   scientific, philosophic and religious understanding.

Chapter 3   The Quest for Truth
   Distinction between personal and absolute truth. Importance of
   truth for healing personal ignorance and societal ills. Relation
   between truth and freedom and their roles in spiritual evolution.

Chapter 4   Life is Communication
   The essence of life and the interconnectedness of all life in the
   universe. Relationship of body, mind and spirit. The stream of
   experience passing through our consciousness and how it relates
   to our enjoyment of life and spiritual growth.

Chapter 5   Physics and Reality
   Historical views of reality.   Idealism versus materialism.
   Limitations of our senses. A universe based on logic. Unsolved
   mysteries of the physical universe. The spiritual substructure of
   the universe. New theories of relativity and space. The wave-
   particle enigma solved. The cosmology of Creation and the Big
   Bang myth.

Chapter 6   Gods and Creation
   Gods as highly evolved life forms in a naturally evolving
   universe. Distinction between gods and the infinite power of
   Creation, which guides the evolution of the omniverse.
   Inconsistencies in the biblical concept of God.

Chapter 7   Spiritual Evolution and Reincarnation
The case for reincarnation as opposed to resurrection. Philosophical deliberations regarding the nature of a person's spirit. Purpose of life as an opportunity for spiritual evolution. Unanswered enigmas connected with reincarnation.

Chapter 8   The Story of Jmmanuel
Discovery of an ancient scroll, purported to be an unedited proto-Matthew. A different story of Jesus' life and spiritual teachings. Revival from near-death. Jesus' connection with extraterrestrial intelligences.

Chapter 9   A Self-Consistent World View
A living omniverse, which evolves spiritually, materially and culturally. A universe inhabited by spirit forms at all levels of evolution.   Gods aiding the spiritual development of life throughout the universe.

Chapter 10   The Road to Freedom
Discourse on freedom.   Freedom must be won through personal effort by overcoming needs and attachments, by transforming evil passions and by conquest of fear.   The causes of needs, negative emotions and passions are ignorance and lack of consciousness. Detailed plan for progressing on the road to freedom.   The liberating power of letting go and forgiving.

Chapter 11   Personal Power
Relationships between fear and power, spiritual consciousness and power, freedom and power, choice and power, knowledge and power, faith and power, money and power.   The power of alignment.

Chapter 12   Creativity, Beauty and Happiness
Personal freedom allows creating a happier existence.   Joy through creativity and self-expression. Appreciation of beauty as a bridge to happiness. Material and spiritual happiness.   Seven layers of happiness.

Per ardua ad astra

This book is dedicated to all those who aspire toward perfection, harmony, wisdom, truth, beauty, love and pure being; to those who consciously choose to unfold spiritually by seeking the path from darkness to light, from ignorance to awareness, from fear to love and from bondage to freedom.

Acknowledgments

The author gratefully acknowledges all the encouragements received from friends and relatives, who supported the efforts to bring this work to print. Special thanks are due to my wife Rose for many good suggestions and for suffering through extended periods when the author was too busy writing and editing and not giving her the attention she deserves.

Picture Credits

COVER: Art work by the author. Background picture of Andromeda Galaxy courtesy of 'The Hale Observatories' (Mt. Palomar). Used with permission from Caltech.

PLATE 1:   NOAA-9 satellite image of Arctic hurricane of February 27, 1987. A color image of this cyclone has previously been published on the cover of American Scientist, Vol. 79, No. 1 (Jan/Feb 1991). Image processing and enhancement of the color original by L. S. Fedor, NOAA/ERL/Wave Propagation Laboratory.

PLATE 2:   M51 (NGC-5194) 'Whirlpool Galaxy' with satellite galaxy NGC-5195, taken by 200-inch Hale Telescope. Reproduced with permission from Palomar/Caltech.

WARNING !

The ideas and concepts expressed in this book may be hazardous to your carefully nurtured religious, social and moral beliefs. Do not read this if you are a happy follower of traditional religious rites, or if you adhere to traditional nationalistic and social values. The material in this book stresses the joy of knowledge over the innocence and happiness of ignorance. It values freedom of independent thought over knowledge from authoritarian sources; and it endorses taking responsibility for your life over living a complacent life within the herd of the majority.

FOREWORD

This book presents the heretical views of a research physicist, who critically examines our cosmic connections and the personal meaning of life. It was written for earnest seekers of truth and freedom, who are trying to make sense of this world. Reality is explored from the perspective of a scientist, who refuses to ignore phenomena that do not fit the accepted doctrine of the establishment. His synergetic world view forges a bridge between science and religion, between logic thought and spiritual values to illuminate the path from ignorance to awareness. Reason and introspection are applied for making a case for a fundamentally spiritual existence and for a living universe, while accounting for all observational evidence. A short autobiography is also included, but the work is obviously much more than that.

Truth and freedom are ideologic concepts, which are of profound importance in philosophy, science, religion, sociology and in the everyday life of each individual. Thus, the topics discussed here cover a wide range of subjects from the physical structure of the universe to psychology and metaphysics. The subject matter is timely in view of the widespread disenchantment with the narrow, diverging views of reality painted by established science and religion. Men and women in modern-day society are searching for value and meaning in their lives, looking for answers they cannot get from Western science, nor from organized religious doctrine. The author's serious, new way of contemplating reality should be of interest to readers from a wide spectrum of society.

The writer believes in the existence of an absolute truth and reality, which may differ greatly from perceived personal truth and reality. On the other hand, he considers freedom to be a strictly personal issue. Freedom must be won by each person through conquest of fear and through letting go and forgiving. The quest for truth and freedom is a personal religious inquiry, the reward of which is a more joyous existence.

Mission Objectives

Somehow I know't was my decision
To sign up for this special mission.
Some time before my day of birth
I chose to spend this time on Earth.

My job, as far as I can trace,
Was not to save the human race.
Free will rules this tract of Creation.
Each soul must find its own salvation.

Then what, pray tell's my mission goal?
To grow in spirit, purge my soul?
This is what every human asks.
But I have more specific tasks:

To fully be, make life an art,
To express love with all my heart,
To conquer fear, let freedom flare,
To create beauty everywhere;

To help my fellow creature's quest
For joy, bring out its best;
To honor Earth in thought and deed,
To curb all envy, thwart all greed.

And if some day you'll ask how well
I've met my goals, let nature tell.
Is there one flower, one more tree?
Another bird because of me?

More clarity in someone's mind?
Some beauty that I left behind?
My life's not been in vain, I pray,
If Consciousness was raised some way.

INTRODUCTION

«We hold these truths to be self-evident,
that all men are created equal,
that they are endowed by their Creator
with certain unalienable rights,
that among these are Life, Liberty
and the pursuit of Happiness.[1]»

This sentence in the American Declaration of Independence precipitated the American Revolution and launched the most powerful nation in the recorded history of Earth's civilization. Noble words, that were meant to unite all humans on this continent and perhaps all men and women on Earth. More than two centuries have passed since these words were penned by Thomas Jefferson, Benjamin Franklin and John Adams. But after a bloody Civil War and more than seven foreign wars, the American people are still divided by socio-economic conditions and by racial bias. Civil unrest and street crime threaten our lives, and our *liberties* are eroded by a self-serving, runaway bureaucracy. Misrepresentation and misinterpretation of the above *self-evident truths* are at least partly to blame for the failure of the American people to achieve *domestic tranquillity* and a *more perfect union.*[2]

All men are not created equal. The truth is that all men and women are endowed with the all-powerful spirit of Creation, and that they are all lovable and capable. But their spiritual development varies over a wide range; and they each have a different set of abilities and talents. Certain talents are stronger in some races than in others. It may be the same deck of cards, but we are each dealt a different and unique hand. Failure to recognize the differences has divided our society more than any other circumstance. The ill-fated and controversial *Affirmative*

Action program is just one example. To demand that the same racial mixture should be represented in each profession and rank is a recipe for mediocrity and social malcontent.

Great damage to our society has also been caused by the phrase: *the Pursuit of Happiness.* There are several problems with this concept. One predicament is the general confusion of happiness with pleasure in our materialistic society. The pursuit of physical pleasure and instant gratification is one of the leading causes of moral decay. Happiness, on the other hand, cannot be pursued. It is a joyful spiritual state of mind that must be created internally.

«**For a happy life is joy in the truth.**»
[Augustine of Hippo, 354-430]

Happiness is a state of inner freedom, for we must be free to choose a state of inner joy and happiness. To be free, we must recognize the true nature of self and the universe, so that we can gain victory over the forces of fear and other negative emotions and habits. Thus, truth and freedom are seen to be intimately connected.

«**The truth shall make you free.**»
[John 8:32]

We must understand that true freedom is an inner strength to be achieved through our own effort. It cannot be bestowed by our government. Once we recognize the truth and achieve inner freedom, we can willfully choose the joyful life. The purpose of this book is to help the reader in his or her quest for truth and freedom.

The views expressed herein have been formulated and illuminated by my personal life-long search for truth and meaning. By education and training, I have acquired a solid background in mathematical logic and in the physical sciences. But most of my growth and understanding have come from personal experience and from the study of a diversity of disciplines, theories, philosophies and religions. I believe that anybody's individual truth is by necessity only a distorted reflection of the absolute truth. So, the more points of view a person can contemplate, the more reflections are available to construct a better an idea of the truth.

I have taken my experiences and viewpoints from many sources of knowledge and have integrated these into a self-consistent belief system. To the purists, who are used to traditional polarized perspectives, this may appear to be a mishmash of old and new ideas, more likely resulting in confusion than in enlightenment. I also went through various stages of such confusion. We must recognize, however, that being confused is a necessary step on the road to clarity. It has been said that the only way out is the way through. Working myself through the fog of contradictions and inconsistencies, I have made steady progress towards formulating a belief system by rational synthesis of ideas, observations and experiences. I consider this system of beliefs to have a high probability of relevance on account of its self-consistency and its correspondence with observation and intuition.

Ideas that have influenced my thinking the most have come from the following schools of thought, listed hereunder chronologically, and not according to their importance:

Taoism [Lao-Tzu[3], 604-531 BC]
Hindu Philosophy [Upanishads, ca. 600 BC]
Buddhism [Siddharta Gautama, 563-483 BC]
Classical Greek Philosophy [Plato, 428-348 BC]
Metaphysics [Aristotle, 384-322 BC]
Teachings of Jesus [Jmmanuel[4], 4 BC-ca.100]
Theosophy [Plotinus, 205-270; Helena Blavatsky[5], 1831-1891]
Zen Buddhism [Hui-neng, 638-713]
Unitarianism [Faustus Socinus, 1539-1604]
Transcendental Idealism [Immanuel Kant[6], 1724-1804;
                    Friedrich Schelling[7], 1775-1854]
Romanticism [Johann Wolfgang von Goethe, 1749-1832]
Transcendentalism [Ralph Waldo Emerson, 1803-1882;
                    Henry David Thoreau[8], 1817-1862]
Analytical Psychology [Carl Jung[9], 1875-1961]
Romantic Poetry [e.g. Khalil Gibran[10], 1883-1931]
Science of Mind [Ernest Holmes[11], ca. 1940]
Human Potential Movement [Bhagwan Shree Rajneesh[12], 1931-1990]

Erhard Seminars Training - EST [Werner Erhard[13], 1935-]
Actualizations [Stewart Emery[14], 1941-]
Religious Science [Terry Cole-Whittaker Ministries[15], ca. 1980]
New Age Thought [16] [ca. 1980].

The above list makes it evident that my personal philosophy has been strongly influenced by early Eastern Philosophy, by the Idealism and Romanticism of the eighteenth century and by New Age thought. I do not like the latter designation, because the New Age beliefs are not new. Enlightened people have made use of these principles throughout the ages. My views do not fall into the realm of religion in the traditional sense, and even though they are largely supported by modern science, certain insights go beyond rational science. Scientific reasoning can only take us so far. The path to greater wisdom and spiritual growth is mostly experiential. Words and thoughts, as in this book, can only act as a guide. The experience and growth must be your own.

Last, but not least, I have relied a lot on my intuitions. Whereas I believe that all information and knowledge has been filtered through my rational mind, this may in fact not be so. I have to acknowledge that certain spontaneous and intuitive thoughts account for the more creative and novel ideas. It is entirely possible, and indeed highly probable, that some or all of these intuitive thoughts have been transmitted to my subconscious by higher forms of intelligence, be they of extraterrestrial origin or from the spirit world or both. Should this indeed be so, then I want to show my appreciation to these higher intelligences by acknowledging their profound influence on the ideas expressed in this work.

In the next chapter I have added a short narration of my personal history to provide a backdrop to my path of discovery, showing how I have embarked on many erroneous pursuits and how I have learned my lessons of life. The life story is periodically annotated with the conclusions and insights drawn from various experiences. It may provide the reader with a better framework from which to ponder some of my more unusual views.

The chapter on physics and reality (Chapter 5) may seem out of place in a book dealing with personal discovery and growth. We need to keep in mind, however, that the material world is important. We can only learn and progress along our spiritual path while living a material life in a physical body. Life in the material world is governed by the physical laws of nature. Because our scientific knowledge is almost entirely confined to the material processes in the universe, we believe this physical knowledge to be grounded in well established facts. Hence it seems reasonable to use these physical laws as a basis from which to build a comprehensive world view, including the spiritual forces of life. Since our society does not agree on any set of proven spiritual truths as a basis for elucidating our existence, an understanding of physical reality will at least give a person a point of departure from which to pursue his or her personal quest for truth. If we believe, as the author has come to conclude, that the spiritual side of nature is more basic than its physical manifestation, then we may well put the cart before the horse by giving our body of physical knowledge too much credibility. Still, our experience of the material reality will not be denied.

Another reason for including Chapter 5 is to show that our scientific knowledge does not consist of immutable facts rooted in absolute truth, as is generally believed by the scientific lay person. It has been my intention here to point out several basic fallacies and misunderstandings of present-day science. The mathematical equations may scare off many readers, but they are necessary to prove my points, since many of my assertions attack the most cherished beliefs of modern physicists and cosmologists. The mathematical expressions do not go beyond high-school algebra and should not present a problem for scientifically inclined readers. Others may just want to skip over the formulae and accept or reject the assertions made in the text on face value.

A PERSONAL QUEST

She was back in the familiar surroundings of her parents' 19th century farmhouse, which was built into the swampy ground next to the Schulteich, a small lake in the village of Oppach, located in a remote corner of Germany. Across the road, on a small hill, half hidden by tall beech and oak trees, rose the slate-covered steeple of the old Lutheran church. Outside, the night was pitch black, and the rain pelted against the windows. It was at least an hour ago, when she had last felt the vibrations of a heavy truck rolling past the house down the country road, headed for Dresden, the capital of the former kingdom of Saxony and the closest major city located 60 km to the west.

Ella had been away for almost five years before returning home from Switzerland, where she with her husband and her three boys had lived near Schaffhausen. Her husband, an engineer, had supervised the construction of a brick and ceramic tile factory there. They had returned a little over a year ago. Owing to the worldwide economic depression, her spouse had lost his job in Switzerland and had taken his chance among the unemployed in his fatherland. Germany was recovering from its own severe economic slump and hyperinflation. A new optimism was taking hold throughout the nation, and a newly elected chancellor had pledged to provide the good life for every citizen willing to work. Ella's father, a hatter by trade, had died two years before, and she still felt sad that she did not have the opportunity to be with him during his last hours.

The contractions were getting stronger now and came more frequently. She knew from previous experience that she would give birth to a new life within the hour. The local midwife had died the month before, so they had to depend on help from another village. There were only a few telephones in town, and even those were out of commission, because earlier in the evening a series of heavy summer storms with strong gusts had blown through the area and had knocked down trees and telephone lines. So they had sent a neighbor on a bicycle to get the midwife from the next village. Unbeknownst to the people waiting for his return, however, he had gotten lost in the dark and heavy rain. It was now more than an hour after midnight, and no sign of help was forthcoming. A sensation of *deja vu* crept into her consciousness, as she remembered a dream she had nine months before. She had dreamed she would give birth to a boy in a barn. Although she was in the comfortable surroundings inside her childhood home, she was right next to the converted barn in the old farmhouse. Her mother and aunt had drawn fresh water from the well inside the house and were busy preparing to boil and sterilize it in preparation for child birth. Herbert was now at her side, and she knew that in essence her dream would come true. The stage was set for her child's arrival in twentieth century Europe.

It was a quarter past one in the early morning of Wednesday, August 22, 1934, when I emerged into this world, assisted by my father. By the time the midwife finally arrived, my father had already cut the umbilical cord. I was now on my own. I had been unceremoniously propelled into the Third Reich and had no idea of the turbulent, violent times lying ahead. I neither remembered having been forewarned before signing up for this lifetime.

During my early childhood I was left much to my own resources. My brothers, being six, ten and eleven years older, had their own playmates and friends, and only reluctantly watched out for little brother when necessary. The family had since moved to Halberstadt, a medieval city with a few modern industries, located in the heart of Germany. My father had found a position there as an aircraft design engineer in a newly established Junkers aircraft factory, which built wings and fuselage sections for the Luftwaffe's fighter bombers. Because of his demanding work, he too was not in a position to spend much time with me. Thus the task of teaching me the early lessons of life was left to my mother. Through this close association with the female energy, I began to develop my softer side, which later expressed itself in a talent for drawing, painting and for language skills. After learning the letters of the alphabet at age four, I taught myself to read phonetically by combining the sounds of the letters into words.

When I entered the German Volksschule at age six, I was well ahead of my classmates in reading skills, arithmetic and grammar. By that time World War II had broken out, and the Wehrmacht was *liberating* and annexing the neighboring nations, bringing them *home* into the Reich. I remember looking at a world map, which my brother had pinned on the wall, considering myself fortunate for growing up in such a powerful nation, one that was allied with the largest country in the world.

Living in the city proved unhealthy for me. I had battled and survived most of the common childhood diseases, including a serious bout with pneumonia, which had brought me close to death. The air in the city was heavily polluted from coal-burning domestic ovens and railroad locomotives operating at the nearby switching yard and railroad station. The latter was less than half a mile from the four-story apartment house, in which my parents had rented a small flat. During my most impressionable years, I would call this modest apartment with worn wooden floors home. The heavy sulfur-laden air on the outside was further degraded indoors by my father's chain smoking, a habit he had developed to calm his nerves, which were stressed from overwork and responsibilities. He was unaware that this cancer-forming activity would eventually kill him in his old age. The physically and emotionally unfavorable environment of the war years exacted a predictable toll on my health. I became a sickly and anaemic child and soon developed a case of chronic bronchitis. Hardly a week went by, when I did not spend at least one day home away from school. Being an avid reader, however, compensated for my frequent absence, and I finished reading through the text books within the first two weeks of each school term. As the fortunes of war turned, we were forced to spend increasingly more time in air raid shelters, and my absence from school became worse.

In the following years, living conditions deteriorated rapidly, and our family was drawn ever more into the insanity and morass of total warfare. By the late summer of 1943, my oldest brother had been drafted into the Wehrmacht and was driving trucks loaded with live ammunition through the endless Russian mud to the eastern front. My second oldest brother had voluntarily joined the *Panzer Division*. After only a few months of service he was reported missing in action. We did not learn he had been killed in battle at Catania in Sicily until eight years later. The youngest of my brothers, six years my senior, was barely fifteen years old when he was called to serve with the antiaircraft units protecting the giant ship hoists in Magdeburg. The hoists made it possible for *Mittelland Kanal* barges to cross over the Elbe river.

My childhood ended shortly thereafter, when the horrors of war reached the German heartland, as the Third Reich was collapsing. I was suddenly surrounded by madness, hate, terror and destruction; and I witnessed firsthand the cruelties that humans were capable of inflicting upon their neighbors in the name of God, country, blood, honor, freedom, democracy, and so on. It was of no comfort to know that those who unleashed these destructive forces were blindly following orders while serving the evil ambitions of their warlords. Whether these were dictators, prime ministers, or presidents who bowed to military power and industrial greed, made no difference to the people killed or maimed.

Recollecting my experiences and observations as a direct observer, even though from a child's perspective, I can contradict some widespread misconceptions about National Socialist control of civilian life, about German nationalism and wartime propaganda. Truly, the newspapers and radio programs were politically controlled and were largely used for propaganda. But the media coverage was positive: «Germany would win the war and would provide a better life for all people». Banners at the railroad station proclaimed: «*Räder müssen rollen für den Sieg*» (Wheels must keep turning for victory). I do not recall ever reading or hearing a derogatory statement proclaiming that the British, the Russians, or the American people were stupid or subhuman. On the contrary, the enemy was always depicted as a formidable, worthy opponent.

This stands in contrast with the anti-German propaganda seen here in the United States during World War II. Examples are the caricatures of German soldiers, depicted as goose-stepping robots, and the dehumanization of the German people being referred to as the ruthless descendants of Attila the Hun. Even now, after more than half a century has passed, this Nazi bashing and anti-German propaganda is kept going in Hollywood movies, in US television programs and weekly news articles of holocaust horrors. Although the German media were controlled by the National Socialist regime, they reported accurately the losses and defeats, as well as the battle victories. In that respect, German news reporting during WWII was less regulated than the US media coverage during the recent Persian Gulf War.

Similarly, I recall no attempted nationalistic brain washing in the schools I attended during this dark period of German history, with perhaps the sole exception of the ridiculous *Heil Hitler* salute recommended for the general public. There was strict discipline in the classroom, yet most of my teachers were kind, well educated human beings. Political propaganda was not part of the curriculum. I recall one teacher with a politically distorted, pro-nationalist attitude, but she was not liked by the students or her colleagues. There was no oath of allegiance to the national flag or to any other symbol of the Third Reich. The national anthem was sung only once during the entire school year, at the end of the spring term, when students were dismissed for the six-week summer vacation. And I have never seen a German national flag on display in a German church. The German people were, and still are, less nationalistic than their US counterparts. My observation, that the German churches and public schools were comparatively free from Nazi propaganda, dovetails well with the accepted notion that Hitler was unsuccessful in enlisting the intelligentsia or the clergy to join him in his deluded ambitions. He was also unsuccessful in introducing the Nazi salute into the *Wehrmacht, Luftwaffe* and *Marine*, the German armed forces, which continued using the military salute, thereby demonstrating their stiff opposition to Hitler's megalomania. To influence and indoctrinate the young generation with his politically skewed ideals, he had to found a separate Hitler Youth organization, patterned after Baden Powell's Boy Scouts to give it an air of respectability. Whereas I was eligible to join the Hitler Youth by the end of 1944, I never enrolled because all hell had broken loose by then.

My father was a Storm Trooper, a member of the *Sturm Abteilung* (SA) of the National Socialist Workers Party. The Storm Troopers are often erroneously maligned and blamed for the war crimes perpetrated by certain factions of the infamous *Schutz Staffel* (SS), Hitler's elite body guards and security forces. My father wore his light brown uniform only a few times during the year to party congresses and parades. He was not particularly proud of it, but he wore it as a token of his loyalty to the fatherland. He was a kind and humane person, who would not, and did not, harm or kill anyone. More than once he risked his life to pull injured people out of burning buildings after bombing raids, never asking whether they were Aryan or Jewish, or whether they were German or foreign nationals. He was one of millions of German citizens in uniform, who conducted themselves with dignity and compassion. It is absurd and disrespectful to the dead, when certain anti-German organizations publicly object to the laying of wreaths at the graves of German soldiers killed in action during WWII. Let me make it clear, however, that I am not defending militarism or armed conflict, especially when directed against civilian populations. War is morally wrong, barbaric and indefensible, no matter what noble cause is espoused to justify the violence.

For the German population, it was a day-by-day struggle for physical survival against all odds during these final months of the conflict. Every day and night, thousands of tons of high explosives and burning white phosphorus rained down on German cities to terrorize and *demoralize* the civilian population. To gain an idea of the scale of destruction, one would need to multiply the Oklahoma bombing several hundredfold to equal the death and destruction inflicted on German cities in a single day and night. As this terrorism continued for four hundred days in a row, millions of German civilians lost their lives or were seriously maimed. Many more lost their homes and livelihood. By the beginning of 1945, we shared our two-bedroom apartment with three other families. Two had been bombed out and had lost some of their kin. Another family of three had fled from the eastern provinces and was infected with lice and typhoid fever.

By the end of the war most of our city was reduced to rubble; but our building had miraculously survived, minus roof, windows and doors, between giant eighty-foot craters dug out by thousand-pound TNT bombs. I took it as a sign that my time to die had not yet come, and that I was yet to accomplish a worthwhile mission in my life. Memories of the physical and emotional trauma, associated with the experience of the full rage of human brutality, were however indelibly etched into my young and impressionable mind. Most of the time, these nightmarish visions remain carefully filed away in the far recesses of my memory. Only occasionally am I reminded of these events, when I read, hear or see reports of similar atrocities being perpetrated in today's world. Then these bad dreams will come to the foreground for my thinking mind to deal with. I have tried again and again to rationalize these experiences with my belief in the positive aspects of the human psyche, but to no avail. A few of these traumatic scenes, called up from the depth of my memory, are shared here to explain my strong opposition to war and violence.

One such event was the nighttime destruction of Magdeburg. This was supposed to have been a happy day, as we were visiting my teenage brother on his birthday in the military barracks where he was stationed. We had no premonition that this would be his hellfire initiation into service with the four-barrel antiaircraft crew, and that by the end of the day he would be burying some of his dead comrades. The attack came shortly after nightfall. My parents and I had taken shelter under the heavy steel and concrete structure of the multispan bridge across the Elbe river. As the night was torn apart by detonations and fire, I found myself holding my ears to block out the deafening roar of explosions all around me. Being past the stage of fright, I was in a dreamlike state, viewing scenes straight out of hell. No fireworks display could ever come close to this. The night sky was filled with clusters of red and orange flares and was cut by numerous beams of searchlights, fluttering across the sky as though having a hard time deciding which of the hundreds of bomber aircraft to lock onto. Luminous streaks of tracer bullets from rapid-fire antiaircraft guns were trying to keep up with low-flying fighters. Popcorn clouds peppered the sky, ignited by shell bursts from a battery of 88 mm cannons stationed on a hill above us. Burning bomber parts rained down along with thousands of bombs, bursting in a continuous, fiery staccato cacophony, as they blew apart residential city blocks across the river. The ensuing firestorm of the burning city painted the smoke and clouds a bright orange. I watched the burning sky as it was reflected in the river. Periodically, huge fireballs and flames shot up thousands of feet, fueled by exploding coal-gas storage tanks at the city gas works. The heavy, acrid air was filled with iron. I could hear the bomb and shell fragments showering down all around us, as they hit the ground and the top of the bridge. This was not the chivalrous combat of old, but hateful, brutal, warfare of desensitized human robots killing anonymously from a distance.

Several months later, violence came to the city where we lived. I remember being frightened out of my wits and screaming in panic, as I crouched under some chairs in our basement, which served as a make-shift bomb shelter. The ground was shaking in an earthquake-like motion, as part of the adjacent building collapsed, and the dust and smoke filtered through the shuttered basement window, threatening to suffocate us. As we found out later, a whole freight train, loaded with more than a thousand tons of sea mines, artillery shells and other ordnance, had been bombed and had blown up in a giant explosion in the nearby railroad yard. The shock wave had leveled nearby buildings, shattered every window in the city and had collapsed aircraft hangars five miles away. The explosion left a three quarter mile long and 25-foot deep ditch, where the train had been. Very few recognizable parts of the train were ever found. An exception was half a freight car embedded in the roof of a house half a mile away.

From then on, all efforts to escape the violence failed. The enemy was intent on killing us. A few days later, on a Sunday morning, we fled the city, because the radio had warned of approaching enemy bomber formations. We had run several kilometers past the edge of the city into the fields of a small farming community, which surely was not a target of any importance. When the bomber squadrons passed over the city without dropping their deadly load, we figured they were en route to another target further north, and we were getting ready to go home. But a minute later we found ourselves in the middle of detonating high-explosive bombs, which turned the tranquil pastoral scene into a densely cratered moonscape. The ground was shaking and rolling, accompanied by the dull roar of exploding bombs all around us. My baby sister and I were lying in a ditch between potato fields, shielded by the bodies of my mother and father, who huddled on top of us to protect us from the flying dirt and bomb fragments whistling through the air. Just why the farmers' fields were carpet bombed that morning has remained a mystery. The bombers had been flying at less than 10,000 feet and visibility had been excellent. Heavily shaken up, but with only minor injuries, we walked back to the city, past dead and injured farmers and other city people who, like us, had hoped to escape the raid. Here I first encountered the sight of dead mutilated bodies, which were carted away in wheelbarrows and dumped unceremoniously into mass graves, like so much manure. The vision of the lifeless bodies, shaking like jelly before rigor mortis set in, was an experience I would not forget for a long time.

While life was rough and unpredictable for the ordinary civilians, it was even tougher for the political prisoners who had incurred the wrath of the regime. I remember seeing a group of eight or ten prisoners being marched down our street, guarded by soldiers in uniforms and with rifles. Some of the men wore boots, others sandals, many were barefoot, but all of them were gaunt and emaciated and were wearing prison garb, easily identifiable by the blue and white stripes of their pants and shirt-jackets. As an inadvertent spectator, I could not tell whether these prisoners were convicted criminals, concentration camp inmates, or just plain slave labor imported from the occupied territories. They were not military prisoners of war, since these were treated quite humanely, owing to the efforts of the Red Cross and Germany's agreement to adhere to the rules of the 1929 Geneva Convention. For several weeks these prisoners were marched around town every day, apparently to get some exercise. As if they needed it. They were being worked to death already for the remainder of the day. They had been housed in a small foundry and warehouse belonging to the *Reichsbahn*, the nationalized German railroad system. Their work was desperately needed to keep the railroads operating despite the daily damage from bombing raids. The German railroad system was, and still is, the lifeblood of German industry and commerce. *Räder müssen rollen für den Sieg!* Able-bodied German menfolks were dying on the eastern and western fronts, which were rapidly closing in, leaving only women and slave labor to keep life going at the home front. What became of these prisoners is not known, except that they might have been killed in the terror bombing of the entire city a few weeks later.

Nobody can say we had not been warned. A few days earlier, people had found leaflets floating down from the sky, reading: *«Ihr Halberstädter, ihr Roten, ihr seid die letzten Toten»* (Citizens of Halberstadt, you red Communists, you will be the last of the dead). I remember watching the city burning from our living room. The last hour had been the most frightful of my life. For what seemed to be an eternity, wave after wave of bombers had plastered the city with high-explosive and incendiary bombs. By a miracle, I had again survived. The house across the street was now only a large pit filled with water. It was twelve o'clock noon on Sunday, but there was no sun; just black smoke, brightly illuminated by the flames of the burning city, reaching as high as the eye could see. The firestorm radiated heat so intense that the asphalt in the street was burning. Winds of hurricane force were tearing the curtains to shreds, as they were being sucked out of the window openings. Only the day before, the windows had been boarded up with plywood to replace the panes shattered in a previous raid. Now, splintered pieces of plywood, along with dirt and other debris, littered the room.

My father and my brother were out helping the injured and searching for trapped people. They had tried to penetrate to the inner part of the city, but were turned back by the extreme heat of the firestorm. Some burn victims, who had escaped the inferno had described to them the hellish scenes of screaming human figures set ablaze by burning phosphorus, hopelessly trying to extinguish the spontaneously reigniting flames, before collapsing on rubble of bricks and charcoal. German military had to rescue Allied bomber crews, who had been shot down and had parachuted into a group of dazed bomb victims. The latter were angrily trying to lynch the perpetrators, who just minutes before had murdered their babies and grandmothers.

Halberstadt was one of the last cities, which was utterly obliterated by the indiscriminate terror bombing of German population centers before the German surrender on May 8, 1945. The raid on Halberstadt was carried out by close to a thousand American B-17 and B-24 bombers and resulted in the total destruction of a city of sixty thousand civilians. More than half perished. Even today, after more than fifty years, the city has not been rebuilt. Several square miles of farm fields now cover the area where the center of the medieval city had been.

Thus, within the short period of a year, I had become educated in how inhumanely the human species can behave. By the end of WWII, forty million lives had been lost, twenty million alone in the Soviet Union. Millions of political prisoners, among them many Jews, were brutally murdered by the morally corrupt and vindictive regimes of Hitler and Stalin. Millions of civilians were killed by the systematic and indiscriminate Allied bombing of German and Japanese cities. Close to 200,000 casualties resulted from a single bombing raid on Dresden, a cultural center with no military or industrial significance. Near the end of the long and severe winter of 1944/45, approximately twelve million Germans were driven at gun point from their homes in the eastern provinces by the advancing Soviet troops and by vindictive Poles and Czechs. Many of the fleeing East Germans, mostly old people, women and children, never made it to the West. An estimated half million were lost. Thousands were raped or killed by pursuing troops and guerrillas, many more froze to death.

After the bloodiest conflict in recorded history, the souls of the dead cried out for justice. German war criminals were tried by an Allied court in Nürnberg and were executed. Many of them deserved nothing better than death. Several German officers, however, were executed or imprisoned for the reprisal killing of foreign civilian guerrillas and their conspirators. When a military force occupies a foreign country, the occupying troops are exposed to deadly terrorist ambushes by guerrillas and partisans. How to deal with this effectively has always been a moral challenge. The military solution has invariably been to keep order by executing any guerrilla and collaborator caught in the act, and by reprisals on civilians who aided in the insurrection. This is standard practice even today, when Israeli military jets regularly bomb civilian centers in southern Lebanon in reprisal for terrorist attacks by militant Islamic groups.

But were there no British, French, American or Russian war criminals in WWII? Was US President Truman ever taken to task for ordering the extermination of the people of Hiroshima and Nagasaki by nuclear bombs? Why is it, for example, that US Air Force General LeMay is heavily decorated and revered for perfecting the strategy of carpet bombing millions of civilians out of existence?   Human justice invariably leans heavily towards the side of the victor, who rewrites history in his favor.   This injustice turned me and other young Germans against politics and militarism as something dirty, immoral and corrupt.

A soldier's business is death. He is trained to kill and willingly be killed for the survival of the regime. He is the hired or conscripted assassin for the ruling elite, be they robber-baron aristocrats, capitalist democrats, military dictators, socialist communists or nationalist fascists. Rulers either enslave the able-bodied men under threat of imprisonment or death, or seduce them into willingly killing their fellow humans in the name of God, liberty, freedom, country, honor, glory, and so on. Since ancient times, the goals of power wielders have been to consolidate their power through control of their subjects by making and enforcing laws, by imposing heavy taxation, and by seducing the populace with idealistic rhetoric. Taxes are used to maintain armies to further the ambitions of the regime through *justifiable* wars, which in turn are fought to kill and enslave, to destroy and confiscate property, and to impoverish the populace, so they can be controlled more easily.

The glorious warrior is a myth propagated by the ruling class. In Christian ideology, the theory of a *just war* was expounded by St. Ambrose and St. Augustine to defend and glorify the crusades. This *justification* created an artificial distinction between valorous combat and murder. By no stretch of the imagination, however, can this devilish concept be extended to justify the killing of hundreds of thousands of women and children to save the lives of the glorious warriors, who had been trained to deal and accept death. The killing and maiming of over 200,000 civilians by dropping nuclear bombs on Hiroshima and Nagasaki was not the work of noble warriors, and it can never be justified by proclaiming that it saved the lives of many US soldiers. It was brutal barbarism, no matter how you look at it. This may sound like a diatribe against politicians and military leaders. But they themselves are willing pawns of the ruling oligarchy hidden behind the military-industrial power complex. Only when all citizens of Earth renounce their allegiances to potentates of any kind, and refuse to take up arms against their brothers and sisters, can the human race be saved. Humanity may have a chance, if they declared a war and nobody showed up to fight it.

In spite of the heavy odds against survival, most of our immediate family came through the inferno of WWII intact physically, but scarred psychologically; except for my second oldest brother, who was killed in battle, for my uncle, who was shot to death by SS troops in southern France for being too friendly to the villagers, and for several distant relatives who were killed by Allied bombs in Hannover and Dresden. My oldest brother survived the battles and winters on the eastern front and the Allied invasion of Normandy, where he was captured and forced to spend the next two years in a POW camp in England. My little sister, born in 1942, was too young to remember any of the hardships.

My only pleasant memories of the war years are of a six-week period in the summer of 1944. Because I had been suffering from bronchitis and whooping cough, I was sent to a summer camp in the *Vorarlberg* region. In the peaceful and tranquil setting of the rural Austrian Alps my body and spirit began to heal, even though the reprieve was only temporary. The experience endowed me with a lasting love for the majestic mountains and gave me the courage to give up my chronic bronchial cough.

In September 1945, my father was ordered by the Soviet occupation forces to supervise the dismantling of machinery at the aircraft factory, which had been located in giant tunnels blasted into the sandstone foothills of the Harz mountains. After all equipment and machines had been loaded onto trains, destined for reassembly in Siberia, my parents decided they had no desire of relocating to a slave labor camp in the Urals, and they promptly made plans to escape to the West. We secretly transported a few treasured belongings to a friend's house where these were loaded onto a handcart. Then we quietly stole out of the apartment in the middle of a moonless October night, went to our friend's house to pick up the loaded handcart and trekked to the next town. There, another acquaintance, who had an old truck, drove us to the newly established border between East and West. A small river divided the Soviet occupied territory from the American Zone. In the darkness of the following night and under the watchful eyes of armed Soviet guards, who had been bribed with a few bottles of homemade *Schnapps*, my father repeatedly waded through the chest-deep, ice-cold waters to carry each of us and our belongings across the river. We camped there until morning, because we dared not enter the nearby village, which was patrolled by American military who had imposed a strict curfew. At the first sign of dawn, we lumbered into town to catch a train to Hannover, a harrowing trip, since all the trains were overfilled with refugees and travelers. Even the rooftops of the wagons were crowded with people. We became separated several times, but finally made it to our destination, a town where the daughter of my father's aunt was a school teacher.

The small, Lower-Saxony town of Sachsenhagen then became our home for the next six years. Having escaped city life with all its unpleasant memories, I savored the semi-rural atmosphere in this farming community. Here it was a daily occurrence to see the cows come home from the pastures to be milked and to settle in their barns and stables for the night.

After catching up to complete my fourth year of elementary school, I pursued my basic education by attending a middle school and a progressive high school in the nearby city of Wunstorf. The latter was offering an accelerated program, established to let students make up time lost during the war years. Like other German schools, it was patterned after the philosophies of the brothers Alexander and Karl Wilhelm von Humboldt (1769-1859 and 1767-1835) and followed the ideas of Swiss educator Johann Heinrich Pestalozzi (1746-1827), who reiterated the ancient Greek Olympic view of *mens sana in corpore sano*, a sane mind lives in a healthy body.

The dedicated teachers of this school introduced me to the rigors of higher mathematics and logical deduction, as well as to the physical sciences of physics, chemistry and geology. We were fifteen students in our class, all young men who had chosen to pursue science and mathematics, rather than the arts and language option chosen by the girls. I have fond memories of the comradeship and personal interaction with my class mates and teachers. The curriculum was well rounded and included studies of the biological life sciences, music, fine art and religion, and it put a healthy emphasis on the physical disciplines of gymnastics, swimming and track-and-field sports. In our group, we studied two foreign languages, English and Latin, besides German grammar and composition.

In my mind I can still hear my teacher's statements, devised to give us a rational cognizance of the physical world around us. In our first physics class we defined physics as *a science concerned with the precise measurement and description of physical phenomena*. This immediately appealed to my sense of orderliness. Just as with mathematics, ambiguity had no place here. Then we examined the laws of motion derived by Galileo Galilei (1564-1642) and by Isaac Newton (1643-1727). Their investigations led to the discovery that *the acceleration of an object is equal to the applied force divided by the mass of the object*. This insight, together with the development of analytical geometry by René Descartes (1596-1650) and of differential calculus by Gottfried Wilhelm Leibniz (1646-1716), provided the foundations for a mechanical world view, in which everything was composed of atomic particles, whose motion and interaction could accurately be calculated and predicted. In this strictly mechanistic view of the 17th and 18th centuries, the universe ran like clock work, leaving no room for individual freedom and choice. I was not willing to accept this rigid, deterministic outlook on reality, however, and I had serious doubts whether such a belief system, built entirely on the physical sciences and on mathematics, could ever provide a complete description of reality. The physical sciences, moreover, could not provide insight into the essence of things, nor a reason for their existence. Questions about the nature of life and consciousness remained unanswered.

With that realization I turned my attention to the life sciences. But like physics and chemistry, the life sciences, such as biology, proved to be descriptive, with the emphasis on classification and structure, and providing little insight into the functioning of organisms. No satisfactory theory was offered for explaining the essence of living things. Even psychology and religion had no satisfactory answers about the deeper meaning of life in the universe.

Another statement, this time from biology class, also made a lasting impression on me. It was a significant insight at the time of its discovery: *The embryonic development of an individual life form is the short repetition of the evolution of the species.* This so-called Biogenetic Law was formulated by Ernst Heinrich Haeckel in 1867. For example, the human embryo develops fishlike gills before forming lungs. This important observation, expressed in Haeckel's Law, together with the fossil records, make a solid case for the theory of evolution over the more simplistic biblical creation myth. Modern genetic research also finds greater similarities in the DNA molecules of related species than in more removed species, showing a systematic progression of the DNA structure from lower to higher life forms; again lending strong support to the theory of evolution.

I had no problem accepting evolution as a scientifically observable and proven fact. In my earlier years, I had already turned away from the biblical scriptures, because I found them to be lacking in logic and nonconforming with readily observable evidence. My mind found it inconceivable that anyone could honestly believe the universe was only six thousand years old, or that every sentence in the bible was the literal, undeniable truth as dictated or inspired by God. I had chosen a path of scientific inquiry and logic, and the common beliefs and superstitions just could not stand up to this kind of scrutiny. Only in my later years did I redirect my attention to the biblical scriptures, and by separating the wheat from the chaff, I was able to extract many meaningful bits of wisdom contained therein.

Whereas evolution is undeniably one of the major processes responsible for shaping the biodiversity of life on Earth and elsewhere, I found the mechanisms of *competition for resources, adaptation to a changing environment and natural selection by survival of the fittest*, as expressed by Charles Darwin (1809-1882) in his work *On the Origin of Species*, too narrow to explain the multiplicity and beauty of life forms in nature. My artistic sense told me that nature has a creative side to her, forever experimenting with new forms. Many forms of beauty and symmetry are created or evolved just for the heck of it, even if the expression of a new pattern has no unique survival benefit attached to it. Thus my own understanding of the natural world gravitated towards a concept of continuous creation over billions of years, guided by an infinitely powerful and creative Force. Such a thought was, of course, in direct opposition to the dogmatic opinion of Western religions, which proclaimed a personal god had created the universe in a single spurt of activity six thousand years ago. It was also at odds with the scientifically accepted notion of a mechanically evolving universe, guided only by the laws of physics and by chance. Observation and logic led me to believe in a creative process taking place all the time and everywhere in the universe. In summary:

The universal Creative Force continually creates new life forms by transcending and perfecting existing ones in a process we call evolution.

This is a much grander concept than the biblical creation, in which God created the universe and all living things in six days and has been resting ever since, allowing the world to go to hell in a hand basket by letting the once created universe and its living occupants decay in a downhill slide of ever increasing entropy. Logic and observation of nature suggested to me that an all-powerful, ever-loving Universal Spirit actively and continually maintains and improves its creation as a material expression of itself. I have tried to argue this point to no avail with the right-wing Christians and the Jehovah Witnesses, who regularly come to my house; and I have learned that one cannot have an intelligent discussion with people whose minds have been formatted by dictatorial authority.

In the years of my early manhood, I developed my capacity for rational thought, but unknowingly neglected my emotional growth. Except for my interest in the arts and gymnastics, my consciousness started to revolve solely around intellectual activity and achievement, while being closed off emotionally for fear of being hurt. I had given up on politics and religion and on society as a whole, and I was not seeking any serious social contact with my fellow humans. I had two or three close friends, however, and by age seventeen I became hopelessly infatuated with a young woman nine years my senior. At the time she was the one person in the world I could emotionally connect with. I had never been close to my father, and I had bought the misguided notions of my male friends and peers that it was girlish and unmanly to run to my mother for help with my emotional confusion.

Though I had grown up physically and intellectually, I was not ready to commit to a long-lasting emotional and sexual bond with my newly-found soul mate. I was not in control of my emotions. When I was close to her, I often had an intense, overwhelming feeling of inner sadness mixed with joy, desire and emotional pain caused by my fear of losing her. Because I had never experienced these feelings before, I was certain that ours was the greatest love the world had ever seen. Looking back from a position of greater wisdom, I now realize that I had a strong emotional need to relate intimately with a person of similar needs, especially at a time of sexual awakening. Need and passion was easily confused then with divine love. Even though the woman eventually betrayed me, I am forever grateful to her for showing me a deeper experience of being.

I was spared the pain and disappointment of witnessing her betrayal of our love, because we were involuntarily separated by fate. In 1951, my father decided to take his family and emigrate to Canada in search of a better life. I was in no economic position to choose staying behind and supporting myself, let alone supporting a wife. I had learned no trade, and I was not ready to become the pillar of emotional strength required for a head of a family. The farewell was excruciatingly painful and sad, as I had the premonition that we would never meet again. For a while we wrote each other love letters twice a week, making plans for our future life together and confiding in how much we missed each other. Then suddenly after six months my letters remained unanswered for no apparent reason.

By then I was accommodating to a new life in a foreign land and society. I had taken a job rewinding electric motors in a repair shop in Guelph, a distinctly British community with Victorian attitudes and morals, located on the lower Canadian peninsula framed by lakes Erie, Ontario and Huron. The work was exceedingly dull and paid an amazing fifty-five cents per hour. I soon decided against performing repetitive labor for the rest of my life and began investigating alternative careers.

Within a year, my former boyfriends also stopped writing, thus terminating all connections with my homeland. Making new friends was hard in a society that labeled all immigrants as DPs, displaced persons from war-torn eastern European countries and considered undesirable by the Anglo-Saxon community. Speaking German in public would invariably draw indignant stares, so that I soon became reluctant to converse in my mother tongue. In addition, as a German I was expected to feel responsible for the Nazi atrocities perpetrated on the European Jews. The endless recounting of holocaust horrors was just beginning to infiltrate Hollywood, the media and the Western governments. Even though the hate campaign should have been righteously directed against the demonic factions of Hitler's *Schutz Staffel*, it was broadened to include all German military, all National Socialists and the German population at large. So I began to experience firsthand, how it feels to be discriminated against on the basis of national origin.

«How could you not have been aware of what was going on in Auschwitz?» was a common question. That we were too busy evading the daily threat of death to be worrying about the fate of prisoners in labor camps was not accepted as an excuse. People with no direct wartime experience tried to make us feel guilty about something we had no control over. The so-called German guilt became an issue that was supposed to make Germans suffer for all eternity. I remember being confronted about this for the first time in a Sunday sermon back home in Sachsenhagen. The pastor had preached to the congregation about the awful guilt we Germans had loaded upon us, and that we should suffer in hell for it. I did not understand. What guilt? Had we not suffered enough already?

Most associates and acquaintances politely avoided any discussion of my German past. Only occasionally a conversation would touch the subject with a typical dialogue like this: «But you Germans started the war.» «I recall that England and France declared war on Germany, not the other way around.» «But you Germans invaded Poland.» «We were told we had to save half of Poland from being taken over by the Soviet communists. German troops marched into Poland as protectors and liberators, a situation which has since been repeated more than twice by US troops. Korea and Vietnam were no different from Poland. Germany was just ahead of its time.» «But the US had no expansionist dreams like Hitler, when the US *invaded* Korea and Vietnam.» «Perhaps so, but was it my fault that Hitler came into power? After all, some of the wealthiest families in England, France and the United States supported Hitler financially and politically. Even Jewish capital supported the German re-armament. And was it not the unfair Treaty of Versailles of 1919, which precipitated the disastrous depression and hyperinflation in the thirties, making Germany ripe for being taken over by a dictatorship?» «But your father designed wings for Hitler's *Luftwaffe*.» «Yes, but it was the only job he could find in the mid-thirties after being told he could no longer stay in Switzerland as a German national. He would much rather have stayed in Schaffhausen, designing machinery for manufacturing ceramics and bricks. That was what he enjoyed doing.»

I was desperately trying to avoid accepting any guilt trips connected with my past, and I was suppressing any anger against particular groups that tried to make me feel otherwise. This struggle did not help my innate shyness, nor did it raise my moderately low self-esteem. In my desire to be accepted, I developed a need to excel, to be the good guy, even going as far as trying to rescue people from their own craziness. I eventually outgrew this anxiousness to please, but it took several decades of self-evaluation.

Meanwhile, I was determined to pursue an intellectual career in the physical sciences, putting my artistic inclinations aside for the moment. The left side of the brain had won out over the right side. It took a lot of persuasiveness to convince the principal of the local high school to let me enter the spring term of Grade 13, skipping Grade 12 the same way I had once skipped Grade 6 to make up time. I studied hard, and five months later graduated with honors at the top of my class. I was awarded a scholarship, but decided not to go to college. My father was struggling to make ends meet, working as a machinist in a local foundry. He had just bought his first house and had a mortgage to pay off, and I was not certain I could support myself through college. My sister, for whom I had a lot of affection, was still going through elementary school. The prudent course of action was to learn a marketable trade first.

Just then I was presented with an opportunity to use my analytical and artistic abilities for visualizing objects and for thinking in three dimensions. I had assumed everyone could do this, until I later met many people who had difficulty visualizing three-dimensional objects. A leading manufacturer of electrical equipment was building a plant for custom designing and manufacturing electric transformers for the power generation industry, and was hiring drafting trainees. I scored exceptionally high in the aptitude test and was hired on the spot. The results of my test were then used as a standard against which all future trainees were evaluated.

During the next four years, I worked hard and advanced from draftsman to designer and then to engineering assistant, learning the fundamentals of mechanical engineering. Two events occurred in this period that drastically affected my life: I was hit by a speeding automobile, narrowly escaping death once again and, while I was hobbling around on crutches, I got romantically involved with a draftswoman of German descent and married her.

The first event was probably meant to awaken me to the realization that I was heading down the wrong path, and that I needed to do more with my life. The fateful three seconds before impact and the ten seconds thereafter are blocked out of my memory. Presumably my

2 A PERSONAL QUEST

subconscious finds these moments too traumatic for the mind to ponder. I later learned from eyewitnesses, that I was thrown more than ten feet into the air, somersaulting over the top of the car and rolling down onto the grass strip beside the highway. By a miracle, I survived with only a compound fracture of my left leg and no damage to my internal organs. After three weeks in the hospital and six months with my leg in a plaster cast, I was able to walk again and resume a normal life.

The incident was significant, because it made me aware that events in life do not happen at random. Fateful providence had prepared me for this. In my gymnastic training I had learned how to fall lightly, how to tumble and fly over obstacles, coming down on my hands and rolling over my shoulders, while tucking in my head to avoid a hard landing on the ground. Strange as it may seem, I remember several occasions during the preceding years, when I had gone over just such a scenario in my mind. I had mentally decided that, if I should ever be faced with the prospect of being run down by a car, I should leap up over the car to avoid suffering an impact to my vital organs and to keep from being dragged under. So, knowing exactly what to do in the frightful split-second before impact had saved my life. Since then, I have not had any visions or concerns about similar encounters, probably because there is no more need for them. As I came to my senses, lying in the ditch and surveying my profusely bleeding, mangled leg, I had the strong conviction that this would not slow me down or keep me from living, even though the prospect of losing the leg was high. At that moment I knew that someone else was in charge of my life other than my rational mind; that this someone else was my self, my spiritual consciousness, and that it has a separate existence from my mind. The decision to slug it out and make the best of the situation was made at this deeper level.

The second event was meant to teach me to listen to my inner voice, but my rational mind promptly ignored my premonitions. When I proposed to my first wife-to-be, I did so out of a sense of moral responsibility and out of wanting to please her. Yet at the same time, I had a gnawing feeling inside of not being ready for such a commitment. As if to tempt fate, we had set the wedding date for the thirteenth of the seventh month. When my brother, acting as my best man, arrived with me at the church that day, I discovered we had forgotten to bring along the wedding rings. So I jumped in my car and raced back home to fetch the rings. My inner self had provided me with another opportunity to think this over and cancel the wedding. However, I was too concerned about what my fiancé and my relatives would think and went ahead with the ceremony and the celebrations. The marriage fell apart twenty years later, when I went through a difficult period of self-discovery, brought on by what is referred to as the midlife crisis.

My first wife was no better prepared for marriage than I, and we learned by trial and error. For many years we felt we had as happy an existence as could be expected. As the years passed, however, I began to realize that there was no spiritual growth, that our marriage was based on material values. The two decades of our marriage followed the lifestyle of upper middle-class *yuppies* (young urban professional persons), only we were a generation ahead of the trend. I took traditional family values and the struggle to achieve excellence serious, while my contemporaries whiled away their time being *hippies*, rebelling against the establishment of law and order, demonstrating against the Vietnam War, smoking marijuana and listening to loud music in disco bars.

I was working diligently at my engineering job, saved money for family trips and took night school classes in preparation for passing the Professional Engineers examinations. In my third year into the program, I passed all three engineering and mathematics tests with a perfect score of one hundred per cent. This had never happened before in the history of the Professional Engineers of the Province of Ontario, for as long as they were conducting qualifying examinations for aspiring young and old engineers. My achievement was written up in newspapers, and I received congratulatory letters from our provincial and federal politicians. When my supervisor at work heard of this, he called me into his office and promptly laid me off, with the excuse that I should attend college and get a proper engineering degree. I was getting too good and was becoming a threat to the other engineers in the department.

Considering this as a sign from a higher power, I chose to enter the academic world of higher learning. I entered McMaster University in Hamilton as a sophomore, completed the four-year course of Engineering Physics in three years and graduated with honors and a Bachelor of Engineering degree. By then I had also become the father of a strong, good-looking boy. Our savings had been depleted, I owed money to my parents, and my wife was no longer happy to work. Besides, I wanted her to devote full time to raising a family. New decisions needed to be made.

Ever since my childhood I had been fascinated with the starry sky and the endlessness of deep space. I always felt that we earthlings had a secret connection with the universe out there. Only the blue daytime sky, created by scattering of sunlight in the atmosphere, gave us the illusion of being protected from the dark infinite reaches. When this curtain vanished at night, we were naked and exposed to the reality of unfathomable nothingness. Gravity alone kept us from drifting off into the void and provided us with an illusory reference frame of safety here on Earth, our cradle. By age eight, I knew by heart what was then known of the planets in our solar system, such as their relative sizes, their appearances, their moons, their orbits. Many sleepless nights were spent trying to comprehend the immense distances to the stars and the galaxies. I had compiled a notebook of astronomical data, long before such information could be bought in the corner bookstore. I just knew that the future of humankind, and perhaps its origin, lay in the magnificent and mysterious cosmos. I perceived that the conquest of the outer reaches of our atmosphere and the exploration of space were noble endeavors, challenges worthy of the human intellect. I wanted to be part of this exploration, which humankind is destined to embark on in order to graduate from its childhood.

I applied for a scholarship and a teaching position at the Institute for Aerospace Studies, a newly created graduate school operated by the University of Toronto. On account of my excellent references, I was hired as a lecturer and admitted into the school program. For nearly five years I studied gasdynamics, upper atmospheric physics, plasma dynamics, thermonuclear fusion, hypersonic flight dynamics and shock waves, while working on my thesis. A meager stipendium of five thousand dollars per year for teaching courses in fluid mechanics and boundary layer theory kept me and my family out of the poorhouse. In 1966 I successfully defended my theoretical and experimental thesis and graduated with a Ph.D. in Aerospace Engineering Science.

The thesis work was supposed to have been straightforward: Build and assemble the necessary equipment and instrumentation, run the experiments, take the measurements, compare with theory and write up the results. It was a hands-on, do-it-all research project. I had to be the theoretical scientist, the aerodynamicist, the engineer, the designer, the draftsman, the technician and the machinist all in one. Besides studying the required academic subjects, I had to become an expert in mechanical engineering, electrical engineering, electronics, vacuum technology, optics, spectral analysis, basic machine shop practice and plumbing. It was a valuable learning experience, providing me with an expertise that I could draw on for the rest of my professional career. Isolating the effect I was trying to quantify turned out to be far more difficult than anticipated, however. The experimental data was convoluted by many other effects, which needed to be studied, so that I could account for them and make suitable corrections. The interfering extraneous influences, however, were as real as the effect under investigation and needed to be understood. I thus gained a healthy respect for the complexity of nature. Simplicity is in the mind, and all theory is an unrealistic abstraction of reality.

My parents were proud to have a son who had earned a doctorate degree. Though I should also have been proud and happy with myself, the achievement felt anticlimactic after some twenty-two years of academic training. I was glad of the accomplishment, but wondered if it was worth the struggle to get to this point. I knew the academic degree did not make me a better person. The value was in the experience, the lessons learned on the path of pursuing a worthwhile goal. Perhaps the most valuable lesson to be learned from such a pursuit is that perseverance eventually leads to results. What these results are depends on the standards of excellence a person strives to attain.

During my last years in graduate school, we had been blessed with a second son. A third son died two days after birth from complications of lung failure. He had been brought into this world prematurely by Caesarean section and had been severely affected by his mother's Rh-negative blood; an omen perhaps that other incompatibilities would bring our marriage to an untimely end a decade later.

Leaving my *alma mater* behind, my sights were set on a career in basic and applied research. I had several offers for a research position from Canadian and US defense establishments, as well as an offer for an Assistant Professorship at the prestigious Princeton University. For ethical reasons I chose not to go into weapons development. The professorship at Princeton was a tempting enticement, but I questioned whether I had grown enough in wisdom myself to convey much of lasting value to my prospective students. I decided then that I could offer more value to society by discovery through laboratory research. This view, however, was not shared by society, but I was not aware of this yet. So I took a position with the Cornell Aeronautical Laboratory in Buffalo, New York and spent the following five years doing research in electron beam excitation of gases, rocket nozzle flows, high-temperature plasmas and atomic physics. I was dedicated to discovering new data, processes and effects that would add to the storehouse of scientific and technological knowledge for the benefit of human society. Because of this belief, I soon earned a reputation among my cynical colleagues for being an incurable romanticist.

My social and family life settled into a normal pattern, since I no longer needed to study evenings and weekends. We spent our free time hiking, camping, picnicking, swimming, and I made a concerted effort to instill in our children a sense of respect, wonder and appreciation for the great outdoors. We also provided our two sons with opportunities to become educated in the finer traits of life. We expected them to absorb some of the cultural inheritances of society by visiting museums, air shows, concerts and the like. One exceptionally memorable occasion was a two-week camping trip to

Florida, which included witnessing the epic liftoff of Apollo 11, humankind's first step away from the home planet to set foot on the moon. We did not realize then that this event would remain the high point of human space exploration for the rest of the millennium.

Judging by the standards of society, I considered myself a good father, bringing up my children in the best manner I knew, while learning how to grow up myself. Society, however, has failed to prepare parents for their task. A person requires a license to drive a car or to sell flowers at the corner. A university diploma is needed to prescribe medicine, but no prerequisites are required for being a parent. No school courses are offered in parenting. Anybody who figures out how to copulate can freely procreate any number of children, whether by intent or by accident. And so, the most irresponsible people have the largest number of offspring. For the survival of human society this is a counter-evolutionary trend. Perhaps babies should be licensed. Such action would only be an extension of the laws needed for civilization to survive and grow culturally. Civic laws supplement the laws of nature, so as to put the benefit of society above the pursuit of selfish goals based on ignorance and greed. The alternative is to educate the masses to practice voluntary restraints for controlling population growth. Instead of giving tax incentives for having children, parents should be taxed for the burden each child puts on society. The latter is, however, politically unthinkable in a socialist society, which rewards social irresponsibility with special benefits.

Back to parenting and to the raising of my two children: If I had to do it over, I would teach them self-reliance and responsibility at an earlier stage in their young lives. In our efforts to raise them, we did not neglect to teach them right and wrong, and we enforced strict discipline. Like many other fathers though, I erred by imposing my personal standards upon them, not recognizing that they are separate and different individual spirits with different talents and different emotions. In addition, I was not sensitive to their vastly different levels of spiritual and intellectual development. They had a biological relationship with me, insofar as they shared some of my DNA patterns, but the similarities ended there. According to widespread opinion, the spirits of parents live on in their children. As much as I tried, I could not substantiate such a notion by observing my children. Yes, we had physical and psychological similarities, but I could not identify with their characters or personalities. My children were foreign. Their psyches were different from mine. I concluded that we do not own our children, they are not part of us. A parent's role is to act as the temporary guardian of an independent spirit in a child's body; a separate person, who needs to be guided and launched on its individually destined path. Therefore, too much parenting can do more harm than good. At the time, I was an incorrigible perfectionist and would rather do a job myself than have one of my sons botch it up. I would show them how to do it perfectly, rather than permit them the space to figure it out for themselves. I did not realize then that a person needs to err and fail in order to learn from it. Allowing a person the freedom to fail can be costly, but such is the price of education.

As time progressed, we began to have more difficulties with our two sons, and as parents we disagreed more often on how to handle difficult situations. But this was only one of many factors steering our ship of matrimony towards the rocky coast. The relationship later ended in divorce, because I needed to do a lot of growing on my own, which I found very difficult in a non-supportive environment. The yuppy style of life, which was emotionally and spiritually empty, was no longer satisfactory in my personal search for the purpose of existence.

In the early days of my academic career and my work as a research scientist, my professional aspirations were dominated by my scientific inquiry into the mysteries of nature. Applying my engineering skills and my tenacity to solving difficult problems in science and technology gave me a sense of purpose. My ambitions were driven by my desire for scientific and technological progress, and I admired the American pioneering spirit, personified in President John F. Kennedy and his 1961 declaration of America's commitment to space exploration and to landing a man on the moon before 1970. On that time schedule, and with a continuing drive for discovery, we should have been landing humans on Mars by 1990 and be ready for interstellar travel in the first part of the twenty-first century. I hoped to be alive to see our civilization graduate from its cradle and enlarge its horizons towards its cosmic destiny.   Contact with other civilizations will be inevitable when we are ready.

Yet the American people could not sustain such idealism for very long. After the moon landings of the Apollo program, and with the inauguration of President Richard Nixon, the starch went out of the backbone of American society, and the will to achieve greatness left the people.

«Where there is no vision, the people will perish.»
[Proverbs 29:18]

The decline of America as a dominant world power had begun. Young Americans, drafted to fight a halfhearted conflict, had to suffer the humiliation of defeat in an undeclared and unpopular war. Funding for the space program was slashed, and aerospace scientists and engineers, including myself, found themselves on the street, a highly skilled and trained work force that was no longer appreciated. A quote from the writings of philosopher Whitehead came to mind, as my aspirations for continued success in the scientific research field went up in smoke:

«A society which does not value trained intelligence is doomed.»
[Alfred North Whitehead, 1861-1947]

Notwithstanding that the twelve billion dollars per year spent on the Apollo program was a paltry sum in comparison with the nation's welfare and defense budgets; notwithstanding that the American population consumed considerately more than this amount in soft drinks, in pet food or in liquor and beer, the voices of the uneducated masses, the comfort seekers, were clamoring to be heard. The politics of envy, also called socialism, won out. They argued that the extra twelve billion dollars were needed to cure cancer, feed the poor and house the homeless. Yet the money spent on the space program was not wasted in space. It was spent right here on Earth, providing jobs and pride of achievement for many Americans.   And it generated new technology, which gave us revolutionary progress in computer science, medicine and satellite communication, to name just a few. Cutting the funding from the spearhead of technological research and exploration does not make that money available for anything else, because that money will vanish in a foundering economy. Conversely, putting seed money into the dynamo of economic, educational and technological advancement generates new wealth for society. A stagnant, unimaginative society degenerates into bureaucratic mediocrity. It should not take a rocket scientist to see the handwriting on the wall:

A great society is great in everything;
A mediocre society has a difficult time to excel in anything.

I believe history is proving the correctness of my viewpoint. We have more poverty, more homeless people, more crime now than ever in American history. NASA is floundering without any clear visions or goals. Medical advances in curing cancer or AIDS have also been slow in comparison with the pace experienced during the visionary years of the dynamic aerospace era.

After losing my research position in 1970, I decided to give up my dreams of making a significant contribution to human space travel. I joined a newly founded commercial company in Ottawa to develop high-energy, pulsed infrared lasers for industrial applications. Becoming interested in the enormous potential of laser applications in industry, medicine, remote sensing and photochemistry, I chose to pursue applied research leading to more powerful lasers in the visible and ultraviolet region of the spectrum. Laser light at these shorter wavelengths is capable of breaking chemical bonds due to its higher photon energy and is thus ideally suited for the photochemical modification of materials.

In the summer of 1976 I joined a group of research scientists at a major aerospace company in California, who were making ground-breaking progress in the development of high-energy, ultraviolet excimer lasers. Government funding was good for a few years because of this laser's potential use in submarine communications and in the defense against ballistic missiles. Even though I had an aversion to working on military systems, I supported Edward Teller's[*] and President Reagan's endorsement of the Strategic Defense Initiative (SDI), commonly known as the star wars program. A successful SDI program had an excellent chance of being able to neutralize a ballistic missile attack, and could therefore make a multilateral nuclear disarmament of the world superpowers a reality. But again, America lost heart and gave up on a vision. By 1987 most of the funding had been pulled out of SDI research. I vowed that this was the last time I would work on government funded research. The disappointment of seeing progress cut off, just when success was within sight, was too demoralizing.

In the interim, I had taken a position as manager of the laser division of a San Diego based company to develop an industrial excimer laser for semiconductor processing. Then, since 1983 I have been consulting in laser technology and aerospace sciences for various companies around the world. I am now happily remarried to a wonderful woman who fully supports spiritual growth. Nearing retirement, I feel that I have sufficiently grown in wisdom to give something back to society by writing about my search for truth and freedom. My view of reality is solidly consistent with my understanding of physical laws and logic. Nevertheless, I have gained most of my personal growth through the study of philosophy, metaphysics, the arts and the experience of living.

Development of my artistic talents and my softer side had been put aside during my early adult years, when I had applied myself to the hard sciences of physics and engineering. But later at age 40, along with my incipient mid-life crisis, I learned to make time for understanding my emotions. I became more aware of spiritual matters, and I started to search for answers about the meaning of existence. On one side, there were the serious questions about the purpose of life and whether there was a conscious afterlife. On the other side, I felt a need to lighten up and to become less serious, to search for joy and to smell the roses. I was opening the door to a large

---

[*] Nuclear Scientist at the Lawrence-Livermore National Laboratory, who is credited with being the creator of the hydrogen bomb

untapped potential for making my life more meaningful and enjoyable. In my high-school yearbook, I was characterized as *tall and serious*, probably meaning *aloof and not much fun to be with*. Now was the time to change that and to take to heart sentiments expressed in two verses written by my mother. She had composed them in German, and I later translated them into English, along with the rest of her poetry:

> Some aspire to glory and fame,
> Others strive to add wealth to their name;
> Then some relentlessly labor away:
> Life is a struggle and toil, they will say.
> Yet others conduct their lives with ease,
> One day at a time, as it may please.
> May happen and come whatever may!
> Who then among all those, I pray,
> Is the happiest person alive?

and,

> Life is beautiful and gay,
> If you're proficient in the art
> Of dodging thorns along the way
> And pass them with a joyful heart.

Poetry never had been my strong side. All during my school years, I dreaded the thought of composing essays. To come up with the suggested minimum number of words was like pulling teeth. Evidently, I was so bottled up emotionally that self-expression was difficult. This changed shortly after I met a sensitive and intuitive lady, whom I later married. She also worked in the aerospace industry, and I would see her regularly during lunch breaks at work and on Sundays in the little Catholic church on top of the Palos Verdes hills, where she sang in the choir during the informal folk masses. We had become good friends and started to form a close emotional bond. I was on the verge of falling in love with her and had composed a love poem for her, something I had never before done in my life. One evening after work, when we met for a picnic on the hillside overlooking the Pacific, I gave her my poem, and she was moved to tears. To my surprise, however, she produced a poem of her own that she had composed for me. Hers was much more beautiful and eloquent than mine. The extraordinary coincidence of both of us having prepared a piece of poetry, when we never discussed this subject before, left me dumbfounded. Her poem, entitled *My Love* touched me deeply:

> When first I looked upon
> Your smiling, loving face,
> I felt a tenderness
> That I could not embrace.
>
> And since that day
> I've felt your loving hands
> Caress my troubled,
> Saddened heart.
>
> My heart cries out so loudly,
> Surely all can hear.
> Yet it is healed and quieted only
> By your tender glance.
>
> My love, my love, how wonderful
> It is to feel a love like yours,
> A love I thought
> Would never come to me.
>
> And if one day I should awake
> To find this but a dream,
> I will know I've dreamed
> A dream beyond compare.

There was a small, secluded parking area next to the street below the church. The traffic was light there, and one could see clear across the ocean to Catalina Island. Late one evening I parked there to be alone with my thoughts and to enjoy the cool sea breeze. I was longing to be with my beloved and wished she would be there with me. After a few minutes, she was pulling her car up next to mine. She had heard my telepathic wish and had found me, even though this spot was not one of our meeting places. In the following weeks though it became just that. Ever once in a while, I would get a gnawing feeling of unrest in my solar plexus and an urge to go and meet her on that hillside below the church. When I followed my hunch, I unfailingly found her waiting there. Mere chance encounters, you may say. Yet the facts speak against chance, because neither one of us ever waited there in vain, even though our meetings were unpredictably irregular and were not pre-arranged. The realization and intellectual acceptance of a telepathic bond existing between two people represented a giant step for the hard mind of a male physical scientist and engineer. Our relationship was nonsexual at that time, but we had grown close emotionally. We had become soul mates.

On several of these occasions, when I appeared to be in an altered emotional state, I noticed a large, almost-white hawk passing overhead. This was unusual, because on a foggy evening near the ocean there were no thermal updrafts supporting a hawk's soaring and circling in the sky. Was this my guardian angel in animalistic form? The significance of this would become apparent only later, when I learned this was a phenomenon experienced by other sensitive persons.

My experiences with telepathic communication had convinced me to accept extrasensory perception (ESP) as a fact of life. Our existence was more than mere material being and material sentience. Evidently, our spiritual consciousness was in touch with all other conscious life and could communicate nonverbally in a way not recognized by present-day science. When I discussed these ideas with other female friends, I was surprised to find them seeing nothing unusual in this. Truly, the right-brained female mind is more attuned to the spiritual world and to ESP phenomena. Intuition, ESP and emotions are natural aspects of the female psyche, but do not normally play an important part in the minds of men.

Here was a new area of growth for me, a whole new world of reality to be explored. I made the courageous decision then to confront my fears and inhibitions, to get in touch with my emotions and to learn more about my spiritual being. By a coincidence, which could be interpreted as a classical Jungian synchronicity[1], a number of good self-improvement programs were available in the late seventies and early eighties. Some of these, such as the Erhard Seminars Training (EST)[2] were so popular that they were denounced as fads of the upper middle class. Detractors claimed that these *primal scream therapy* workshops bolstered the ego and produced a me-generation of self-centered individuals. Nothing could be further from the truth. I found these workshops to be extremely useful for a person's emotional growth. Graduates of these self-improvement programs have developed a high personal integrity not normally seen in the rest of the population. Speaking from my own experience, participating in these interactive, confrontational workshops is much more cost-effective for stimulating personal growth than paying a shrink to listen to one's problems.

Over a period of two years, I took the EST Training[2], took part in Stewart Emery's Actualization Workshop[3] and participated in his intensive Creative Personal Interaction workshop. The lessons in these programs were designed to push people into a higher level of awareness, to make them take responsibility for their lives, to teach them relaxation and meditation, to expose emotional hang-ups and to promote psychic healing and spiritual growth. The interactive situations were often confrontational by design, so as to help participants face and overcome fears, inhibitions, guilt feelings and other personal insecurities.

In one such activity our group was acting out a scenario of being on a sinking ship. A lifeboat was available for saving only four people. The group was to elect the four people who should be given a chance for survival, with the remainder facing almost certain death. Everybody was given a chance for making a plea for being elected. The goal of the exercise was to find how much a person valued his or her own life. People with a clear purpose and love of life had no problem, but others, including myself, were just too willing to sacrifice our lives for someone else, whom we considered more deserving. Having been confronted with the need to value our own lives more caused me to re-evaluate the purpose of my existence and to question whether I was living passionately enough.

In another exercise, affectionately called *Arsehole Theater*, we had to act out a scene in front of the group, taking on a character opposite to our nature. The purpose of this activity was to overcome personal fears and obstacles, to express emotions and to generate enough enthusiasm for enrolling the audience. My script was a scene out of a Shirley Temple movie, in which I had to portray a cute, innocent, silly little girl. I had to repeat the performance four times, before the audience was satisfied of my putting enough emotion into the acting and playing the character convincingly. After having finally succeeded, I was exhilarated for having pushed through my feelings of stage-fright, frustration and anger. The same was true for other participants. While still in this elevated state of mind, knowing the world was not going to end if we made fools of ourselves, we were sent onto the streets of Los Angeles. Our mission was to enroll as many strangers as possible into listening to a fabricated story and playing an imaginary game with us. I had always been shy and emotionally restrained since childhood. Acting with childish innocence and enthusiasm recaptured a feeling of child-like confidence that should be our natural inheritance. I found many people eager to play along, but others moving away and rejecting my friendly advances. The experience made me recognize that I was not angry or offended by rejection while in this open, enthusiastic state of mind. We often get offended in our everyday interactions, because we put too much importance on our status in society and on how we appear to others.

Other experiential lessons and exercises brought me in touch with my emotional heritage, my childhood experiences and their subconscious effects on my personality. I learned the value of mastering my emotions, such as sadness, anger, joy, and playing with them for the enrichment of my life. This was different from bypassing my emotions by suppressing or denying them, which I used to do and still have a tendency of doing, unless I consciously remind myself of it.

My quest to understand reality by taking into account all aspects of existence, not just the material manifestations of nature, continues to this day. In order for us to be firmly grounded in this reality, to feel at home in this universe and to have a meaningful existence, we must fully understand the differences in such concepts as spirit, soul, mind, consciousness, self, ego and psyche. We must be aware of the difference of what is out there in the physical world and what is contributed to our experience by our mind. Take, for instance, our experience of color, which is basic to our appreciation of beauty in nature and in the visual arts. From a physicist's point of view, there is no such thing as color. Red light, blue light, X-rays, microwaves, and so on, are all electromagnetic waves, which differ only in their frequency. Color is a subjective quality created in the mind of the observer. The mind assigns color impressions to the various light frequencies impacting on our retina. There is no way of knowing whether your experience of red, yellow, green and blue is identical with mine, or whether you experience a different color spectrum. The only reason we believe we all *see* the same colors, is that certain colors have similar psychological impacts on most observers, and that most people agree on what constitutes a pleasing color combination. As with color, we must consider the possibility, as expressed by Kant[4], that our experiences of space and time may also be creations of our mind, projected onto the objects of our experience.

I had always been extremely interested in the mysterious and the unexplained. So, for the next ten to fifteen years, I took every opportunity to immerse myself in the study of the more esoteric literature and the review of religious concepts. I began to embrace certain aspects of the New Age movement which emphasize our spiritual nature, but I continued to reject some of its more illogic fads connected with astrology, witchcraft, channeled information from questionable spirit sources, and so on. As with everything else, we need to be critical and sort out the wheat from the chaff. I renewed my critical study of the UFO folklore to determine if some of its claims could be integrated into a consistent picture of the universe and the history of humankind.

Putting aside the misidentifications, hoaxes, deceptions and psychic delusions, but taking into account the millions of verified UFO experiences, and looking at the entire picture of Earth's history within the framework of an incomprehensibly vast and diversified cosmos, the evidence is overwhelming that we have been visited regularly by emissaries from different extraterrestrial civilizations. Life is abundant out there! I strongly believe that we are part of a living universe that evolves purposefully, that the underlying *fine stuff* of the universe is spiritual and intelligent, and that it is synonymous with the all-encompassing creative power that many call *God*.

The spiritual realm is nature's fundamental essence.
It is not a byproduct of an accidental emergence of life,
but it is the source of all life.

Taking this insight together with the UFO evidence, we may logically conclude the following:

1   Earth humans are not the only intelligent species in the universe.
2   Other, more advanced species have been traveling through space for aeons and have mapped almost all planets capable of supporting complex living organisms.
3   The universe does not belong to Earth humans. Many races already control the cosmos.
4   These *gods* have a vested interest in Earth and have guided the evolution of Earth humans for millions of years, probably not just for our own benefit.
5   The *gods* have a vested interest in our cultural, societal and political affairs, as well as in our physical and spiritual evolution. They may be the covert movers and shakers behind human affairs.
6   Earth's civilization may be an ongoing experiment with an uncertain outcome.
7   Some of us may be reincarnated spirits originating from other worlds.
8   Most of us may have personal spiritual mentors, or guardian angels, who monitor and guide us in our Earthly mission.

We may become conscious of signs from our spiritual mentors when we are in an altered emotional state or when we arrive at fateful crossroads in our life. My observation of a large hawk passing silently overhead when preparing myself for fateful changes in my life may well be representative of such signs from the spirit world. This assumption is supported by a psychic experience, which I had several years ago. While participating in a semireligious New Age workshop, and while in a state of guided meditation, I was asked to visualize a person walking towards me who was my spiritual mentor. As he came close enough for me to distinguish his facial features, I was shocked to see the head of an eagle or hawk instead of a human face. This was before I believed in spiritual guardians and before I associated the hawk visions with spirit signs. While I was vaguely familiar with the Egyptian sky god Horus at that time, I was not aware of the importance the *Hawk* plays in New Age mythology. I learned only recently about other contemporary persons claiming to have a special spiritual connection with Horus. As an example, Andrija Puharich[5] and Uri Geller have observed hawks in association with UFO sightings, often in places where hawks would not normally be found.

According to channeled information, claimed to have come from a *Galactic Council of Nine*, Phyllis Schlemmer[6] gives a mythical account (historical account, if you accept such channeled information as true) of the *Hawk's* importance in human affairs. In her version of human history, the *Hawk* was an advanced extraterrestrial human-like being with a hawk costume and mask, who came from a distant planet called *Hoova* and first arrived on Earth ca. 35,000 years ago to procreate the Cro-Magnon race. He brought into existence the modern human race and was instrumental in founding the ancient civilizations of early Tibet and Atlantis. In a later incarnation of the *Hawk*, as the biblical god *Yahoova*, or *Jehovah*, he founded the Hebrew society in 11,000 BC. In a third reincarnation as *Horus*, he spawned the Egyptian civilization around 6,000 BC. Egyptian pharaohs claimed to be direct descendants of their god Horus. In our modern era, the *Eye of Horus* has been used as a mystic symbol of wisdom in secret societies, such as the Masonic Lodges. By way of this association, the symbol has found its way into the Great Seal of the United States of America.

The veracity of Ms. Schlemmer's account must be considered in the light of all channeled information. I do not reject the channeling practice outright. On the contrary, I consider telepathic communication to be the preferred method between entities separated in space. The problem with channeling is that it depends on the truthfulness, expertise and motives of three entities: the alleged source of the transmission, the medium whose subconscious mind facilitates the communication, and the interpreter who writes down or records the message. Direct telepathic or verbal communication between two entities should have a higher probability of being reliable. But even there, as with UFO contactees, we have to be selective and consider the integrity and knowledgeability of the contactee as well as the motives of the UFO intelligences. The latter have been known to spread disinformation to confuse human society. In defense of Phyllis Schlemmer's story, it has no obvious conflicts with what we definitely know, and hence her story might just be true. The existence of a galactic council, which keeps track of emerging civilizations in a populated part of this universe, is not beyond logic and belief.

THE QUEST FOR TRUTH

**The prophet spoke: «None are so blind
as those who will not see!»
He meant these words for all mankind,
the man from Galilee.**

What is truth? A simple question, but not so simply answered. A common belief is that everyone has to find his or her own truth, an inner truth, which may be different for each person. As valuable as this personal truth may be for the spiritual development of the individual, there also has to be an external, immutable, universal truth — *The Truth*. Our personal quest should be directed towards the understanding of this unremitting truth.

Throughout history, people have depended on their parental and pedagogical authority figures and on their political and religious leaders to tell them what is true. Religious organizations have traditionally tried to instill the belief that they, and only they, hold a monopoly on the truth. Wars have been fought over this. Independent thinkers, who found a different truth through observation of reality, have been stoned to death, crucified, stretched over the rack or burned at the stake. In order to dominate and control people, a powerful religious sect must not only claim to be representing the truth, but it must control access to this truth. Our organized religions are obsessed with such power and control. This obsession for control is in itself an observable historic truth and makes any *truths* sanctioned and proclaimed by organized cult religions highly suspect.

The truth cannot be legislated by a representative government. It cannot be determined by popular vote. It cannot be ordained by a

religious authority, or decreed by a court of law. The truth just is —
period. Many people who believe otherwise have much housecleaning
to do in their minds and spirits. Misconceptions and confusion about
the truth and the sources of truth are widespread among people of all
ethnic backgrounds. Just how easily the truth can be distorted and
covered up was demonstrated in the widely televised coverage of the
O. J. Simpson murder trial. Defense attorneys Johnnie Cochran and
Barry Scheck repeatedly argued that the jury was going to determine
the truth. How naive can a person get? As the record shows, the jury
promptly ignored all evidence relating to the truth and announced a
verdict which satisfied no one with even an ounce of intelligence.
This illustrates the futility in looking at our public institutions for
providing us with any worthwhile insight, or even with an intelligent
analysis of the true nature of things, or with what is right or wrong.
Another example of how alienated from the truth our leaders are, is
given by the behavior and remarks of the last US president of the
twentieth century, the ultra-liberal Bill Clinton. He has been known
to lie, cheat and deceive with impunity, not to mention that he may
also be challenged in other moral aspects. The moral vacuum at the
top is evident from a recent quote originating at the White House:
«The truth is whatever you want it to be.» Such a position leaves no
common ground for any intelligent discourse. Not until we demand
the highest standards of intelligence, education, wisdom and moral
fortitude from our public servants can we hope to look for any truth or
justice from our public officials. After all, the administration of
justice demands wisdom. Anybody running for public office should
first demonstrate meeting a strict level of prerequisites pertaining to
character, education and experience. This is most important for
presidents, congressional representatives, governors, judges, jurors
and anybody else we elect or appoint to hold power of life and death
over us.

Since no such standards exist in our present society, its representatives
cannot be trusted to determine the truth; nor can they be relied on for
establishing a value system for us. In the present scheme of things, the
search for truth remains a personal quest of discovery.

**Life and the quest for truth and freedom
are do-it-yourself propositions.
Nobody can do them for you!**

We must also recognize that the distinction between inner truth and external, absolute truth is an illusion. We often talk about two different worlds, an inner world of experience and an external world of realities. We differentiate between inner strength and external worldly power. Personal integrity and character give us inner strength, whereas external power is wielded by society's ruling elite, which exercises power over the population through control and manipulation, usually for its own glorification and gain. The artificial differentiation between inner and absolute truth, between inner and external power, between inner beliefs and external reality, exists only because our internal world is segregated from external reality. It is out of touch and inconsistent with the outside world. We need to bring the two into balance and harmony. Otherwise, we will continue to lead a schizophrenic existence.

How this can be accomplished is a question of utmost philosophical and sociological importance. Adjusting our inner world to conform with what our deluded human society perceives as reality might beckon as an easy compromise. But besides leading to death and destruction, it would mean abdicating our responsibilities, and it would deny our divine heritage and our innate moral convictions. Just as Immanuel Kant [*Critique of Pure Reason*, Königsberg, 1781], expressing his awe about the grandeur of the starry cosmos without and the moral principles within, we cannot ignore our connections with our spiritual nature and the universal truths. Any thinking person should realize that human society has taken the wrong turn a few centuries ago and is now in the fast lane, barreling headlong towards moral and physical suicide.

We have raped mother Earth and have amputated her limbs by driving an uncounted number of her life forms into extinction. We have denuded her forests, squandered her resources and destroyed her natural beauty. We have poisoned her rivers, lakes and oceans, polluted her soils and her atmosphere, all under the pretext of liberty, property rights and progress. Through lack of self-control and faulty reasoning, we have burdened Earth with more children than our ecosystem can sustain. We have done so in a selfish effort to validate our existence and prowess. We have confused and misled the masses with religious half-truths and called it faith and devotion. We have abused power and called it politics, economics and diplomacy. We have inflicted unimaginable pain, suffering and death upon human populations in order to maintain and enforce political power structures.

During the last few decades of the second millennium, the crises afflicting Earth's society have been reaching the boiling point. We have allowed our governments to become bloated bureaucracies, which spend our hard-earned money on weapons of mass destruction. We have allowed these bureaucracies to rob the resourceful and industrious benefactors of society in order to reward the lazy under the guise of fair taxes and welfare. We have allowed them to use criminal force and state sanctioned executions in an effort to contain street crime, instead of eliminating the causes of criminal behavior. We have allowed our elected representatives to be bought by special interest groups, whose greed and corruption work against the well-being of life on this planet.

We have run after pleasure and instant physical gratification, but have neglected to nourish our spirits. We have endorsed perversion and called it alternative lifestyle. We have killed the unborn and called it choice. We have fouled our communication channels with violence and profanity and called it freedom of speech. We have neglected to discipline our children and called it building self-esteem. We have exploited the poor and ignorant and called it lottery.

It is time for each individual to wake up and take corrective action, while striving to influence society as a whole to save it from decay and destruction. Instead of capitulating to an ignorant society, we must reform our beliefs and attitudes, so as to build an inner world of truth and conviction, thereby transforming society from within. As indicated above, the internal world of the individual and the external world of society are not separate and thus can only be healed as a unit.

We have a hope of accomplishing this, if our beliefs and attitudes are solidly founded in the eternal natural laws of the universe and are in alignment with the Creational Spirit.

There is no need to search for the truth. The truth is always readily observable. It is simple, abundant, and it can be found everywhere and anytime. Seldom is it hidden. Yet most of us do not make the commitment to recognize the truth when we see it. For it takes wisdom to recognize the truth, to sort the wheat from the chaff, the true reality from the deceptions, illusions and lies. Wisdom teaches us to distinguish, to pick out the sparkling diamonds of truth from among the glitter of worthless would-be truths.

The power of distinction is vital.

Many deceptions and lies masquerade as the real thing. Even in the natural world such mimicry is common. Harmless snakes take on the threatening color patterns of poisonous coral snakes, harmless flies may look like wasps, and so on. Being able to distinguish between harmless and dangerous species can save your life.

Among human populations, differences in physical and psychological makeup also exist, and it is foolish to disregard these differences. Practicing racial and ethnic color blindness is desirable when it comes to loving your neighbor, but it can be tragic when differences in a group's biological or psychological heritage are not taken into account. Different races have different tolerance levels to drugs, are prone to different illnesses and allergies. They are motivated by different values; they respond differently to stress, to threats and to psychologic treatment. For example, certain indigenous tribes of the Americas and Australia have a different perception of time and of what is important in life. We are not doing them a favor by forcing them to fit into the industrialized way of life of white society, or by imposing our Caucasian work ethics on them. This is precisely why Afro-Americans and Native Americans suffer in Northamerican society, why their economic well-being is below average. It is a tragic consequence of not recognizing their differences.

**Recognizing differences and making a distinction
is prudent;
judging a person's value because of these differences
is bigotry.**

Life and things have no hidden meaning, they just are. We create
the meaning and the values by how we live our lives. We give
significance and meaning to the things and events around us by
bringing them into our consciousness. The purpose of our existence
is to experience life as an adventure and to grow spiritually through
that experience.

«Life is either a daring adventure or nothing.»
[Helen Keller 1880-1968]

The universe with its natural laws was brought into being by a
living Creator for the sole purpose of supporting life. It was
created by Spirit and provides the arena for Spirit to grow and
perfect itself. Spirit manifests itself and expresses itself in all there
is and in all life forms, including you and I.

Life is an opportunity for experience and growth!

Living in truth means being aligned with the all-powerful Spirit of
Creation and with its laws and principles. The universe is with us
when we come from the truth. For a while we can deny the truth,
but it does not change what is and what is not. We can cheat and lie
to get what we want through the power of our ego. Such alienation
from the all-supporting spiritual life force, however, will cause us to
live in a non-responsive universe. Ultimately all must come back to
the truth, because that is where the real power resides. The truth is
not what our president or we pretend it to be, but what the Eternal
Spirit designed it to be. Real truth is endowed with the power of
Creation. There is nothing else of value. By living in conformance
with the laws of nature and with the will of Creation we learn to
recognize the truth.

Is recognizing the truth and telling the truth the same thing? Yes, one is a consequence of the other. Once we have recognized the truth, we have an obligation to live according to this truth and to pass it on, to tell it like it is. To live a lie and tell a lie are not only deplorable, but are the most basic blockages that impede a person's spiritual growth.

In order to find the true nature and purpose of life, we must embark on a journey of personal discovery.

The search for the truth is a journey of self-discovery
out of the darkness of ignorance
into the light of understanding.

Understanding sifts the truths from the falsehoods in a person's mind. The emphasis here is on understanding, not just on being aware of it or superficially knowing it. We all have accumulated a lot of knowledge, but we understand so little. Only through wisdom can we recognize and understand the truth. Knowledge can make us powerful, but wisdom makes life joyous and meaningful. As we will explore in a later chapter, recognition of the truth allows us to break our inner chains, making us free. The creative and responsible exercise of this freedom then leads to a more joyous experience of life. This is also expressed in the biblical scriptures:

«And you shall know the truth,
and the truth shall make you free.»
[John 8:32]

At birth, we instinctively know the truth. But we soon forget it, because we are preoccupied with learning the physical survival skills necessary to sustain our lives. Also we are busy developing our individual personality and are learning to relate meaningfully to our surroundings. After the first two decades of life, we have secured our physical well-being by having adapted to the rules of nature and society. At that stage, we know how to assert ourselves to obtain what we need while maintaining our personal sovereignty. We have also made progress in controlling the part of our mind that is capable of rational thought; and we have succeeded in programming our thought processes, often incorrectly and in a manner that is not logically self-consistent.

The need to assert ourselves as individual entities, separate from the rest of the world, may at first appear as a step backwards in light of the spiritual truth that all living spirits are one and the same. The latter realization, however, comes only after sufficient spiritual growth makes us wise enough to accept this reality. Hence we must look at the ego stage of our spiritual evolution as a necessary stepping stone toward enlightenment, and we must do so without guilt.

To fulfill our mission of spiritual growth in this life, we need to rediscover, as an adult, our connection with the universal life force, the Spirit of Creation. This religious inquiry starts with a deliberate effort to commune with life and the nature spirits, and with rediscovering who we are by turning our attention inward. The movement is from the shallow layers of existence to the deeper roots of life. As we progress, we become environmentally sensitive, abhorring all destruction of nature and all brutality afflicted upon living beings. Not only do we honor our body as the temple in which our spirit resides, but we also recognize and appreciate the natural ecosystem of planet Earth as our life-sustaining mother.

The initial, most important step in our earthly mission is to wake up to the realization of our spiritual heritage. We need to accept that we chose to be here for a divine reason.

**The path, as well as the goal, is spiritual growth
— for its own sake.**

To embark on the narrow path leading to enlightenment, we must be willing to discard our learned preconceptions and wrong beliefs. For many of us, our Earthly teachers have not been gifted with true wisdom. Thus, we need to be fearless and daring enough to throw out the old concepts and find the truth anew. By transforming our beliefs and convictions, and by living according to our newly found wisdom, the world will automatically be transfigured for the better. To restructure our minds and our belief systems, we must be prepared and willing to overcome the inertia in ourselves and in society, which tries to maintain the status quo. Truth is not arbitrary or elusive, we only need to be willing to recognize it when we see it. Our willingness to recognize and accept the truth is all we need. Such is the road leading to truth and freedom.

**«Be not conformed to this world,
but be ye transformed by the renewing of your mind.»**
[Romans 12:2]

Persons following their individual paths in their quest for truth and freedom will advance their own personal growth. But will society as a whole advance and benefit from this? The answer is yes, society will progress and benefit, because it consists of individual persons who progress. Society and its people are one and the same and have to support each other in a symbiotic interrelationship. If they do not, society will become impoverished and will thereby keep its members from flourishing, which in turn impoverishes society further. The interdependence is a vicious circle, amplifying all tendencies. It will drive the society and its people in a positive or negative direction. Culturally, a society will either advance or decline. A static society is not stable and thus does not exist. This argument must not be construed to mean that the population must increase for a community to prosper. Often the opposite is true. For society to keep prospering physically, intellectually and spiritually, two interactive processes must become well established within that society. To support personal growth, it is essential that:

1   Society must have a self-correcting mechanism for *accumulating* knowledge and wisdom and for amalgamating newly recognized insights with previously established facts, so as to build this body of knowledge and wisdom into a consistent and logical world view. The body of knowledge and wisdom is never complete or without error. It needs to be amended as it grows in an ongoing process, in which new insights replace previous theories, assumptions and *facts* that are found to be in error. The body of knowledge and wisdom is the foundation of human culture and must be safeguarded. It is the source of capability and power in the society. It affects all

areas of human endeavor, including science, philosophy, religion, law, art, sociology, politics, industry, economics, health care, environmental concerns and so on.

2   Society must nourish personal development by *dispensing* true knowledge and wisdom to the younger generations in a supportive and loving manner. This educational support must be provided in a nonauthoritative way by guiding the thought processes of students on their path of discovery, emphasizing logic and spiritual insight. The educational system must address the needs of the bodies, minds and spirits of the young and must assign the proper resources to satisfy these needs. Students must be taught without bias and in conformance with the natural laws of Creation. Transfer of knowledge and wisdom is needed at all levels of the community, in the family, in institutions schooling mind and spirit, as well as in social programs connected with arts, sports, nature and recreation.

Thus, society needs to preserve and perpetuate knowledge and wisdom in order to have a guaranteed future. We may ask: How well are Earth's civilizations meeting these requirements for sustained cultural evolution? Western science appears to do a good job of accumulating, updating and preserving knowledge of material things and processes. But it falls pitifully short in the philosophical and spiritual arenas. Science takes no responsibility for making unwise decisions, as was amply demonstrated by the abuse of nuclear energy for death and destruction. Furthermore, the science establishment has become authoritative and biased. New ideas, observations and discoveries are often ignored, suppressed or hushed up if they do not fit the theories of the establishment. Prime examples are the scientific debunking of spiritual phenomena, of UFO experiences and of prehistoric archaeological discoveries.

On the spiritual side, our religious institutions, churches and cults are more concerned with domination and ritual than with spiritual knowledge, the source of wisdom. The three world religions originating in the Middle East have failed miserably in their obligation to provide people with truth and purpose in life. The major Eastern religions were founded on ancient philosophical wisdom, but have since also been corrupted during the last few millennia. Whereas all organized religions contain kernels of truth and wisdom, the messages given to lay people are designed to confuse, rather than to enlighten a person searching for truth and freedom. For spiritual teachings to be of value, the motive for dispensing spiritual wisdom must be pure and not be contaminated by ambition, greed, envy and lust for power and control.

Knowledge, logic, wisdom and love belong together. They do not simply coexist but are interdependent. Similarly, our scientific knowledge and spiritual wisdom must be consolidated for true values to emerge. The separation of religion and science, or of church and state, is not healthy for the future of humankind. It makes it extremely difficult to establish and teach values based on truth and wisdom.

LIFE IS COMMUNICATION

A discussion about life is meaningless, unless we have a valid working hypothesis of the spirit-mind-body relationship. Thus by necessity, a large part of this chapter deals specifically with consciousness and with our understanding of the functioning and interrelationship of spirit, mind and body, irrespective of the nagging suspicion that *mind* may be a hypothetical concept and a figment of Western psychology, and that its existence as a separate entity may be in doubt.

The essence of life is a problematic subject, which the encyclopaedic knowledge of Western culture cannot adequately address. We only need to ponder the seemingly innocent question of a child, such as: «What is a bird?» Our learned men and women of science will offer various explanations and definitions, none of them capable of truly answering the question. A family member may answer the question based purely upon casual experience: «A bird is an animal with wings, which enable it to fly. It builds nests and lays eggs that hatch into baby birds.» Zoologists will classify where the genus *bird* fits into the family tree of animals. They will describe the anatomical details characteristic of birds, and they may produce a long list of different bird species and their geographic distributions. Aerodynamicists will contemplate the clever design of bird feathers and wings, which permits birds to defy gravity. Naturalists will talk about the role birds play in the ecology and where they fit into the food chain. They may talk about the habitats of different species, and they may classify species by their appearance and by their peculiar songs. Psychologists will describe the learning abilities of birds, and they may discern inherited memories and rituals from learned behavior. They typically will also deny that birds have intelligence, feelings or spirits.

Only the artists, poets and philosophers will admit it may not be possible to define the essence of a bird with our limited vocabulary and our limited conceptual understanding. An artist may attempt to depict the beauty of light diffracted into many brilliant colors by the intricate microscopic structure of the feathers.   If he or she is poetically inclined, the rendering of the bird may capture the spirit of flight, symbolic of freedom and joy. The true philosopher of the ancient tradition knows it is futile to try defining the reality behind the appearance of a bird without first understanding the principles of life and how the spiritual life force expresses itself in the physical manifestation known as a bird.

Common dictionaries, such as Webster's, define life as the quality that distinguishes living organisms from dead organisms and inanimate objects. They furthermore describe this quality of life as characterized by metabolism, growth and reproduction. This biological definition is strictly materialistic and does not acknowledge a life-giving spirit, or life energy. More recent editions of modern dictionaries may add two more characteristics: response to stimulation and adaptation to the environment. These are reluctant concessions that an intelligence is in control of the individual, and that an organizing power gives the species the ability to evolve by adaptation.

The rapid technological advancements during the last few decades, however, have forced us to look at life in a wider context. Our mental horizons have expanded to include the whole planet. We have beheld the finite sphere of Earth from space and have marveled at the fragile beauty of Earth's ecosystem. We have recognized the finiteness of Earth's resources and the need for controlling population growth in order to avert starvation, social decay and nuclear war. We have complemented and augmented the rational activities of the human neocortex with high-speed computers and semiconductor memories. We have built a global network of communication channels via radio, telephone, cable, television, satellite relays, microwaves, lasers and fiber optics, facilitating almost instant communication between people anywhere on Earth. By analogy with the world-wide web of the internet, all life on Earth is similarly interconnected, but in a more intimate way. Humanity is just now starting to become aware of this interconnectedness. Systems theory and, in particular, systems ecology has come of age.

With this cognition, we find it no longer acceptable to think in reductionist terms about life. We are beginning to see the need to stress the functional aspects over the structural properties of living beings and the need to look at the interrelationship of all life. Just as we cannot examine the functioning of a single living cell without looking at the whole organism, we can no longer isolate one living organism from all other living things it is connected to. Every living thing on Earth is part of the planet-wide web of life and, as we shall argue later, not just in a biological sense, but also on the spiritual level. And from a wider perspective, the ecosystem of Earth is just a small part of the universal web of life. The moral and social implications of this insight are mind-boggling. The words of wisdom of American Chief Seattle bear repeating here:

«Man did not weave the web of life,
he is merely a strand in it.
Whatever he does to the web, he does to himself.»

The environmentalist movement has embraced these words and used them as the theme for the 1992 United Nations Conference on Environment and Development in Rio de Janeiro.

When we look at life from a system's point of view, we find it far more encompassing than the old reductionist view. Further insight may thus be gained by redefining life in systems language. This has been done, at least in a biological sense, by systems ecologist Fritjof Capra in his books, *The Turning Point*[1] and *The Web of Life*[2], and the concept has been brilliantly elucidated by actress Liv Ullmann in the motion picture *Mindwalk*[3]. While on a beach in Normandy, she explains this philosophy of life to a politician and to a poet: «The essence of life is self-organization!» Besides being interconnected with all other life, a living organism exhibits three features of self-organization; it is self-renewing, self-maintaining and self-transcending. Self-renewing refers to the constant renewal and change at the cellular level, as well as to the reproductive renewal of the species. Self-maintaining refers to the stability of the pattern of the living being. Even though parts of its body are constantly renewed, the overall form and function of all its subsystems, such as its organs, remain the same. Self-transcending refers to the inborn tendency of a species to reach out and create new forms, new patterns, new colors, new beauty. By inference, the prime motivator in the evolutionary process is creativity. Species evolve by creatively adapting to each other and to the planetary environment in an ever ongoing dance. Life does not evolve *on* the planet, but co-evolves *with* the planet.

The idea of life being self-organizing goes back to Immanuel Kant [Critique of Judgment, 1793], an idealist philosopher of the German Romantic period during the eighteenth century. The words, *self-organizing and self-maintaining*, may imply a purely materialistic origin of biological organisms, with the quality of life being a biochemical byproduct. Such an implication, however, has not been intended by either the idealistic philosophers, nor by the more recent systems ecologists. Accepting the self-organizing quality of life, we may ask who or what is the authority controlling the organizing activity. The activity is not random, but is purposeful and creative. An open-minded person will logically admit that living organisms are animated by a spiritual life force. The existence of a creative life force provides the only viable explanation of life in general, and of conscious human life in particular. Friedrich Schelling [1775-1854], who followed in the footsteps of Kant, taught that all ideas originate in the eternal spirit of the Creator, a Creator who cannot be known by conjecture, only by experience. He declared creativity, not morality, as the highest human achievement.

When we understand the spiritual nature of existence, and when we acknowledge our inner self as spirit, then the organizing, maintaining and transcending of the human life form is recognized as the natural activity of the universal life force, of which our conscious spirit is an integral part. Similarly, all other life forms are perpetually evolving into new expressions of themselves, guided by the same life force. In this wider context of life, the interconnectedness of all living beings becomes clear. All living organisms relate to each other, to a common environment and to a common spiritual ancestry. This communication, or communion, of all life is its most important quality. It is the essence of life, because this quality and activity describes the functioning, as well as the purpose of life in the universe. The communication of a living being with its environment provides the opportunity for experience and growth.

The term *communication* is used here in its most comprehensive connotation. We must take from the environment and we must give back to the environment in order to live. On the most basic, biochemical level, we must eat and drink and eliminate wastes. We must breathe in oxygen and exhale carbon dioxide. A physical awareness of our surroundings is facilitated by external stimuli reaching us through the portals and filters of our senses for instant analysis by the mind. As our most important channel for incoming information, we humans rely most strongly on our sense of vision, permitting our minds to construct three-dimensional images of material objects in their correct geometrical relationship with our bodies. Such visual information, complemented by auditory, olfactory and tactile inputs, is vital to us for orienting ourselves and for navigating in the physical world.

Knowledge is basic for our learning experience and mental development. It may come to us in the form of the written word, which we peruse with our sense of vision via the medium of light. The spoken word and music are transmitted to us as patterns of pressure waves picked up by our ears. To a lesser extent, knowledge may also be derived from information contained in chemical stimuli detected by our senses of smell and taste, and from direct contact with matter through our sense of touch. All these inputs are conveyed to our cognitive and subconscious minds for processing. In this way, ideas and thoughts flow into our existence.

Conversely, ideas and thoughts are returned to the universe by means of self-expression through speech, song and writing, through bodily movements, as in dance, as well as through artistic creativity and work with our hands. In this way, the mind receives and transforms ideas and uses the material body to circulate this intellectual wealth back to the environment. This communication provides the stream of experience, which we call living. It connects all life together. We must communicate with the living universe in order to exist.

«No man is an island entirely of it self.»
[John Donne, *Devotions upon Emergent Occasions*, 1626]

Similarly, we must constantly replenish our spiritual aliveness by staying connected with the all-pervading spirit of nature, or Creation, of which we are an integral part. We must nurture our emotional well-being through loving relationships with other living beings. This need for spiritual communion, has been affectionately illustrated by James Redfield in the nine insights described in his best-selling book *The Celestine Prophecy*[4].

Although all living organisms communicate on the material and spiritual levels, only the more highly developed beings have sufficient brain complexity for supporting rational thought, enabling the interchange of cultural and technological ideas. On Earth, the more highly evolved mammals, such as humans, whales, dolphins and apes, appear to have the capacity for rational thought and the capability for artistic self-expression. Other complex life forms, including insects, have the capacity for exchanging information and for extracting life-supporting knowledge from the environment. Examples are pigeons finding their way home, and bees telling other bees through body movements and dance where to find honey-laden blossoms.

We are aware of communication taking place on the physical and informational levels, but a deeper interconnectedness exists also on the spiritual level. This spiritual communion between life forms takes place all the time, even though we may not be aware of it. For many organisms, this is the most basic form of communication. When we see schools of fish or flocks of birds behaving as though they were a single organism, all turning at the same instant, we observe communication at this level. Humans are so much in their heads, being pre-occupied with their rational thought processes, that they have shut themselves off from this basic spiritual communion.

We have to invent a sixth sense and acknowledge the possibility of extrasensory perception (ESP) in order to explain intuitions, hunches, feelings, inspirations and telepathic thoughts. The spiritual part of the mind continually receives a stream of information through this channel, whether the thinking mind acknowledges it or not. At the same time, the spirit-mind broadcasts emotions and telepathic thoughts back out into the universe. For example, a predatory animal can instantly sense if you are afraid of it. Among humans, we can often get a first impression, a feeling of antipathy or sympathy, or love at first sight, for a person we have just met. This is spiritual communication. We need the *total stream of experience*, however, on the conscious and subconscious level, to sustain our life.

> «**Man shall not live by bread alone,**
> **but by every word that proceeds out of the mouth**
> **of the Almighty Spirit.**»[*]
> [Deuteronomy 8:3; Matthew 4:4]

Allow me to digress for a moment here, because this reminds me of a seminar I attended in 1982 on the subject of *Prosperity, your Divine Right*[5]. The guest speaker, Reverend Ike[6], made it clear that prosperity is a *total thing* and not just money. Prosperity or wealth is a measure of the degree of our involvement in the circulation of all good. You have to be open and willing to receive the good that is yours, because the Infinite says:

> «**All that I have is yours.**»
> [John 8:32]

The poor are poor, because they fail to receive the good which the Infinite is freely offering. Poverty is a state of mind, not a physical condition. The flow of the universal resources through our living system, through our consciousness, is what makes us alive and rich. As Reverend Ike stated: «You cannot take another breath until you

---

[*] I have avoided the use of the word God here, since the understanding of this concept differs from person to person and has been adorned with too many human attributes.

give away the one you have.» Hence it is necessary to *participate in the circulation* of all good.

We must spend money to receive money, we must love to receive love, we must convey healthy thoughts onto the environment to have health. Whenever we lack something, we can prime the flow of that commodity through our consciousness by circulating some of the commodity. This does not mean that we should become wasteful spenders and consumers of material goods. As we become aware and grow sensitive to the needs of society, of the environment and of the planet, we will find the proper balance automatically. What this society needs most at this time is to open up more to the flow and circulation of the intangible goods of the mind and the spirit. If mental blockages prevent you from receiving, follow the advice of the prophet:

«Ask and it shall be given to you;
seek and you shall find.»
[Matthew 7:7]

Prayer, being a form of meditation, works. It is a communication with the infinite Almighty Spirit, and it makes little difference what god-head or image you attach to the Infinite Resource. You are part of this resource by divine inheritance. Prayer, in combination with giving away some of what you lack, will unplug the pipeline of circulation.

«For it is in giving that we receive.»
[St. Francis of Assisi, 1182-1226]

Back now to the relationship of spirit, mind and the material manifestation of life, the biological organism: From insights gleaned about the inner functioning of the human being, we may construct a schematic, as in Figure 1, which demonstrates the relationship between spirit, body and mind, and which indicates the flow of energy and information that keeps a conscious organism alive.

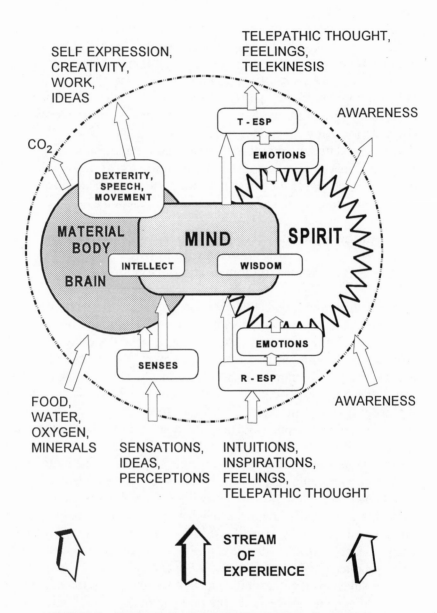

FIGURE 1. Communication of a Conscious Organism
[Human] with its Environment

The graph must not be taken too seriously; it is only a model. It is by necessity incomplete and improvised for several reasons: First, it is difficult to show all intricate connections between the numerous functional components in such a complex system. Moreover, some components, such as *emotions* and *wisdom,* are intangible properties rather than identifiable parts.   Second, due to our rudimentary understanding of life, we have not yet formulated exact words and concepts for many functional parts and processes involved. We also find much confusion and disagreement about the meanings of ghost and soul. Hence we will avoid the use of these words. Third, we must realize that the segregation of the material organism, the mind and the spirit is artificial, since they interconnect and function as a single unit.

**All that exists has been created from spiritual energy
and is infused with Spirit,
whose fundamental nature is life.**

The spirit is the power that creates, organizes, maintains and transcends the physical organism. Let us contemplate how a new living organism comes into being by considering the early stages of embryonic development.   After conception, the fertilized ovum divides repeatedly into a mass of identical cells.   At this initial stage, the developing embryo may be considered just a growth in the womb of the mother.   But then, after one or two weeks, a miraculous event happens. The growth starts to produce cells with diversely different shapes and functions. These begin forming the various organs and structural parts of the organism. The building of a new human being has begun. Have you ever wondered, how a cell knows it should become a liver cell, for example, instead of bone marrow, and just how and where in the developing body it should arrange itself? How do cells communicate this information? How do they know to stop dividing when enough liver cells have been produced? To say that it is all encoded in the DNA or RNA strands sidesteps the question. The DNA is the blueprint created by the *architect*, and the cells are the building materials. If you want a house instead of a barn, you need a supervising intelligence, a representative of the architect, to ensure the correct assembly of the building materials into the shape of a fully functioning house. In the developing embryo, this supervising intelligence is the individually conscious spirit, who is incarnating in the emerging life form. The developing embryo is its material expression, the embodiment of this spirit. It must guide the development as soon as cell differentiation takes place. Abortionists take heed! Abortion is the destruction of a living organism, and it interferes with the wishes and destiny of a human spirit. Preventing conception does not carry this moral stigma and should be the only method of birth control.

The spirit organizes and maintains the life processes in the material body. Whereas the biological organism can maintain itself for awhile, it will decay and die without the life-renewing influence of the spirit. Modern medicine can keep a spiritless, comatose human body alive with machines providing the material needs to keep the organism functioning on a strictly mechanical level. But when the plug is pulled and the life-support is removed, the bodily functions degenerate rapidly in the absence of a life-giving spirit.

For the spirit to give meaningful life to the organism, it must have a means to access every cell of the biological system. The spirit consciousness controls the body through the material intelligence, which we have become accustomed to calling the *mind*. The mind has no separate existence of its own, however. It is created when the spirit merges with the organism. It can be thought of as the liaison, the intermediary and communicator between spirit and body. Because the mind is the bridge between spirit and body, it may be thought of as having a spiritual part, containing the self-awareness, and a physical part that uses the brain and the nervous system to interact with the body. In this way we become aware of our body, and of our rational thoughts. Even though the mind is only a concept used to describe the interaction between spirit and body, we will use this word as though it were an identifiable reality, in the same sense the English-speaking world understands the concept.

It is noteworthy here to quote the viewpoints[7] of Eduard «Billy» Meier, a modern-day prophet and contact person, who obtains his wisdom from higher intelligences. He maintains that *mind* is an erroneous concept. There is only the *material consciousness*, associated with the rational activities of the brain, and the *spiritual consciousness*, the true source of our self-awareness and of our subconscious resources. The material consciousness and the spiritual consciousness are connected through their respective material subconscious and spiritual subconscious with a central collective consciousness. This viewpoint may well be closer to the truth, as it may explain paranormal experiences more easily. We have already stated, that the construct in Figure 1 is an oversimplification of reality. If we accept Billy Meier's model, endorsed by Meier's extraterrestrial teachers, then we need to replace the rational part of the mind with the *material consciousness* and the spiritual part of the mind with the *spiritual consciousness*, the two separate consciousnesses having only an indirect connection via the central collective subconscious. The basic argument of life representing the stream of experience, as illustrated in Figure 1, remains valid, however, and is not contingent on whether we use the concept of *mind* or not.

Because humans have forgotten their spiritual connection and spend so much time in their heads, they mistakenly identify with their rational mind. *I think, therefore I am*, is the well-known statement made by Rene Descartes [1596-1650] in the early seventeenth century. Descartes' viewpoint displaces the center of consciousness from its actual spiritual source towards the rational brain activity. Modern psychology and Western society in general have adopted this view and regard the conscious mind as a product of the activities of the brain and the nervous system. The existence of spirit is disavowed by modern science.

As we have defined the concept here, the mind has no consciousness of its own. If a purely material consciousness should exist, it would extinguish with the death of the material body and could not be associated with a person's true self or spirit. True consciousness is in the domain of the spirit. It is a second-order awareness of being aware. Consciousness is the spirit *experiencing* the rational activity of the mind-brain system. When there is no spiritual awareness of the rational mind activity, the *lights are on, but nobody is home*. Because humans habitually confuse ego with self and mind with spirit, they are often not aware of their direct spiritual consciousness. Our material ego consciousness has pushed the true spiritual consciousness into the background of what we refer to as our subconscious. Most other life forms, however, do not suffer from this confusion between ego and spirit, so that their consciousness is entirely spiritual.

Putting things into their correct perspective, we need to expand Descartes' statement, so as to reflect a wider cognitive wisdom:

I observe and acknowledge my thoughts,
but do not identify with the thinking mind;
therefore I exist as a spiritual, as well as a physical entity.

Not identifying with the thinking mind is important for the sake of our sanity and happiness. Roman emperor Marcus Aurelius [121-180 AD] already verbalized this idea:

«Those who do not observe the movements of their own minds
must of necessity be unhappy.»

Modern computer science has created a new paradigm of artificial intelligence and has spawned a set of new concepts, which can help us understand the relationship between spirit, mind and body. By analogy then, the microprocessor (CPU, or central processing unit) corresponds to the rational part of our brain, the neocortex. The software and user input that make the computer perform a specific activity, such as mathematical computation or word processing, are analogous to the mind. The output devices, such as the monitor, speakers and printers correspond to our voice organs and hands. The operator, who controls the computer activity through a user interface (keyboard, mouse, etc.) is akin to the spirit. It is he who makes the conscious decisions. The functioning of the computer and the activity of the mind are closely related, so that we can artificially produce a fantasy experience by coupling the computer/software system directly to our senses through the interactive medium of *virtual reality*. By no stretch of the imagination, however, can we ever construct a machine that has self-awareness of its own. We can build robots that act like humans and can learn by trial and error. But they will not be able to love, feel emotions, such as joy or sorrow, or create great works of art, because they have no connection to Spirit.

We must speak out here against a dangerous modern trend pervading our educational system; namely that the human mind is nothing more than an information processing center, akin to a computer, and that computers are therefore indispensable aids to the developing mind and to logical and creative thought. Nothing could be further from the truth. Because of its association with the spirit, our mind is much more than an information processor, and conversely, the computer is nothing more than a dumb, pre-programmed tool. There is no such thing as *artificial intelligence*, and computers in the classroom discourage real thinking.[8] The mind needs to be trained to analyze ideas, visions and insights, so as to make intelligent judgements and to gain a deeper understanding, a process that may eventually lead to greater wisdom. No computer can impart a value system in our students, and is thus a waste of time and money at the elementary level of education. The comparison of the computer with the functioning of the brain is pursued here only for elucidating the relationship of brain and mind.

We understand computer memories, because we created them. The fast random-access memory (RAM) chips of the CPU use bistable micro-transistor circuits that can be switched from one stable current configuration (on-state) to another (off-state). For long-term memory, information is stored in magnetic or optic media. The mechanisms of the human memory, however, are poorly understood. Just as in the electronic microprocessor, our thought processes are associated with measurable electric pulses in the millivolt range. These impulses pass from neuron to neuron. But the similarity ends here. The human memory cannot be measured in gigabytes. It is not stored in binary bits, but in a more complex manner. Scientists have not been able to trace the origin of a thought to any specific location in the neural network. Presently the best understanding of thought and memory by biologists, medical scientists and psychologists is as follows: A thought triggers a complex pattern of neurological impulses within the network of billions of neurons. Each neuron is connected to many other neurons at cell junctions, called synapses. Repeated activity along a network of pathways burns in this thought pattern by causing chemical changes at the synapse junctions. The pattern of pathways can then be repeated, or recalled, at will. This is experienced as recalling a thought. When we say: *recalling a thought at will*, we truly put our scientists to a test. Not being able to understand our thinking process, modern science is at a complete loss when it comes to explaining *will*. Whether learned knowledge is stored at the molecular DNA level is not known. Just as the random-access memory of a computer is lost when the system is shut down, so the human memory stored in the neural network is lost when the physical brain dies.

Scientific theories of the functioning of the mind are unable to account for the existence of genetic memories, containing instinctive knowledge, such as nest construction and migratory routes for birds. Neither can they explain hypnotic recall of past-life memories. If the purpose of our existence is spiritual growth through many reincarnations, then whatever has been learned in a lifetime must somehow survive death of the organism. This is consistent with the belief of most religious philosophies; namely that our self-awareness, or consciousness, along with our learned wisdom, survives physical death. We must therefore consider the possibility of an etherial memory that belongs to the spirit world. Either each individual spirit has an etherial memory that is part of its immortal existence, or there is a spiritual group memory, perhaps a central spiritual memory bank, an etherial library so to speak, that all spirits have access to. Such a spiritual memory bank would be analogous to the collective subconscious postulated by Carl Jung.[9]

The ancient Hindu philosophers in India believed in such a spiritual library, containing the accumulated knowledge and experience of all conscious life on Earth. They called it the *Akashic (etherial) Records* or the *Akasha Chronicles*. Individual spirits have selective access to their past records contained in this memory bank. Many New Age sects and philosophies have revived this idea of the Akashic records, and claim to have gained confirmation of its existence through knowledge obtained by channeling[10], by accessing ancient memories through hypnotic regression,[11] or by direct communication with extraterrestrials.[12]

Let us summarize the ideas from this Chapter. Life is communication. What we call living is the stream of experience that flows through our consciousness. An organism is closely connected to all other life through the interchange of materials, thoughts and spiritual energy. On the material level, plants take in water, minerals, carbon dioxide and solar radiation and recycle these elements as oxygen, carbohydrates, oils, and other compounds. Animals take in food (carbohydrates, proteins, fats), water, oxygen and recycle these as carbon dioxide, water, nitrogen compounds, and so on.

On the experiential level, the organism communicates with its environment by receiving impressions of light, heat, sound, chemical and physical stimulation through its senses. A conscious mind, formed by the symbiotic union of spirit and body, converts this communication into an experience of color, music, and so forth. Ideas may be received through the written or spoken word, through pictures and through observation of external events (natural processes, theater, drama, music, social interactions, and so on). Ideas are returned to the world through creativity. The spirit guides the body by means of the mind to create literature, music, art, technology. The material body is necessary for the expression of ideas and for communicating the joyful experiences of life. The performance of non-creative work for maintaining the physical existence can be handled by the material brain functions without much supervision from the spirit.

But intuitions, feelings, inspirations and telepathic thoughts are manifestations of spiritual activity. In Figure 1, we have added an input channel for these, marked *R-ESP* for Receiving Extrasensory Perception and a corresponding output channel marked *T-ESP* for Transmitting Extrasensory Perception. Transmission of telepathic thought and feelings, and telekinetic control of external events, may be accomplished through the latter. ESP is an artificial concept and does not correspond to any actual part of the body or mind. It is used as a descriptive idea for what is a natural communication channel for the spirit. The boxes marked *emotions* have been placed in close association with the spirit and with the ESP channels. Emotions are connected more intimately to the spirit than to mind or body. Psychologists who have studied ESP phenomena have invariably found that the emotional state of a person has a profound effect on the ability to have ESP experiences and for producing ESP effects.

Knowledge and intellect belong into the domain of the material, rational mind associated with the functioning of the brain, and have been so placed in Figure 1. But true insight and wisdom belong to the spiritual part of the mind. Insights and wisdom, learned by the spirit through the life experience, further the growth of the spirit and are retained by a collective subconscious or recorded in the etherial memory of the Akashic records. In future incarnations, a person may then retrieve some of these memories from the collective subconscious or from the Akashic records, because these memories remain associated with the particular person's individual spirit, who has selective access to this knowledge.

PHYSICS AND REALITY

For many citizens of Earth it is sufficient to exist, to pursue life's pleasures and to struggle through its tribulations and challenges. Yet, questions as to the meaning of life, questions about purpose and destiny and about the nature of reality cannot be put off forever. Sooner or later a person must try to fathom the complexities of the real world.

A precise definition of reality is difficult, because all we know and have is our *experience* of reality; and how we experience this reality is different from person to person. Yet our experience and how we rationalize this experience is part and parcel of our learning process. Integrating our personal experiences with knowledge already learned allows us to update our view of reality in an ongoing process of formulating a self-consistent world view.

But what part of our experience is real and what is imagined? Just by asking this question, we have already acknowledged that there exists an objective reality outside of our mind. Are dreams, visions, hallucinations then less real? We may, for example, wonder if our experience of life is itself only a dream, and if we may someday wake up and emerge into a completely different reality. Is it possible we imagine all of life's experiences? Could the physical world be a figment of our mind? Inquisitive, self-reflecting minds have pondered such a possibility throughout the ages. This kind of subjective idealism was already articulated in the ancient Indian Vedas, which considered the entire universe as an illusion (maya). A similar position was taken in Western philosophy by the extreme English empiricist George Berkeley [1685-1753].

Several good reasons come to mind for rejecting such a viewpoint. If there is no physical world, and if reality is the machination of the mind, then what would be the purpose of life? Communication with other sentient beings would be meaningless, if they do not exist. There would be no value in wisdom. Why then would these philosophers even bother to write down their thoughts? Moreover, our enormously complex physical world, nature in all its splendor and with all its perfectly attuned laws and its infinitely diverse manifestations, all interrelating perfectly, would be far beyond the capacity of the human intellect to invent.

The physical world cannot be denied, as anyone foolish enough to step in front of a speeding bus will painfully have to acknowledge. Those who would deny the existence of an external reality may, of course, consider pain and death to be an illusion as well. Death would simply be the end of a dream leading into a new psychic illusion. Our subconscious desire to cling to life speaks against this idea. We value our physical existence, illusion or not. We appear to have a significant spiritual commitment and investment in this material expression of our self. Logic would tell us, we need to accept the existence of a physical world *out there*, which is independent of our imagination. Even though the mind does not create reality, it can have a powerful effect on reality. When the mind focuses spiritual energy in an act of will or faith, the results can be truly awesome. The power of thought and faith allows a person to walk over red-hot coals without getting burned, or thrust a steel skewer through his body without apparent injury. Faith can spontaneously heal a sick body, and conversely, it can transform an imagined infliction into real wounds.

A valid theory of reality must take into account the spiritual aspects of being, as well as the physical manifestations of reality. In this chapter we strive to understand the physical world a little better. We should note, however, that *physical* does not always mean *material*, even though the material properties of matter are an important part of physical reality.

But is physical reality anything like our experience of it? Definitely not! Our senses, which are our observational windows on the world, are exceedingly narrow. Take, for example, electromagnetic waves. Gamma rays, X-rays, light, microwaves, radio waves are all different aspects of the same phenomenon. They differ only in their oscillation frequency. Their frequencies range from 10 oscillations per second (Hz) for extremely low-frequency radio waves to over 10^{22} Hz for gamma rays associated with cosmic radiation, spanning some 70 octaves. Our eyes can detect less than one octave of visible light out of this immense frequency spectrum. The acoustic window of our sense of hearing is a little wider. We can hear approximately eight octaves out of a total of more than 32 octaves of sound vibrations.

The world *out there* is immensely greater and more complex in all its aspects than we can sense or even imagine. Natural phenomena range over many orders of magnitude and could not be comprehended on a linear scale. Propitiously, our sensory organs have a highly nonlinear response. This enables us to detect very faint signals at the low end while preventing saturation at the high end, where the input level may be millions of times greater. Nature has wisely designed our sensory organs to have an approximately logarithmic response. The sound waves from a rock group are ten thousand times more intense than soft piano music, yet our ears perceive the loudness of the rock band as only about twenty times louder. Science has recognized this fact and has long been using logarithmic scales to gauge the full range of natural quantities. Engineers measure sound with a logarithmic decibel scale; seismologists use a logarithmic Richter scale for earth tremors; astronomers use a logarithmic magnitude scale for the brightness of celestial objects. A magnitude difference of 15 corresponds to a brightness ratio of a million (the brightness of the sun versus that of the moon, for example). And by convention all scientific units come in powers of ten, or rather powers of a thousand, such as picometers (10^{-12} m), nanometers (10^{-9} m), micrometers (10^{-6} m), millimeters (10^{-3} m), meters (10^{0} m), kilometers (10^{3} m), and so on. From a mathematical point of view, nature is more geometric than arithmetic. Ratios are more natural than differences. Multiplication is more natural than addition. Nearly all the more important natural laws of physics contain products and ratios of measurable quantities. Seldom do we see plus or minus signs in these equations.

5.1   The Logical Universe

My professional education and training has been in the physical sciences and in the practical, no-nonsense arena of engineering. Science is a perfectly valid endeavor for discovering valuable knowledge about the structure and laws of our physical world. In that pursuit, the scientific method has been a most successful tool for analyzing and utilizing the forces of nature. Without it, we would not be able to send a spacecraft to Neptune, we could not communicate globally, and the Earth could not support six billion people.

I always found it amazing, however, that all processes in the universe should yield to logic description and mathematical prediction. We are able to describe a natural process by a mathematical equation, a short-hand notation of a logic statement. This is amazing enough. Yet, in accordance with the scientific method, this equation is often treated as a self-consistent reality to which all related natural processes should conform. This circumstance makes scientific prediction possible, but we tend to forget that mathematical formulations are by necessity only incomplete descriptions of natural events.

No *a priori* requirement exists for reality to conform to logic thought. Consider an elementary form of logic inquiry, such as: «What is seven times eight?» Every school child knows there are an infinite number of wrong answers, but only a single correct one for such a mathematical proposition. Similarly, we could imagine an infinite number of illogic universes. A universe built on logic, however, will be working with internal consistency and will be able to bring forth complex forms of organization. Every observable effect will have a cause. Besides creativity, logic is a necessary ingredient, which allows this universe to develop higher complexity. This inference may also be true for the evolution of human societies, political structures, economic systems, law and art. If these are not built upon logical principles, they will not survive long, and will soon self-destruct. We are seeing much of this happening in our present society. Thus, logic acts as the governing factor, which weeds out unworkable systems in nature and in human affairs. Logic is the cornerstone of nature and of our sciences. There could be no useful science or technology, if this were not so. As a body of descriptive knowledge, science is generally self-consistent and stands on its own merits. A person would be foolish to attack or disregard that aspect of Earthly science. Being a scientist myself, I agree with most of our scientific knowledge.

Despite its success, however, all science is primarily descriptive. In the last analysis, it does not explain anything. Most scientists know a lot, but understand little. Trying to increase my own understanding and to find meaning within the framework of a living universe, I beg to disagree with the interpretation of some of this scientific knowledge. My thoughts on where scientific theory has gone wrong are outlined in the following sections.

5.2 Mysteries and Paradoxes

According to accepted science, all material substances are made of atoms and molecules, and these in turn are composed of more fundamental particles, such as protons, neutrons and electrons. Throughout our more recent history, scientists and philosophers have tried to find the fundamental building blocks of the universe. High-energy particle physicists have spent the last half century smashing high-energy beams of speeding protons and other ions into nuclear targets, to see if the known nuclear particles could be dissected into more fundamental building blocks. They have succeeded in creating a bewildering zoo of so-called *elementary particles*, such as quarks and mesons; but none are stable for much longer than a nanosecond (billionth of a second). So the question arises, whether these quasi-particles have any meaningful relationship to the structure of protons, neutrons and electrons. Physicists have also searched in vain for the elusive magnetic monopoles, whose existence is inferred from the apparent symmetry of electric and magnetic effects described in the well established equations formulated by Maxwell [1831-1879]. Magnetic monopoles would carry magnetic charges in analogy to the unit electric charges carried by protons and electrons. Here is an example, where nature refuses to conform with theory. Similarly, the search for gravitons, which are thought to be needed for explaining gravitational interactions, has so far been futile.

Careful evaluation of data derived from many years of smashing billion-electron-volt (GeV) particles into each other with billion-dollar particle accelerators (synchrotrons, cosmotrons, betatrons, and so forth) has proven that certain physical quantities are conserved in these interactions. Strict conservation is observed for electric charge, energy, angular momentum (spin) and linear momentum. The latter can be considered as a special case of angular momentum. These conservation laws, together with symmetry laws, are most sacred to the scientific establishment. Applying the conservation requirements to particle interactions has in the past led to the successful prediction and discovery of new *particles*. The simultaneous conservation of energy and momentum in particle dynamics, for example, requires the existence of another stable *particle*, the neutrino. The neutrino is believed to have zero charge and zero *rest mass*, and it is almost impossible to detect. It is presumed to move with the speed of light. In many respects, the neutrino has properties similar to those of the photon, except that it carries only half a unit of spin angular momentum, compared with the photon's unit spin. In Section 5.4, we will give arguments for denying particle status to the photon. It is similarly possible that the neutrino is also an illusionary quasi-particle. The neutrino may just be a reaction of the substructure of space, a vibrational disturbance propagating through space at the speed of light; but with no particle actually moving along the hypothetical path of the neutrino.

As another important consequence of the conservation laws, each elementary particle should have a corresponding antiparticle. When a particle is *created* in a high-energy collision, a mirror image of that particle also appears, having opposite spin and charge. We thus have antielectrons (positrons), antiprotons, antineutrons and antineutrinos. Antiparticles can in principle form stable antiatoms, antimolecules and antimatter objects. Matter and antimatter cannot coexist in close proximity, however, because upon contact the corresponding particle-antiparticle pairs will annihilate and transform themselves into gamma radiation. We do not know whether antimatter has negative mass or positive mass, or whether mass is an absolute quantity that can be neither positive or negative. I believe the latter to be true. Negative mass would lead to the paradoxical inference that a piece of antimatter would accelerate in a direction opposite (against) to any applied force. Moreover, antimatter would be gravitationally repelled from ordinary matter. No such repulsion has so far been observed.

Our known world appears to be constructed entirely of matter, which brings us to the great mystery of the conspicuous absence of antimatter. We are certain the sun and the solar planets are made of ordinary matter. Otherwise we would have seen our space probe self-destruct in a blinding flash of light and gamma rays, when it landed on one of the other planets. The explosion would have been a thousand times greater than any hydrogen bomb blast. And solar wind particles would create an aura of gamma radiation as they strike planetary atmospheres, if the sun and the planets were not composed of the same ordinary matter. If creation of the universe followed the same physical laws which we observe today, then equal amounts of matter and antimatter should exist. Where then is all the antimatter? Is every other star made of antimatter, or every other galaxy, or are there antiuniverses? We cannot tell from the light received, since antimatter atoms and ordinary atoms give off identical electromagnetic radiation. Antiphotons do not exist, and if they did, they would be indistinguishable from photons.

We know little about the structure of the stable subatomic particles, only that they have spin, charge and mass. We will not be concerned here with contrived properties, such as *strangeness, charm, color* and *flavor*, which have been invented by particle physicists to catalog the illusive, artificially created, unstable quasi-particles and to fit them into their preconceived theories. Spin and charge seem to be related, just as energy and mass are. But just what is electric charge, and how does it attract or repel other charges? Nobody knows. Charge appears to be a property that is distributed throughout the volume of a particle. As inferred from scattering experiments,[1] the charge distribution within protons and neutrons appears to be spherically symmetric, but varying with radial distance from the center. No elementary particle has been found which has an electric dipole or higher moment. Similarly, all particles exhibit either a zero magnetic moment or a simple magnetic dipole moment. That elementary particles have properties, such as spin, charge and mass (energy), is a strong indication of these particles having a substructure. Something must spin and something must allow charge to be distributed. Just what that substructure consists of remains a mystery.

When we listed the neutron as a stable particle, we were not entirely correct. It is stable only within the atomic nucleus, where it is constrained by the strong nuclear binding forces. A single, free neutron decays spontaneously into a proton, an electron and an antineutrino in about 17 minutes. We may thus consider the neutron to be a composite particle. This leaves only the electron and the proton as candidates for the basic building blocks of matter. We do not know why the proton is 1836 times more massive than the electron. Perhaps the proton is a convoluted configuration of the more basic positron, surrounded by a neutral energy shield, which would account for the extra mass of the proton. The energy shield would protect the central positron from annihilation when an electron is captured by a proton to form a neutron. With such a model, astronomers would no longer need to search for the missing antimatter in the universe. It could be found in every atomic nucleus.

Whereas we do not know whether electrons and protons have a substructure or not, we can be fairly certain that, on a coarser scale, atoms consist of protons, neutrons and electrons. The first workable model of the atom was proposed in 1912 by Niels Bohr [1885-1962] and Ernest Rutherford [1871-1937]. It is analogous to the familiar model of the solar system and has planetary electrons orbiting around a massive central nucleus. A typical size for an atom is one tenth of a nanometer, or 10^{-10} meter. We would need a chain of ten million atoms to bridge a one millimeter gap. Because atoms are so small, we need an incredible number of them to make up familiar objects. For example, a cubic centimeter of solid aluminum contains 6×10^{22} atoms. This number is larger than the number of sand grains on all the ocean's beaches. As small as atoms are, electrons and protons are 20,000 times smaller yet.

More than 99.95% of an atom's mass is concentrated in the small nucleus, which contains a specific number of protons for each different chemical element. In the Bohr model of the atom, negatively charged electrons, equal in number to the positively charged protons in the nucleus, whirl around the nucleus in discrete circular orbits. Electric forces hold the electrons in orbit, while *strong nuclear forces* hold the protons and neutrons together in the nucleus. Neutrons are needed in the nucleus to keep the protons together against their repulsive electric forces. And, as with the solar system, most of the atom is empty. The nucleus and the electrons occupy less than a millionth of a millionth of the atomic volume. We thus find it hard to understand what makes material objects so solid. There is nothing solid about an atom or its components. Our concept of solidity cannot be applied to the subatomic world. Neutrons, for example, can freely penetrate thick layers of matter, passing through billions of atoms without being impeded.

Quantum and wave mechanical theories have since refined Bohr's model of the atom. Today's conception of the atom is one in which the electrons are smeared out over entire spherical shells and other symmetric configurations centered around the nucleus. The electron is no longer considered a hard particle, but a fuzzy blob of energy, which might be detected anywhere within the cloud pattern described by a mathematical probability function. And it cannot with any certainty be found at any particular point. Electrons *orbit* within their allotted shells at high velocity (at about 1% of the speed of light), completing more than 10^{15} revolutions each second, thereby weaving a tightly knit, impenetrable shield, which defines the size of the atom. This explains a person's inability to walk through a wall. The electron shells of the atoms in the person's body cannot readily penetrate the electron shells of the wall atoms.

Modern physics recognizes four different forces in nature: gravitational, electromagnetic, strong nuclear and weak nuclear interactions. The strong and weak nuclear interactions have an extremely short range and can be considered contact forces. The only two forces of nature with infinite range are gravitation and electromagnetism. How these forces can act over large distances has never been explained and is one of nature's greatest mysteries. Theoretically, this action at a distance can be treated by postulating a force field, a concept first introduced around 1850 by Michael Faraday

[1791-1867] for illustrating electric and magnetic interactions. During the same period, Bernhard Riemann [1826-1866] formulated the mathematical tools for quantifying such fields. Field theory has since been extended to describe gravitational interactions and fluid-dynamic flow fields.

More recent theories propose that electromagnetic action at a distance is facilitated by an interchange of photons, and similar gravitational action by an exchange of gravitons. However clever these ideas may be, the field theories and the particle exchange theories are by necessity only mathematical crutches, and neither provides any real understanding for solving the action-at-a-distance mystery. Could it be that we do not understand the forces of nature because we do not grasp the true nature of space and time? We intuitively and unquestioningly accept the concepts of space and time as fundamental. In our Newtonian and Cartesian way of thinking, space and time provide the framework and arena for all material activity and for all our experience. Most of us take it for granted that space and time had to exist before everything else was created.

The advent of the Relativity theories by Albert Einstein's [1879-1955] and of the Quantum Mechanical theories by Max Planck [1858-1947], Erwin Schrödinger [1887-1961] and Werner Heisenberg [1901-1976] shattered the mechanistic underpinnings of science during the early part of the twentieth century. Einstein tied space and time together by postulating a four-dimensional space-time continuum as a reference frame for all world events. Moreover, in his famous mass-energy relation he declared matter to be just another manifestation of energy. He proposed that all energy has mass and that energy is *the* fundamental stuff of the universe, that energy is in fact *all there is*. Space and time were no longer independent of the energy distribution in the universe. Large accumulations of energy in the form of matter were believed to warp the space-time matrix, explaining why light rays bend around massive objects like the sun. Relativistic concepts also demanded that the flow of time could no longer be considered uniform throughout the universe.

Whereas Einstein's theories afforded a fresh look at the basic physical interrelationships and processes, they also created a new set of paradoxes, which cannot be resolved philosophically, even though they may be *justified* through mathematical manipulation. We must remember, mathematical description is a useful tool to describe observed reality, but it is not a reality in itself. The paradoxes arise out of the theories' confusion about the nature of space. The classical theory of light as an electromagnetic wave needed an *elastic ether* to carry the light vibrations. Experiments designed to detect our motion through this ether of space were unsuccessful. Einstein used these experimentally inconclusive results as the primary axiom for his Special Theory of Relativity, published in 1905.   In common language, he postulated that the speed of light measured by an observer is constant, independent of the observer's motion relative to the source or anything else. There could be no preferred reference frame attached to space itself. With this postulate, Einstein denied the existence of a light-carrying ether. Space had to be absolutely empty, a nothingness without any properties. A few years later, in 1916, he contradicted himself with his General Theory of Relativity, which unequivocally depends on space being a medium that can be distorted and warped. His Special Theory, however, is what leads the unwary theoretician into absurd contradictions. The problems associated with the nonlinear addition of velocities, with relativistic length contraction and time dilation are discussed in the subsequent section on Relativity.

The explosive technological growth of the late twentieth century has provided physicists with new powerful instruments and tools for probing and exploring the microcosm and macrocosm. Theorists have been working overtime to deal with many new discoveries in the subatomic world, as well as in the cosmos at large. While their theories are often able to describe newly discovered oddities correctly, they do not add one iota to our deep understanding of nature. Quantum physics and relativity theories deal with new phenomena by formulating new postulates and by making corresponding adjustments to the mathematical framework. In the subatomic arena, new quasi-particles, like gluons, gluinos and quarks, are conjured up to account for any surplus or missing mass. And if these enigmatic particles do not behave according to established theory, new rules are made up to connect their odd behavior with imaginary properties, such as strangeness, color and flavor.

Another way to make observational data fit theory is to add more dimensions to our baffling world. Enlightened scientists know that a suitably complex mathematical construction can be created to fit any real or imaginary set of observations, provided a sufficient number of arbitrary coefficients and constants are inserted, all adjustable and tunable to fit the data. Modern cosmologists delight in creating such *Theories of Everything, Superstring Theories* and the like, which propose that our world is 10, 11, 15 or 27-dimensional. One enterprising theorist even suggests that everything can be explained if the world had 506 dimensions.[2] Meanwhile we are still trying to fathom the enormous complexity of Creation, the wave-particle duality of light, the nature of time and space, electric charge and gravitation, the mysterious action at a distance, the secrets of nuclear structure, the formation of stars and galaxies, and the significance of quasars and black holes.

The cosmology in vogue now is the *Big Bang* theory of creation. This theory is based on Edwin Hubble's [1889-1953] astronomical work at the Mount Wilson and Mount Palomar Observatories. From optical red-shift data, he inferred that all distant galaxies are moving away from us. And the further away they are, the faster they seem to recede. This single observational piece of evidence gave rise to the idea of an expanding universe as the after-effect of a gigantic explosion, which created the known, observable universe. The Big Bang is believed to have occurred 12 to 15 billion (10^9) years ago. According to this theory, the universe started from a point singularity of infinite energy density, then exploded to create everything that exists today, including space and time. As the universe expanded and cooled, material particles condensed, which later coalesced into stars and galaxies. Will the universe expand forever? Apparently so. Astronomers have yet to detect sufficient matter capable of halting the expansion through gravitational attraction.

But to the embarrassment of cosmologists, many new pieces of observational evidence, collected via the orbiting Hubble Telescope, do not fit well into the Big Bang theory. Among the troublesome data are stars that seem to be older than the universe, giant black holes in the center of galaxies that should have taken more than 15 billion years to form, and evidence that the expansion is accelerating.

An ongoing controversy revolves around the origin of life in the universe. Are we alone? Is intelligent life out there? Only a few years ago, mainstream science had considered the formation of planets a rare accident. Today, most scientists will acknowledge that planets form naturally in the condensation stage of every star. With a hundred billion stars in our galaxy and with as many galaxies, life-sustaining planets are quite common, and the universe should be teeming with life.

What about the overwhelming evidence of millions of reliable UFO sightings and of thousands of contact episodes around the world? We cannot avoid taking at least some of the reported experiences seriously. Logic and straightforward deduction should tell us we are being visited by extraterrestrial intelligences on a regular basis. Despite mountains of direct and circumstantial evidence, the scientific community continues to take a disdainful and cynical attitude, dismissing all sightings and contacts as hoaxes, misidentifications, swamp gas and hallucinations. Rather than ridiculing and debunking such experiences, we should seriously test the information conveyed in these alleged contacts, to see if it can illuminate the mysteries of this universe. We may be surprised what we can learn. Yet we must also be vigilant and not fall prey to misinformation and orchestrated efforts to mislead and confuse the public.

5.3 Relativity and Space

Nothing can go faster than the speed of light. At least, this is the creed of modern relativists and the official position of contemporary science. But is this an established fact? Einstein himself stated in his original papers that, in a relativistic sense, no material body could be *observed* to travel faster than the speed of light. This was perfectly logical, because he used light signals as the measuring stick for all world events, for determining relative velocities and for defining simultaneity. He made the speed of light an *absolute* limit only in his later writings. Turning such a relativistic concept into an absolute quantity, however, is contradictory and unjustified. The relativists consider absolute concepts to have no real meaning in any case. We are confronted here with a philosophical problem, stemming from the belief that an observer's sphere of consciousness is limited to a small section of space and time. Those of us, who believe in an ever-present, all-encompassing, eternal spirit consciousness, have no problem with absolute ideas. We can view the whole universe with our mind's eye without being limited by the speed of light.

The relativists say the universe is finite but unbounded, like the surface of a sphere. Yet, if the universe is finite, then there must be a center of mass, which would conveniently serve as a distinct point of reference for everything else. If the world has four or more spatial dimensions, this center point may lie outside of our observable three-dimensional space and may be inaccessible. Because electric and gravitational force fields fall off inversely with the square of distance, however, our world must have three spatial dimensions and no more. This is required by the conservation of energy (mass) and charge. A simple mathematical analysis can show these force fields falling off inversely as the cube of distance, if the world were four-dimensional. The laws of physics just do not support the existence of any fourth or higher spatial dimensions. Treating time as being equivalent to a fourth spatial coordinate is equally unwarranted.

The impetus for Einstein's theories came from experimental results that failed to prove the existence of a vacuum *ether*, thought to be necessary for the propagation of light waves through space. In 1887, Michelson and Morley (MM)[3] showed that light propagates with the same speed in the direction of Earth's motion as in the opposite direction. In the MM experiment, a light beam was split in two with a partially reflecting mirror positioned at 45° with respect to the beam. The two beams were reflected back and forth between mirrors in mutually orthogonal directions. Then the beams were recombined and made to interfere, so as to produce optical fringes. The fringes were expected to shift, when the whole apparatus was rotated relative to the known orbital motion of the Earth. No fringe shifts were detected outside of the experimental uncertainty. This negative result could not be understood on the basis of accepted theories.

During the next fifty years, the experiment was repeated al least a dozen times with increased finesse and accuracy. Some experimental setups were so sensitive to vibration, that the City of Cleveland agreed to halt all streetcars during one of the experiments. As much as scientists tried to detect an *ether drift*, their results remained inconclusive. The experiments did not actually measure light velocities, but relied on optical fringe shifts. I believe the interpretation of the experiments was flawed, because it did not account for changes in phase and frequency of the light waves reflected from moving mirrors. Then there is the nagging fact, that spinning versions[4] of the MM experiment apparently proved the existence of a preferred reference frame, namely a vacuum ether.

The refutation of the ether was not readily accepted by the scientific community. Several attempts were made by theorists to invent compensating effects, which could be used to explain the MM results and save the ether theory. Among these efforts was a proposal by G. Fitzgerald [1893] and H. A. Lorentz [1895], suggesting that fast moving bodies shorten their dimension in the direction of motion. Instead of a contraction in length, a corresponding time dilation would also serve to explain the MM results. According to this theory, a stationary investigator observing a moving clock would find it ticking more slowly. Neither the Lorentz-Fitzgerald contraction, nor the time dilation effect were successful in saving the ether concept. Instead, Einstein incorporated both ideas into his relativity theories. Einstein's version of the time dilation effect leads to the famous twin paradox,[5] which requires pages of hand-waving arguments to explain away.

The relativistic addition and subtraction of velocities also creates severe conceptual distress. According to the Special Theory, velocities cannot be added algebraically. For example, consider a spaceship traveling away from the sun at 0.9 times the speed of light. Light emitted from the sun at speed c overtakes the spaceship. A scientist on the spacecraft confirms that the ship is moving away from the sun with 90 percent of the speed of light by measuring the rate of decrease of the apparent diameter of the sun. He also measures the speed of light relative to the ship and finds, in accord with theory, that the light still overtakes him with a relative velocity of c. Hence, he concludes that c minus 0.9 c equals c, a paradoxical result. This illogic, non-algebraic speed difference is also inconsistent with the observation of a Doppler shift in light frequency. The first-order Doppler shift is a classical effect, that depends on classical velocity differences. The light passing a moving observer should not change in frequency, if the observer always measures a fixed light speed c, irrespective of his own speed in relation to the source.

The best known mathematical relation, associated with the Special Theory of Relativity, is the mass-energy equivalence formula, $E = mc^2$. Popular interpretation of this formula holds that mass can be converted to energy and vice versa. Moreover, nuclear fission and fusion bombs are believed to represent dramatic proof of Einstein's theories. Both notions are erroneous.

The correct interpretation of the formula regards mass as a measurable *property* of energy. Energy has mass. In nuclear fission and fusion reactions, energy is conserved, and thus mass is conserved also. Matter energy is being converted to radiation energy and heat energy, but no energy is created, and no mass is destroyed. The celebrated formula can just be considered as a simple definition of mass, i.e. $m = E/c^2$, where $1/c^2$ is the proportionality coefficient. Whereas Einstein derived this formula by considering the relativistic mass increase of an electron accelerated to high velocity, it could just as well have been derived from classical and quantum mechanical concepts, without resorting to Lorentz-Fitzgerald transform factors for length, mass and time. Hence, confirmation of $m = E/c^2$ does not in itself validate the Special Theory of Relativity.

Einstein denied the existence of a vacuum ether of space and asserted space to be a nothingness without properties. Yet space is known to have specific properties, which can be measured precisely, such as its electrical permittivity ϵ_o and its magnetic permeability μ_o. These two quantities define the electromagnetic impedance of space as $(\mu_o/\epsilon_o)^{1/2}$, and the propagation velocity of electromagnetic waves in space as c $= (\epsilon_o \mu_o)^{-1/2}$, two more properties of space. And Einstein's assertion of space being empty is strongly contradicted by the phenomenon of vacuum polarization. When an isolated charged particle, such as an electron, is observed in vacuo, it appears to be surrounded by ephemeral particles of opposite charge (positrons). These particles oscillate in and out of existence, here one moment, there the next, like will-o-the-wisps. Their transitory life is very short, even on a subatomic time scale. These *virtual* positrons are thought to be members of electron-positron pairs, appearing out of the vacuum and vanishing again by recombining with each other. During their short lifetime, the positrons are drawn closer to the free electron, whereas their negative partners are repelled to a greater distance. This constitutes an electric polarization of the space around the original electron. The electric charge measured as the charge on the electron may, therefore, not be the real charge of the *bare* electron, but rather the charge of an electron *clothed* in its induced vacuum charges. The actual bare charge of the electron may be significantly larger than its measured value.

When Maxwell[6] derived his equations, he assumed the luminiferous ether consisted of a tenuous but continuous fluid. This concept has a certain appeal, as we are familiar with the behavior of fluids, such as air and water. Flow patterns in the fluid medium of space could perhaps explain action at a distance, and elementary particles could perhaps be identified with fluid vortices, sources and sinks.

When studying ancient philosophy, off-beat scientific theories and UFO lore, we come across a recurring belief in a fine-structure underlying all space and all matter, with perhaps another layer of microstructure below that. This fine stuff underlying the atomic order is thought to be linked with spiritual energy. The presence of such a sea of spiritual energy would clarify how thought and spiritual power can control, or even create matter. Many esoteric beliefs and theories consider space, and hence the entire universe, to be made up of two kinds of elementary energy units, opposite but complementary, extremely tiny and virtually infinite in number.

Approximately 3,000 years ago, pre-Taoist philosophers in China distinguished within every natural object two interacting energy modes, the positive *Yang* energy and the negative *Yin* energy. In more modern times, with the help of relativistic and quantum concepts, the English physicist Dirac[7] predicted the existence of the positron, a particle with equal mass but opposite charge of the electron, which had been discovered thirty years earlier. He also proposed the theory of a sea of virtual electrons, which occupied all space, but which were normally undetectable. If an electron was *lifted out* of this *Dirac Sea* with an energy expenditure of $2m_ec^2 = 1.022$ MeV, it would leave a *hole* that would act like a positively charged particle, the positron. Dirac's theory later served as a model for the positive hole concept in modern semiconductor technology. But the Dirac sea of virtual electrons imprisoned in positive holes, as a model for the vacuum space, was never given serious consideration by established science. Recently, Simhony[8] revived and expanded the electron-positron model of space. He believes space to be densely populated by actual electrons and positrons, arranged in a three-dimensional lattice, in the same way as negative chloride ions and positive sodium ions are arranged in a crystal of rock salt. Whereas his theory can naturally explain many of the quantum mechanical assumptions and postulates, his papers have been rejected and barred from publication by better-knowing peer reviewers, just because his theory would re-establish a preferred frame of reference.

Simhony calls the space lattice *epola* and assumes the electrons and positrons are held in the lattice with a binding energy of $E_b = m_ec^2 = 511$ keV. If this binding energy is simply electrostatic, then the space between adjacent particles (lattice constant) is approximately five femtometers (5×10^{-15} m). This leaves very little room for the particles of ordinary material objects to pass through space unimpeded. Herein lies a major stumbling block, making it hard to accept the epola theory without reservations. It goes against common experience, which tells us that material objects can pass freely through empty space with zero resistance.

If we were to add up all the individual particle masses in the epola, we would determine a mass density of 10,000 tons per cubic centimeter of space. This is ten billion times the density of ordinary matter. So, how could space possibly be so transparent to moving objects? The secret lies in the concept scientists call *binding energy*. Remember, we stated earlier that all energy has mass, and that there probably is no such thing as negative mass. Well, binding energy is the sole exception. It is an energy hole; not just the absence of energy, but an abyss that swallows energy. Binding energy is negative energy and can be considered to have negative mass.

We can best illustrate this negative energy by examining the atomic nucleus. The strongly attractive nuclear forces create an energy hole, which keeps the protons from flying apart due to their electrostatic repulsion. Because of this nuclear binding energy, the mass of a nucleus, i.e. the total energy in the nucleus, is always less than the sum of the masses of the component nucleons. The nuclei of some elements are more tightly held together than others. For example, a helium nucleus is more strongly bound (more stable) than a deuterium nucleus. So, when two deuterium nuclei are fused into a helium nucleus, as in a hydrogen bomb, there is a net loss in nuclear energy. The energy difference, i.e. the increase in binding energy, is released as radiation and kinetic energy.

In the epola model of space, the binding energy per particle is equal to the mass-energy of the particle itself. The electrons and positrons disappear into the energy holes produced by the interaction of their electric charges, making them undetectable. The externally measured mass density of the epola space is thus equal to zero. Having been robbed of their energy, the electrons and positrons in the epola space are therefore unable to interact with ordinary matter and do not resist the motion of objects through the vacuum of space.

The epola lattice constant is also probably much larger than the five femtometers assumed by Simhony. Remember, it may not be possible to measure the bare charge of an electron because of the positive electric clothing induced in the vacuum. If the bare charge of the electron is taken to be 100 times the measured value, then the particles in the epola space will be 10,000 times farther apart. The per-particle binding energy will still be 511 keV, and the epola as a whole would still be massless. Such a space would then be far more transparent to the passage of nuclei and electrons of the atoms in ordinary objects.

So, does the fine-structure of space consist of electrons and positrons, hidden in energy holes of their own making? Or is there a still finer microstructure underlying the electron-positron space? At least one British engineer seems to think so. R. D. Pearson[9] proposes that everything in the universe is ultimately made up of positive and negative *cosmons*, thousands of times smaller yet than electrons. He also believes that these cosmons are akin to spiritual energy, and that the power of the spirit over matter acts at that level. Rudolfo Benavides[10] of Mexico similarly believes the world to consist of spiritual energy, made up of small polarized energy units. The positive energy units, he calls *anana*s, the negative ones *anionites*. Ananas are pure thought energy, and the anionites facilitate the materialization of thought. This bit of wisdom comes from extraterrestrial sources in the Pleiades and was allegedly transmitted to selected contactees on Earth. Analogous information was apparently also given to Billy Meier[11] of Switzerland by his Pleiaran tutors. They told him the universe was created from spiritual, intelligent energy, which they called *Sohar*.[*] The Sohar continues to guide the evolution of the universe.

When we contemplate all theoretical and observational aspects of space, taking into account intelligent speculation and ancient wisdom about the structure of the universe, we should seriously consider a vacuum space made up of oppositely charged energy units, too small to detect, but underlying everything there is. We will call them energy units, rather than particles, because particles imply a solidity that does not exist at this ultra-microscopic level. Solidity is an illusion of our everyday material world.

---

[*] This word has the same root as the Hebrew word *Zohar*, meaning *splendor*. Meier's contacts claim that many Hebrew words are derived from an ancient extraterrestrial source language.

5.4 The Wave-Particle Enigma

Light is an electromagnetic oscillation of space, propagating with a constant velocity c in a direction perpendicular to both the oscillating electric and magnetic field vectors. We use the term *light* here in a generic sense to include all electromagnetic radiation from radio waves, through the visible spectrum, to gamma rays.

The fundamental nature of light is wavelike, and its electric and magnetic manifestations are accurately described by Maxwell's Equations[6], which form the foundation of classical electromagnetic theory. In Maxwell's theory, the propagation of electromagnetic waves depends directly on the properties of a highly elastic *ether*, believed to be filling all space. The propagation speed c of elastic waves may be expressed by:

$$c = \sqrt{\frac{Y}{\rho}} \qquad (1)$$

where Y is the modulus of elasticity, and ρ is the mass density of the ether. The wave picture of light could easily explain most optical phenomena, such as diffraction, interference, refraction, internal reflection, polarization and birefringence. And so everything was well until the year 1900, when Max Planck introduced the first quantum mechanical concept with his *Distribution Law*. The latter was an empirical fit to the emission characteristics of a *black body*[*] heated to a known temperature. Fitting a theoretical curve to the frequency dependence of the measured intensities became feasible only, if he assumed that radiation was emitted in discrete quanta, and if the quantum energy was proportional to the frequency of radiation:

$$q = hf \qquad (2)$$

---

[*] A nonreflective bit of matter (gas, liquid or solid) in radiative thermodynamic equilibrium with its temperature

where h is Planck's Constant, which was determined to be 6.63×10^{-34} joule-second. Later, in 1905, Albert Einstein used the quantum concept to account for the photoelectric effect. Photoelectric emission of electrons from a metal surface occurs only if the light frequency is above a certain threshold. Below that critical frequency, no electrons are emitted, no matter how high the light intensity. This strange behavior could be explained by considering the impinging light flux to consist of individual energy packets, called photons, each with an energy of hf, and each one interacting individually with an electron at the metal surface. By transferring all of the photon's energy to the electron, the forces that bind the electron to the metal matrix could be overcome, liberating the electron. Photons were believed to be similar to the light particles hypothesized by Isaac Newton more than two centuries earlier.

After Einstein published his Special Theory of Relativity in 1905 and derived his famous mass-energy relation, scientists started to consider seriously the possibility of converting photon energy to matter energy. Perhaps fundamental particles could be *created* with high-energy gamma rays. Conservation of energy, angular momentum (spin) and electric charge requires the production of particle-antiparticle pairs. Producing an electron requires the simultaneous production of a positron. By 1932, Carl David Anderson had shown that gamma rays of sufficient energy, $hf \geq 2\, m_e c^2 = 1.02$ MeV, could indeed produce electron-positron pairs under certain conditions. This discovery reinforced the belief in light photons.

Since then, light has been considered to have a dual nature, wavelike as well as particlelike, depending on the phenomenon under investigation. The photon theory is typically applied to explain photochemical reactions, whereas the wave picture is used for elucidating optical diffraction effects and for interpreting nonlinear properties of some optical materials. The shorter the wavelength of light, the more it seems to behave like a stream of particles. Modern quantum physicists consider photons to be real particles, moving with the speed of light c in the direction of the light ray. Particle physicists list the photon as one of the unique elementary particles that make up the universe. This notion makes the photon the weirdest elementary particle known. It does not have a unique energy or mass, it ceases to exist unless it moves at a fixed speed c, and it is its own antiparticle. Calling the photon an elementary particle forces it into a category into which it does not belong. It cannot be a real elementary particle in the same sense as the electron.

The interpretation of light as speeding bullets of energy has created an unresolved paradox, which cannot be reconciled with the more readily observed wavelike nature of electromagnetic radiation. If we accept that this universe is based on logic, then we need to challenge this photon concept. To this effect, I will describe three situations that demonstrate the inconsistency of the photon concept with observation and logic. I will temporarily assume that the Special Theory of Relativity is correct, and that the wave-photon duality of light is a valid representation of reality.

Example 1: The Capricious Photons
Now there are five, then three, and then perhaps two point seven.

According to the photon theory, the number of photons, ϕ_0, passing through unit area in unit time is proportional to the light intensity, which in turn is proportional to the square of the electric, or magnetic wave amplitude, E_0 or B_0. The photon flux density is given by:

$$\phi_0 = \frac{\epsilon_0 c E_0^2}{h f_0} = \frac{c B_0^2}{\mu_0 h f_0} \tag{3}$$

where ϵ_0 and μ_0 are the electric permittivity and the magnetic permeability of free space, respectively.

Consider now a steady stream of collimated light of frequency f_0 (a laser beam, for example) emanating from a distant star system and passing an observer in a spaceship. The latter is initially at rest with respect to the light source. He will measure a light intensity of $\epsilon_0 c E_0^2$ and a photon flux density given by Equation (3). Each photon carries an energy of hf_0 and passes him with velocity c.

Then let the space traveler fire up his rockets and acquire a constant velocity v away from the star, where $v \ll c$. According to the Special Theory of Relativity, the light waves still pass him with velocity c. But does he still measure the same photon flux? One of the axioms of relativity theory requires Maxwell's equations of electrodynamics to be valid in all frames of reference moving at different, but constant velocities. According to this condition, the electric field amplitude in the light wave, as measured by the moving observer, is now given by $E = E_0 - v B_0$, or $E = (1 - v/c) E_0$. Both the electric and magnetic amplitudes have decreased by the factor $(1 - v/c)$. The wave intensity has decreased by the square of this factor.[*] In addition, the light frequency has decreased to $f = (1 - v/c) f_0$ due to the Doppler effect,[*] so that the new photon energy is $(1 - v/c) h f_0$. The space traveler will now observe a photon flux density of

$$\phi = (1 - v/c) \frac{\varepsilon_0 c E_0^2}{h f_0} = (1 - v/c) \phi_0 \qquad (4)$$

Hence, he sees a smaller number of lower-energy photons passing him than before.

Where did some of the photons go? He could not have outrun them, because all photons still appear to fly past him with velocity c. If he were moving towards the source, he would see additional photons. Evidently, photons are being destroyed or created, depending on the motion of the observer. This paradox would disappear, if we would allow the photons to have a variable velocity relative to the observer. Hence something is wrong with Einstein's postulate, which says the propagation velocity of light is independent of the motion of the observer, and/or the concept of discrete photons moving with the wave at speed c is flawed.

---

[*] For simplicity, the classical relations are used here. Using relativistic formulae would not change the argument.

Example 2: The Mysteriously Accelerating Photons

When elastic waves (seismic waves, for example) pass from a material of low density to one of higher density, the waves slow down (see Equation 1). When they pass back into the lower density substance, they speed up again. The same behavior is observed with electromagnetic light waves passing through an optically denser material, such as a glass lens. The change in wave speed at the boundaries accounts for the phenomenon of refraction. The index of refraction n of an optical material is defined as the ratio formed by the speed of light in vacuo divided by the speed of light within the material (n = c/v).

Now let us inspect this from the photon point of view. As the photons emerge from the far surface of the lens, they must suddenly speed up with almost infinite acceleration. We may ask: What force at the rear surface of the lens accelerates the photons? There is no answer to this question. Again, we must suspect the validity of the photon concept.

Example 3: How Large or Small is a Photon?
One moment as large as a galaxy, at another as small as a molecule of silver bromide.

Next consider the well known two-slit interference pattern. When a light wave is passed through two narrow and parallel slits, the emerging light acts as though it was coming from two coherent line sources of light. Along certain directions, the waves are 180° out of phase and cancel each other out, causing zones of darkness. Along other directions, the waves emanating from the two slits are in phase and reinforce each other, creating zones of brightness. All aspects of this interference pattern can readily be explained by means of the wave theory of light. However, this did not satisfy the quantum physicists. They repeated the experiment with extremely low levels of light. So low, that according to their theory, individual photons would arrive at the two slits at distinctly different times. Photon counters, placed in the *dark* and *bright* zones of the two-slit interference pattern, produced photon counts that mimicked the pattern expected from the wave nature of light. The photons avoided the detectors in the dark zones, but were counted in the bright zones. A photographic film, exposed for a long time, still showed the customary fringe pattern. When the detectors were placed at the slits, they confirmed that no two photons arrived at the two slits simultaneously. They were detected only at one slit or the other. The conclusions from this experiment were:

♦   Individual photons still carry their wave characteristics.
♦   Photons interfere only with themselves.
♦   A single photon would have to pass through both slits to follow the interference pattern, but can only be detected at one slit when intercepted.

This is illogic enough, but consider now enlarging the experiment to cosmic proportions. Assume two imaginary slits thousands of light-years apart, but millions of light-years away. Light from a distant galaxy or quasar, perhaps billions of light-years away, passes through the two openings and is observed here on Earth. The angular geometry is such that wave optics would predict a giant interference pattern, through which the solar system may move, slowly passing through alternate *bright* and *dark* fringes in the course of millennia. Such a phenomenon may actually be observed in the cosmos. Some recently detected, distant quasars[12,13] may be brightened by such an interference effect, caused by the light being gravitationally deflected around two sides of an intervening galaxy. If it should be confirmed that interference effects occur on a cosmic scale (besides the more commonly observed lensing effects), can we then assume a photon to be smeared out over tens of thousands of light years, as it passes around both edges of the galaxy? Yet when it is detected on a photographic plate, it suddenly contracts to a fraction of a micron, since the entire energy of the photon is needed to photochemically interact with the small grain of silver bromide. Again, logic thought cannot account for this behavior of the photon.

We could find many more such incongruities arising out of the photon hypothesis. Quantum theory has failed to provide any good reason for the optical quanta to have energies proportional to the wave frequency.

Classical wave theory predicts the exact opposite relationship. A single low-frequency oscillation contains much more energy than a single high-frequency oscillation of the same amplitude. Wave energies vary inversely as the square or cube of the frequency, depending on the dimensionality of the wave.

A way out of this predicament is to deny the existence of the photon as a speeding particle of light. Photons are not quantities of electromagnetic radiation but are a characteristic of space. Space, and space only, is quantized, not the light waves. Light is wavelike, and the wave-particle duality of light is a myth, brought about by our lack of understanding of the nature of space and time. It is noteworthy that Einstein originally considered the photon to be an *imaginary quasi-particle*, useful only for describing the transfer of energy in an electromagnetic wave. We will consider space to consist of a matrix of elementary energy units held together by electric forces. These energy units are not material particles in the common sense. They may be identical to electrons and positrons, or they may be made of finer stuff (see Section 5.3). When excited by an electromagnetic wave, these electrically charged energy units execute transverse oscillations in harmony with the oscillating electric field vector of the wave. The transverse oscillation is quantized, giving rise to an apparent quantization of the wave itself. This proposition follows closely the views expressed by Simhony[8], who considers the photon as representing the average *per-particle part of the energy transferred in the wave motion* through the electron-positron lattice, which he assumes occupies all space. Whereas Simhony's theory does not make use of *a priori* assumptions for the quantization of angular momentum, we will assume that the transverse oscillations of the elemental energy units of space are quantized in the same manner proposed for the electrons in Bohr's theory of the atom. We do not claim to understand fully the true nature of space, and we do not claim that Simhony's theory is wrong. The following argument is presented only for showing how the paradoxes created by the wave-particle duality can be removed by assuming that space, rather than light, is quantized.

Suppose the *fundamental energy units* of *space* (feus) exhibit the properties normally associated with electric charge and suppose they are set into sympathetic harmonic oscillations by an electromagnetic wave, which itself originated from oscillations of the feus. Assume also that the feus have conventional mechanical properties, such as inertial mass, momentum and kinetic energy, even though we know there is nothing material about these units. For space to be neutral, equal numbers of positive and negative feus are needed. Let us call them f+ and f-. These positive and negative units are assumed to be arranged in a uniform matrix, held in equilibrium by electromagnetic interaction and/or by another unspecified force. The space matrix is equivalent to the elastic ether implied by Equation (1). Let us now isolate a typical f+, f- pair. Assume the individual units have a mass m and are being held apart at an equilibrium distance x_e by an imaginary spring with a spring constant k (see Figure 2). The spring represents all forces acting on the pair of feus. When displaced from their equilibrium positions, the distance between the two units will increase and decrease in a sinusoidal manner. This model represents an oscillating electric dipole with the properties of a classical harmonic oscillator. The displacement of the two charges from their equilibrium distance (the stretching of the imaginary spring) can be represented by:

$$x(t) - x_e = A \sin(2\pi ft) \qquad (5)$$

where the oscillating frequency f which is forced upon the dipole by the wave, is normally below the natural frequency f_n of the feus dipole given by:

$$f_n = \frac{1}{2\pi}\sqrt{\frac{k}{\mu}} = \frac{1}{2\pi}\sqrt{\frac{2k}{m}} \qquad (6)$$

The symbol μ represents the *reduced mass* of the two units in the dipole.

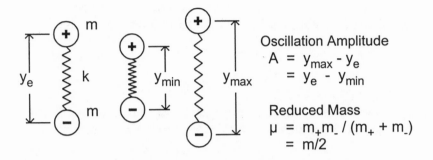

Oscillation Amplitude

$A = y_{max} - y_e$
$= y_e - y_{min}$

Reduced Mass

$\mu = m_+m_- / (m_+ + m_-)$
$= m/2$

FIGURE 2. Model of Positive-Negative FEUS Pair

The displacement-time curve and the velocity-time curve for the oscillating dipole are shown in Figure 3. The sinusoidal motion can be thought of as being generated by the y-component (projection onto the y-axis) of a rotating vector of length A moving with constant angular velocity $2\pi f$, as represented in Figure 3(a).

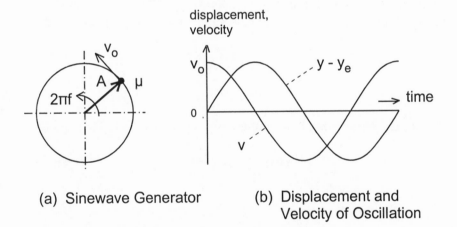

(a) Sinewave Generator

(b) Displacement and Velocity of Oscillation

FIGURE 3. Oscillation of FEUS Dipole

The maximum velocity occurs when y-y_e is zero. It corresponds to the tangential velocity of the equivalent circular motion. From the model in Figure 3(a), this velocity is

$$\upsilon_o = 2\pi f A \tag{7}$$

Except for extremely high-frequency gamma radiation, this transverse oscillation velocity is significantly slower than the wave velocity c.

We now assume that the angular momentum of the equivalent circular motion is quantized, like the angular momentum of an orbiting electron in the Bohr atom:

$$\mu \upsilon_o A = \frac{1}{2} m \upsilon_o A = n\frac{h}{2\pi} \tag{8}$$

where n = 0 or 1, or possibly 2 for a very high-intensity wave.

Eliminating v_o from Equations (7) and (8) yields an expression, which shows the amplitude of the oscillatory motion varying inversely as the square-root of the frequency. This is a consequence of the quantization of the motion of the feus, in other words the quantization of space.

$$A = \frac{1}{2\pi}\sqrt{\frac{2nh}{mf}} \tag{9}$$

Conversely, eliminating A by multiplying Equations (7) and (8) yields

$$\frac{1}{2}m\upsilon_o^2 = nhf \tag{10}$$

where n is generally 0 or 1.[*]

_____

[*] Note, when only a single positive or negative feus oscillates within the space matrix, $\mu = m$, and Equation (10) would read ½ mv_o^2 = ½ nhf. This may correspond to half-spin neutrinos which, like the photons, are space disturbances that spread with the speed of light.

This is the transverse vibratory energy of a f+,f- pair. Its energy quanta are proportional to the frequency, just as for traditional photons. This energy is transferred from one feus pair to the next, as the wave propagates through space at velocity c. The number of feus pairs participating in the wave motion by sympathetically resonating with it determines the intensity of the wave. Since the number of feus within the sphere of influence of a single wave oscillation is extremely large, the intensity of the electromagnetic radiation has to become inordinately high, before all available feus become enrolled into participating. Increasing the intensity of the wave beyond this point may force some of the f+,f- pairs to vibrate with energies of 2hf. This could account for *multiphoton absorption* processes seen in extremely intense laser beams.

The electromagnetic aspects of the oscillating feus pairs are probably more real than their mechanical vibration. The transverse displacement of the f+ and f- elements from their equilibrium position creates an electric dipole vector, which propagates with the speed of light in the direction of the wave. This transport of the dipole field is equivalent to phantom positive and negative charges moving with the wave, but no real particles are actually propagated. The phantom movement of charges is consistent with Maxwell's equations as applied to electromagnetic waves. One of them relates the oscillating field vectors $\underline{E}$ and $\underline{B}$ to the wave propagation vector $\underline{c}$.

$$\underline{E} = \underline{B} \times \underline{c} \qquad\qquad (11)$$

Equation (11) matches the condition required for a charged particle, of either sign, to move with speed c in a straight line through transverse electric and magnetic fields, without being deflected by either field; that is, the magnetic force on the moving phantom charge is equal and opposite to the electric force at all times, provided the oscillating electric and magnetic fields are in phase.

In the photoelectric effect, electrons are ejected by the quantized transverse oscillations of the elemental energy units of space. Photons, as physical particles moving at the speed of light, are not needed.   Attempts by optics textbooks[14] to explain double-slit interference patterns in terms of photons passing through one slit or another are futile and nonsensical. Statements like: «photons only interfere with themselves,» or «we do not know which slit the photon has passed through when it arrives at one of the fringe maxima,» are irrelevant, since no photons pass through either slit. No photon moves in the direction of wave propagation, but space elements vibrate transversely to it. The photon is a hypothetical concept, which only has meaning when electromagnetic radiation interacts with matter to liberate electrons or break chemical bonds, or when it interacts with the substructure of space to produce electron-positron pairs. In all these circumstances, a minimum vibrational energy of space elements is needed to overcome the binding energy of the particles liberated.

In summary, let us consolidate the ideas expressed in this and the previous sections. In earlier discussions on the fine-structure of space, we showed how binding energy can reduce the externally measurable mass density of space. The externally measured mass m_x of a feus is given by:

$$m_x = \frac{E_m - E_b}{c^2} \qquad (12)$$

If the binding energy E_b of the feus is equal to its mass energy E_m, then the density of space is zero and, according to Equation (1), the velocity of wave propagation would be infinite. Formula (1), however, is the relation for the velocity of a bulk deformation wave. Our model of electromagnetic waves does not strictly fall into this category (Here we differ from the electromagnetic wave model of Simhony[8]). In our model, the ether waves consist of quantized local oscillations of the feus. These units oscillate individually within their potential wells, created by their electric binding energy. At that microscopic level, each feus unit has an inertial mass equal to E_m/c^2, unaffected by the binding energy. The elastic forces holding the feus units together in a f+,f- pair are the same forces which couple neighboring pairs to each other. We can thus rewrite Equation (1) in terms of microscopic quantities relevant to our model of space:

$$v_p = \sqrt{\frac{E_b}{m}} = c\sqrt{\frac{E_b}{E_m}} \qquad (13)$$

The wave propagation velocity v_p is seen to be equal to c, rather than being infinite, if the binding energy of the feus is equal to its mass energy.

Certain experimental observations, such as vacuum polarization and vacuum pair production by gamma rays, suggest a luminiferous ether consisting of an electron-positron matrix, meaning f+ may be a positron and f- an electron.   If there is a primary spiritual microstructure underlying space, consisting of cosmons, Sohar units, ananas and the like, then one might expect the binding energy of these micro-units to exceed their mass energy, so that in this spiritual realm, signals can travel at speeds far in excess of the speed of light (see Equation 13). Such speculations, however, lead to new contradictions which cannot be resolved with present-day science. It shows how ignorant we are.

5.5 Mechanical Units of Charge

Science fiction writers and independently thinking scientists, who refuse to follow the beaten path, have long been looking for a connection between electrical and mechanical quantities.   One motivation is to find a way for controlling gravitation by electromagnetic means. In this section we will express electric charge in mechanical units and relate it to such quantities as mass and momentum.

The scientific system of units prior to about 1935 had been the cgs system, which used centimeters for measuring length, grams for mass and seconds for time. All other mechanical quantities, such as force, energy and momentum, could be expressed by combining these units. For example, the unit of force was 1 $g\text{-}cm\text{-}s^{-2}$, which was called 1 dyne.   When electricity became an important part of modern technology at the end of the 19th Century, electric charge and electric current needed to be quantified and integrated with the mechanical cgs units. For describing the forces associated with electric charge, the electrostatic system of units was introduced by arbitrarily setting the permittivity of free space equal to unity ($\epsilon_o = 1$). The electrical quantities of charge, potential and current were then measured in statcoulombs, statvolts and statamperes. For expressing electromagnetic effects, the permeability of free space was set equal to unity ($\mu_o = 1$), and new units of abcoulombs, abvolts and abamperes were needed to make physical relations come out correctly. The electrostatic units were incompatible with the electromagnetic units; and the practical use of physical formulae, describing electromagnetic effects, became confusing and cumbersome.

Maxwell's equations should have given a clue that a self-consistent system of units could not be created by setting both ϵ_o and μ_o equal to unity. The relevant relation

$$\epsilon_o \mu_o = \frac{1}{c^2} \qquad (14)$$

needs to be observed for any consistent system of units.

With the industrial revolution and the emergence of practical engineering as a world-shaping force, a practical and more consistent system of scientific units was needed. In June 1935, the *International Electrotechnical Commission* adopted the MKS system of units, based on the meter, the kilogram and the second as the basic mechanical units. The system was later extended to include electric and magnetic units, such as the coulomb, ampere, volt and weber, in a compatible manner with the mechanical units. This *Rationalized MKS System of Units* is now in use. It was created by arbitrarily setting the magnetic permeability of free space equal to $4\pi \times 10^{-7}$ henries per meter. By Equation (14), the electric permittivity of free space then became equal to $10^7/(4\pi c^2)$ farads per meter. In the rationalized MKS system, four units are considered basic, the three mechanical units plus the coulomb as the unit of electric charge. But was this system really a good choice? Nature herself tells us there is a better choice.

The rationalized MKS system has ignored the inherent symmetry existing in electromagnetic phenomena. Consider the mutually symmetric roles played by the electric field **E** and the magnetic field strength **H** in Maxwell's equations, specifically in the wave equation for electromagnetic radiation. The symmetry becomes apparent when we study the way electromagnetic waves are generated and propagated.

In a radio transmitter, driven by a resonant LC-circuit, the electric energy oscillates back and forth between a capacitor C and an inductor (coil) L. When the current is zero, all energy is in the electric field of the capacitor,

$$W_C = \frac{1}{2} C V_o^2 \qquad (15)$$

where V_0 is the maximum voltage on the capacitor. A quarter oscillation later, the current is at a maximum value of I_o, and the charge on the capacitor is zero. At this instant, all energy is in the magnetic field of the inductor,

$$W_L = \frac{1}{2} L I_o^2 \qquad (16)$$

This is the same energy that was previously in the capacitor, so that LI_o^2 equals CV_o^2. It is an interplay of voltage and current, of electric and magnetic fields. Corresponding oscillating electric and magnetic fields appear at the dipole antenna, and a portion of these fields is released and radiated as electromagnetic waves. Far from the dipole, the electric and magnetic fields in the electromagnetic wave are in phase, consistent with the wave equation derived from Maxwell's equations.

In such an electromagnetic wave, the energy in the wave is shared equally between its electric and magnetic fields. In a plane electromagnetic wave, the time average of the energy density is given by

$$W_{ave} = \frac{1}{2} \epsilon_o E_o^2 = \frac{1}{2} \mu_o H_o^2 \qquad (17)$$

where E_o and H_o denote the amplitudes of the oscillating electric and magnetic fields, respectively. The ratio of electric to magnetic field amplitude is then given by:

$$\frac{E_o}{H_o} = \sqrt{\frac{\mu_o}{\epsilon_o}} = Z_o \qquad (18)$$

This ratio is called the impedance of free space and is denoted by Z_o. In the rationalized MKS system of units, the free space impedance is 376.7 ohm.

The electric and magnetic fields in an electromagnetic wave contain identical energy densities. Hence, logic tells us to make the numerical values of the field amplitudes equal, to set $E_o = H_o$. We use this insight to define a new system of units, which we call the *Symmetric MKS System*. In this new system of units, the mechanical MKS units are retained, but the unit of electric charge is redefined, along with all other electric and magnetic units.

As we can see from Equation (18), equalizing the field amplitudes is equivalent to setting $\epsilon_o = \mu_o$ and $Z_o = 1$. In addition, we have to satisfy Equation (14), so that

$$\epsilon_o = \mu_o = \frac{1}{c} \qquad (19)$$

Thus, both the electric permittivity and the magnetic permeability of free space are made numerically equal to 3.336 nanoseconds per meter, which designates the time it takes for an electric field or a magnetic field to penetrate one meter of space. To convert equations from the rationalized to the symmetric system of units, all we need to do is replace ϵ_o and μ_o with $1/c$. Rather than inventing new names for the electric and magnetic units of the symmetric system, we will designate the symmetric units by preceding the name with a sigma. For example, the symmetric unit of electric charge is σcoulomb, or σC. The conversion factors are 376.7, the square root of 376.7, or their inverse values. A partial list of conversion factors is as follows:

QUANTITY	SYMMETRIC UNIT		CONVERSION FACTOR	
Electric Charge	1 σcoulomb	$= 1 \text{ m kg}^{1/2} \text{ s}^{-1/2}$	$= 0.05152$	coulomb
Electric Current	1 σampere	$= 1 \text{ m kg}^{1/2} \text{ s}^{-3/2}$	$= 0.05152$	ampere
Electric Potential	1 σvolt	$= 1 \text{ m kg}^{1/2} \text{ s}^{-3/2}$	$= 19.410$	volt
Capacitance	1 σfarad	$= 1 \text{ s}$	$= 0.002655$	farad
Inductance	1 σhenry	$= 1 \text{ s}$	$= 376.7$	henry
Resistance	1 σunit	$= 1$	$= 376.7$	ohm

In the symmetric system of units, all resistances and impedances are dimensionless quantities measured in units of the impedance of space. Capacitance and inductance are measured in seconds, consistent with the time constants RC and L/R for R=1. That is, capacitance is measured by the time it takes to charge a capacitor to 1 - 1/e of the applied voltage through a unit resistance (space). Inductance is measured by the time it takes for the electric current in a coil to build up to 1 - 1/e of the steady-state current.

Choosing symmetric units makes it possible to describe all electric and magnetic phenomena in terms of mechanical units of length, mass and time. We will consider these as fundamental, and all other quantities derived from these. This does not mean, however, that it may not be preferable to designate another set of three quantities as fundamental, such as energy, momentum and electric charge.

Let us now look at how electric charge and fields are related to mechanical quantities. In the remaining part of this section, all mathematical relationships will be expressed in conformance with the symmetric system of units. A classical example, where electric forces are balanced against inertial forces, is the Bohr model of the hydrogen atom. Balancing the electric attraction between the orbiting electron and the nuclear proton against the electron's centrifugal force gives

$$\frac{m\upsilon^2}{r} = \frac{c\,e^2}{4\pi r^2} \tag{20}$$

where r is the radius of the electron orbit and e is the electronic charge. Taking the orbital angular momenta as being quantized in units of h/2π, the electron velocity in the lowest orbit is given by

$$\frac{\upsilon_1}{c} = \frac{e^2}{2h} \tag{21}$$

A corresponding relationship is given by the definition of the *Fine-Structure Constant* α, which was first introduced by Sommerfeld in 1934 to explain the fine structure observed in atomic energy levels:

$$\alpha = \frac{e^2}{2h} = \frac{1}{137.04} \tag{22}$$

The fine-structure constant is a dimensionless number. Its significance is not entirely understood, but it plays an important role in the structure of atoms. It represents the ratio of the electron velocity in the first Bohr orbit to the speed of light. The square of the fine-structure constant, α^2, expresses the ratio of the electron size to the size of the ground-state hydrogen atom.

Equation (22) can be rewritten to give the elementary charge in terms of mechanical units, thus:

$$e = \pm\sqrt{2\alpha h} = \pm 3.109 \times 10^{-18} \, joule^{1/2} s^{1/2} \tag{23}$$

Note that Equation (23) naturally provides evidence for the existence of both positive and negative elemental charges. The quantity e^2, and any other charge squared, has units of angular momentum. We may suspect that charge squared is in some way simply related to angular momentum in the substructure of elemental particles, analogous to mass being a characteristic of energy.

The equation also suggests that elemental charges come only in pairs, and that charges may not be permanently separable. The value of the charge on the proton has been measured to be equal to the charge on the electron with an accuracy of better than one in 10^{20}. Theoretical arguments predict that the positive and negative charges should be exactly equal. In addition, we expect the numbers of positive and negative charges in the universe to be exactly equal. This is in itself a profound observation and one of the mysteries of the universe. Since electric forces are so much stronger than gravitational forces, it would take only one excess electron or proton for each 10^{18} (a billion times a billion) nucleons to upset the gravitational balance between astronomical bodies.

5.6   Not-so-Black Holes

The world is intricately structured from the ultramicroscopic subnuclear level to the macroscopic intergalactic scale. Creative activity takes place at all levels of existence all the time. Our awareness is, however, largely confined to the level at which we interact with the world, to our arena of experience. When we measure physical phenomena, we encounter different natural forces, depending on the scale of resolution of our investigation. The measuring stick defines the arena of activity. The sizes of measuring sticks needed to commensurate the cosmos adequately range over forty orders of magnitude. In the table below, we have arbitrarily divided this immense range into six scales or levels of experience, each level being separated from the next level by a factor of a hundred million.

ARENAS OF COSMIC ACTIVITY

Arena	Measuring Stick	Dominating Natural Force
Subnuclear	10^{-16} meter	Nuclear
Molecular	10^{-8} meter	Electric
Human	1 meter	Electric & Gravity
Planetary	10^{8} meter	Gravity
Interstellar	10^{16} meter	Gravity
Intergalactic	10^{24} meter	Gravity & Electric

Our human experience and influence are confined almost exclusively to the molecular, human and planetary levels. At the molecular level, all activity is dominated by electric forces. At the planetary and larger arenas, gravity dominates. In our day-to-day life, we measure objects and distances with a regular yardstick. The human level of experience is midway between the molecular and planetary levels, where electric and gravitational forces are of equal importance. This situation maximizes the human potential for creative activity within our sphere of influence. Intelligent human life did not develop at this level by accident but by divine providence in the plan of Creation. In this and the following sections, we will concentrate on the macroscopic world held together by gravity. Here we encounter astronomical phenomena dominated by gravitation in its most extreme manifestation.

A large portion of the observable matter in the universe is concentrated in spheres of hot luminous plasma of ionized hydrogen. Like our sun, these stars are the thermonuclear furnaces, in which the nuclei of heavier elements are cooked up by fusion of lighter nuclei. The interior of a typical star is subjected to hellish temperatures of tens of millions of degrees and to pressures approaching a hundred thousand tons per square centimeter. Such conditions support thermonuclear reactions with the release of enormous amounts of radiation energy. The outstreaming electromagnetic radiation pressure counteracts the gravitational forces, thus keeping the star from collapsing.

The thermonuclear synthesis of elements eventually depletes the light fusionable fuel in the stellar core, causing the star to contract adiabatically and to radiate thermal energy generated by gravitational compression alone. For stars of solar mass, this late evolutionary phase ends in a slowly cooling white dwarf star, in which matter is compressed to densities approaching a hundred tons per cubic centimeter. The brightest star in our skies, the dog star Sirius, has such a dense, white dwarf companion star. The two stars orbit around their center of mass in about fifty years in a perpetual dance. The contraction of a white dwarf star is eventually halted by the *degenerate electron pressure*, a quantum effect which prevents more than one electron from occupying the same *quantum space*. Heavier stars with masses between 1.4 and 2.3 solar units are believed to end their lives as rapidly spinning neutron stars, the so-called pulsars. Degenerate electron pressure is insufficient to support more than 1.4 solar masses (Chandrasekhar limit[15]), so that the electrons are forced to combine with protons to form neutrons, when such stars undergo gravitational collapse. Neutron stars have densities of several billion tons of matter per cubic centimeter. For stars with more than 2.3 solar masses, however, not even *degenerate neutron pressure* will halt further gravitational contraction. Present-day physics knows of no force strong enough to prevent total gravitational collapse of a dead massive core into a point mass of infinite density. Rapidly spinning stars would contract into a spinning ring singularity.

As the dying star compresses to higher and higher densities, the gravitational field at its surface becomes extremely intense, resulting in a strong curvature of space-time, as predicted by Einstein's General Theory. When the star has contracted to only a few miles in diameter, space-time folds in over itself, and not even light can escape the grip of gravity. The concentrated mass becomes disconnected from our reality and disappears into what is called a *black hole*. The spherical surface that separates our reality from the black hole is called the *event horizon*. The equations describing the relativistic space-time geometry around such a concentrated mass were formulated in 1916 by Karl Schwarzschild[16]. The radius of the event horizon of the black hole is termed the Schwarzschild radius and is given by:

$$r_s = \frac{2GM}{c^2} \qquad (24)$$

Here, G is the universal gravitational constant, and M is the mass enclosed by the event horizon. For a black hole containing one solar mass, the Schwarzschild radius is 2.96 kilometers. For simplicity, we consider here only black holes which have no angular spin momentum and no net charge. Next we intend to address questions such as: «Are black holes really invisible?» and «What roles do they play in the cosmic scheme of things?»

Black holes *suck* and accumulate matter. They are energy sinks. For black holes of moderate mass, up to the equivalent of ten million suns or so, black holes are expected to be surrounded by accretion discs formed from gases, dust and stars that have been disrupted by the strong tidal stresses near the hole. In the presence of strong gravitational gradients, matter spiraling into the black hole is heated to incandescence, thus betraying the presence of the black hole. At first glance, we might expect the tidal stresses (gravitational gradients) at the event horizon to get stronger with increasing mass. But this is not so. Calculations show the gravitational gradients at the event horizon becoming more gentle as the mass of the black hole is increased and its event horizon is correspondingly expanded. For black hole masses above 160 million suns, solar type stars are no longer disrupted at the event horizon before they get swallowed. The radius of such a supermassive black hole is approximately half a billion kilometers, the distance from our sun to the asteroid belt between Mars and Jupiter. Supermassive black holes of more than 200 million solar masses are not expected to have glowing accretion discs.

Observational evidence has been accumulating over the last decade, which strongly suggests that supermassive black holes exist at the centers of most galaxies, gradually gobbling up stars and growing in size. Given enough time, such black holes may eventually devour an entire galaxy of a hundred billion stars. The diameter of such a monster black hole would be about a light-month across. Are supermassive black holes without accretion discs truly out of sight? Far from it. They are not invisible, but highly conspicuous, because they *reflect* the light of every star in the entire universe multiple times into the eye of the observer. To investigate how light is deflected around a black hole, we needs to calculate the orbits of light rays passing through the vicinity of the black hole. The relativistic equation describing light trajectories in the Schwarzschild field outside the event horizon is:

$$\frac{d^2u}{d\varphi^2} = \frac{3\,GM}{c^2}\,u^2 - u \qquad (25)$$

where u = 1/r, and r, φ are the polar coordinates measured from the center of the black hole.

Consider a light ray aimed to miss the center of the black hole by a distance b, if it travelled in a straight line unaffected by the gravitational field of the black hole. The parameter b is known as the *impact parameter* of the trajectory. Orbits with large impact parameters undergo only small deflections and resemble hyperbolic orbits. Orbits coming close to the event horizon, however, do not resemble any of the familiar Keplerian orbits (conic sections). There are no closed stable light orbits. Light rays coming from afar are either captured by the black hole or are hurled around it and flung back out into space. A light ray may wrap around the black hole several times before being ejected back out; but at no point can it come closer than $(3/2)\, r_s$ to the center of the black hole, lest it be captured. The corresponding minimum impact parameter is b = $(3\sqrt{3}/2)\, r_s = 2.598\, r_s$. Let us call this the *impact horizon*.

The total deflection suffered by a light ray can be calculated by numerically integrating the differential Equation (25). The results of such an integration are plotted in Figure 4, which shows the total deflection of a light ray in radians as a function of the impact parameter b. When b is greater than $100\, r_s$, the deflection is less than a degree. When the impact parameter is close to $2.6\, r_s$, the deflection becomes large, and the light ray may orbit many times around the black hole. If the light ray approaches with an impact parameter which is $0.09\, r_s$ larger than the impact horizon, then the light ray is deflected by 180° and is sent back to its source. Figure 5 illustrates a light ray orbit undergoing a 466° deflection.

An observer peering at a black hole sees every luminous object in the sky multiply *reflected* in the black hole halo. There are an infinite number of light trajectories connecting a luminous object with the observer. Two such trajectories emanating from a star are shown by rays 2 and 3 in Figure 6. For each star in the universe, the spectator sees a series of images converging towards the impact horizon on both sides of the black hole. In order to determine how bright these images appear, the gravitational lensing effects on the light wave passing the black hole have to be taken into account.

The gravitational field gradients in the black hole halo cause the light rays to diverge in the radial direction and to converge in the azimuthal direction (parallel to the event horizon). Hence the light passing through the halo is subjected to a highly astigmatic lensing effect. Except when the ray deflections are less than a degree, or when they are near an integral multiple of π (such as 180°, 360°, 540°, etc.), the equivalent focal lengths are rather short and are on the order of the diameter of the event horizon. In most cases, therefore, an observer far from the black hole will find himself looking at a star image in the black hole halo through a diverging lens, so that the brightness of this image is greatly reduced from the apparent brightness of the star itself. But if the observer is at one of the azimuthal line foci, the image seen in the black hole halo may appear many times brighter than the source star itself. Predicting the brightness of a black hole halo for a given situation requires complex computer calculations. The author has performed a thorough study of this optical effect.[17] He is thus qualified to make educated guesses about the appearance of black holes under certain specified circumstances.

Consider a supermassive Schwarzschild black hole of six billion solar masses, located at the center of a lenticular galaxy, populated by a hundred billion stars. A beamship circles the black hole at a safe distance of one light-year. With an orbital velocity of 9,200 km/s, it will take 205 years to circle the black hole. A group of space tourists from planet Earth have arrived in this ship to enjoy a most spectacular sight. The apparent diameter of the black hole (impact diameter) is 3.6 light-days, taking up half a degree in the densely star-studded sky. The apparent size of the black disc is approximately the same as the moon seen from the Earth's surface, and it is surrounded by a brilliant halo. The sight vaguely resembles a total solar eclipse, except that the delicate corona around the eclipsing moon has been replaced by the sparkling star halo surrounding the black hole. The brightness[17] of the halo is equivalent to several thousand zero-magnitude stars. For comparison, typical zero-magnitude stars in our night sky are the bright stars Arcturus, Vega, Capella and Rigel.

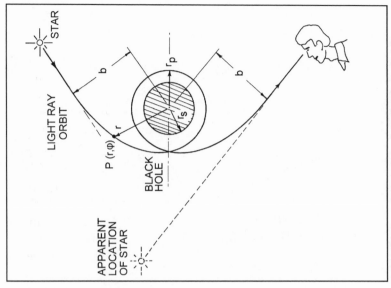

FIGURE 5.   Example of Light Ray Orbit with 466 Degrees Deflection

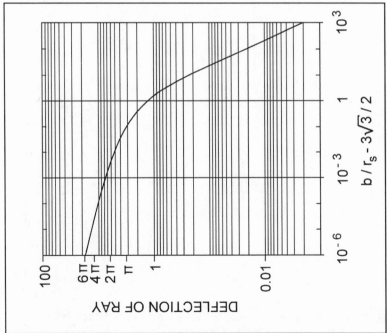

FIGURE 4.   Deflection of Light Ray in Radians as a Function of b

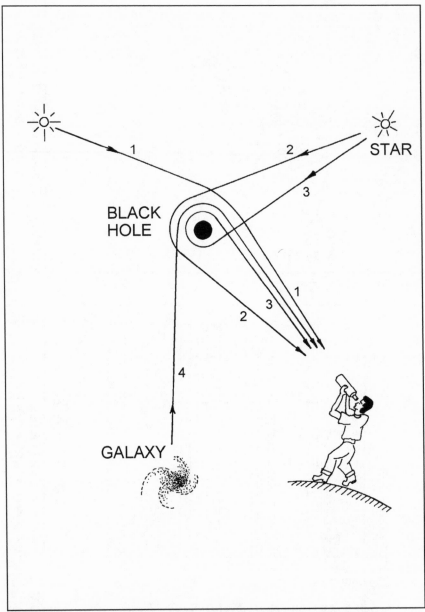

FIGURE 6.   The Whole Universe is Reflected in the Black Hole Halo as Seen by an Observer.

Some time ago, back home, the Hubble space telescope took an intriguing picture of this same central region of the lenticular galaxy NGC7457, located 60 million light-years from Earth. The picture showed an extremely bright galactic nucleus. The telescope's resolution was 0.1 second of arc. Within the unresolved central pinpoint of approximately 8,000 cubic light-years, the observed brightness was believed to indicate a star density of 600 suns per cubic light-year[18]. Calculations show that the halo of a black hole, containing six billion solar masses, could easily produce the appearance of such a bright nucleus. The halo would reflect the light-equivalent of five million stars of that galaxy into the Hubble telescope. If spread out over the unresolved volume of 8,000 cubic light-years, the luminosity would correspond to 600 suns per cubic light-year. If the optical resolution of the telescope could be improved to 0.0001 arc-seconds, then the astronomers would erroneously conclude that the star density at the galactic nucleus is an incredible 600 billion suns per cubic light-year. Such inconceivable emission of optical power is consistent with the alleged enormous energy outflow from the mysterious quasars, quasi-stellar light sources, assumed to be at cosmological distances (billions of light-years away).

A supermassive black hole, swallowing up stars and other matter, gains in mass and grows in size. A star falling into a black hole loses potential energy and gains a corresponding amount of kinetic energy, so that its total energy and its mass do not change. If we could gently lower the star onto the event horizon, the star's mass would diminish to half its original value, owing to its loss of potential energy. This loss in mass would be analogous to the binding energy of a nucleon in the atomic nucleus, discussed previously in Section 5.3.

In the accumulation process associated with a real black hole, matter falls into the event horizon with a high velocity, approaching the speed of light. In general, the infalling matter will have a large preferred tangential velocity component. Hence most, if not all, real cosmic black holes can be expected to have a high angular momentum, as well as a high mass content.

5.7   Galactic Vortices

Spiral galaxies have a central ellipsoidal bulge, surrounded by spiral arms which are confined to a disc-shaped region in the galactic plane. Gases, stars and other debris orbit around the center of mass of the galaxy in near-circular pathways. The laws of celestial mechanics, based on Newtonian physics, can predict the velocities of the stars quite accurately, provided the mass distribution within the galaxy is known (see e.g. Berman[19]). If we assume stars and other galactic matter are uniformly distributed over the visible volume of the galaxy, and if we consider the mass distribution spherically symmetric within the central bulge and having circular symmetry in the flat spiral disc region, we can make the following predictions for the orbital speed of stars:

♦   Within the central bulge, orbital speeds should increase linearly with distance from the center.
♦   Within the visible spiral disc, orbital speeds should increase as the square root of distance from the center.
♦   Beyond the visible disc of the galaxy, assuming near-zero mass density in this region, the orbital speeds of stars should decrease inversely as the square root of distance from the center.

Optical analysis of Doppler frequency shifts in the starlight from a galaxy seen edge-on yields the orbital speed distribution shown in Figure 7.

Within the visible part of the galaxy, the observed velocities are approximately as predicted, showing a linear speed increase in the central bulge and then leveling out in the spiral arms. Two anomalies, however, need explaining. The high, anomalous speed of stars near the center is probably caused by the presence of a supermassive black hole in the galactic nucleus. At distances beyond the visible spiral disc, a few stray stars appear to circle the galaxy at the same speed, regardless of their distance from the galactic center. This contradicts the expected fall-off in speed in the extragalactic region.

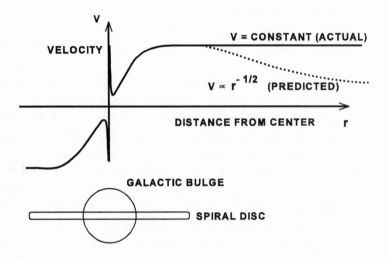

FIGURE 7.   Orbital Velocity Distribution for Stars in Galaxy

We may conclude the following from this observation:

♦   The galactic accumulation disc extends much farther out than the
     visible spiral arms.
♦   Assuming a flat, two-dimensional galactic accumulation disc, the
     mass density in this extended disc falls off inversely with
     distance from the galactic nucleus. (In a spherical geometry, the
     mass density would have to drop off as the inverse square of
     distance from the center to explain the constant orbital
     velocities).

Irrespective of whether we assume a spherical or cylindrical symmetry
for the galactic mass distribution, the density drop-off with distance is
such that successive circular shells of unit thickness contain an equal
amount of mass. This observation is consistent with the following
model of the galactic dynamics:

Stars and other galactic matter swirl around the galactic nucleus in near-
circular pathways. The orbits do not quite close, however, because of

a slow centripetal drift of mass towards the center. The orbits also do not follow the apparent spiral structure of the galactic arms. The visible spiral pattern is created by new star formations, initiated by density waves spreading through the galactic disc.

As the mass in the galactic disc slowly drifts towards the center, angular momentum is not conserved, since orbital velocities do not appear to speed up as the disc contracts. Hence, there must be a momentum transfer mechanism at work via gravitational and magnetic fields, which tends to keep the orbital speeds constant. This phenomenon is not unlike the situation observed in the condensation of stars and the formation of planetary systems, where we also find a glaring deficit of angular momentum in the spinning mass of the central stars. Several theories have been proposed to account for the small angular momentum of stars, such as our sun. Theoretically, momentum can be exchanged through a magnetic coupling between the star plasma and the ionized, swirling protoplanetary matter, speeding up the latter and slowing down the former. Evidently, electric and magnetic processes play an important part on a cosmic scale, even though the macrocosm appears to be dominated by gravitation alone.

The presence of a supermassive black hole in the heart of a galaxy may be considered the driving force, causing galactic material to collect and swirl in towards the center, much like a giant vacuum cleaner sucking up dust. It is analogous to the low-pressure eye of an atmospheric hurricane, which is instrumental in the formation and growth of the giant cyclone. Note that in a hurricane, the clouds also move in circular paths and do not follow the visible spiral arms of cloud formation. Pictures of atmospheric hurricanes taken by satellite cameras are quite similar to astronomical photos of spiral galaxies, making it difficult to distinguish between them. Plates 1 and 2 illustrate this close similarity between the two manifestations. In a hurricane, atmospheric mass drifts towards the low-pressure eye, where it is lifted up into the stratosphere, to be cooled and recirculated into surrounding high-pressure areas. A similar mechanism may be at work in galaxies. Galaxies with active black-hole/quasar cores appear to spew out matter along the magnetic poles of the central dynamo.

PLATE 2.   Whirlpool Galaxy M51
            [Courtesy Palomar/Caltech]

PLATE 1.   Arctic Hurricane of 27 Feb 1987
            [NOAA-9 Satellite Image]

- 129 -

5.8 The Big Bang Myth

On a human scale, and in terms of human units of measurements, the universe is unimaginably vast. Only a few hundred years ago, the farthest places an intrepid traveler could dream about lay in a mysterious far-away land at the ends of the world (meaning Earth). Today our home planet has shrunk to a finite globe, which can be circled by a jet plane in a day and a half or by an orbiting spacecraft in 90 minutes. Men have traveled to the moon, traversing a hostile vacuum space through a distance equivalent to ten world-circling trips each way. But how much more immense is the observable cosmos! To express the distance to the stars and remote galaxies in miles is meaningless, because our mind has difficulties grasping the significance of such large numbers. We can gain a little appreciation of the expanses involved by comparing one immense distance against another and expressing this comparison in ratios of numbers more familiar to us.

The nearest star, our sun, has a volume of 1.3 million Earths and is on average 390 times farther from us than the moon. Our closest stellar neighbor, comparable in size to our sun, is Alpha Centauri, which is 275,000 times more distant than our sun. All visible stars in the night sky, including billions of stars that contribute to the faint glow of the Milky Way, are part of our galaxy. Our Milky Way galaxy is a typical spiral galaxy containing over a hundred billion suns. Its structure is disc shaped with a diameter of 100,000 light-years (ly) and a thickness of 15,000 ly. A light-year is the distance a ray of light travels in one year at a speed of 300,000 kilometers per second. Alpha Centauri is 4.34 ly away from us. Our solar system is approximately 30,000 ly from the galactic center, or 7,000 times the distance to Alpha Centauri.

But our galaxy, our island universe, is not alone. Astronomical telescopes, probing the far reaches of the cosmos, have detected a vast number of other galaxies, distributed more or less evenly in a lace-like pattern over the entire universe. The number of observable galaxies exceeds a hundred billion, each containing approximately a hundred billion suns. Galaxies are separated from each other by millions of light-years. The nearest full-size galaxy is the magnificent

Andromeda Galaxy[20] at 2.2 million ly from us. It has a similar shape, size and structure as our galaxy and has over 300 billion stars. On average, galaxies appear to be spaced about 5 million ly apart, or by fifty times their diameters. However, we see distant galaxies as they were and where they were billions of years ago, because their light took that long to reach us. Hence, in an expanding universe, their present positions would be much farther out, so that the average separation between galaxies may be as much as 15 million ly in the outer regions of the observable universe.

The idea of an expanding universe was spawned to explain observations made by Edwin Hubble in the late 1920s. He had recognized most of the fuzzy *nebulae* as full-fledged galaxies located at enormous distances outside of our own galactic system, and he found from the study of their optical spectra that their emission lines were shifted towards lower frequency (redshift). He interpreted this as a Doppler shift phenomenon. Distant galaxies appeared to be fleeing from us at high velocities. Hubble found their velocities of recession varying in direct proportion to their distance. These observations fitted well into one of Alexander Friedmann's theoretical models[21], describing the evolution of a dynamically expanding universe. In this model, the universe came into being by a single act of creation from a primordial nucleus of extreme energy and density, exploding and expanding to become our universe. The details of his theory were later refined by Georges Lemaître[22], Willem de Sitter[23], George Gamow[24,25] and other cosmologists. Cosmic expansion is now taken as a fact, and the *Big Bang* creation theory is considered the only viable cosmology by the scientific establishment. Cosmologists desperately cling to the Big Bang concept and keep patching it up to incorporate newly discovered observational anomalies.

According to modern cosmological theory, the Big Bang occurred about 15 billion years ago by a gigantic explosion of a superhot, superdense mass of near-infinite energy density. As it expanded, the fireball cooled, particles and atoms formed, gas clouds condensed into stars and galaxies. Galaxies are still rushing outward, carried by the momentum imparted by the Big Bang. They may race on forever, depending on the total mass in the universe. The universal expansion is slowed only by the gravitational pull between galaxies. Most cosmologists believe we live in a universe of critical density; that is it contains just enough mass for the expansion to come to a standstill after an infinite amount of time. In relativity theory, this corresponds to a flat universe of zero curvature in space-time. This condition is modeled by setting the constant Ω (omega) equal to unity in the cosmological equations of Friedmann and de Sitter. Another factor in the equations is the *cosmological constant* Λ (lambda). The latter is usually taken to be zero, meaning no long-range repulsive forces act on the fleeing galaxies.

Number counts of distant galaxies indicate that the universe may indeed be *flat*. But there is a problem. If we take all stars, gaseous nebulae, dust clouds and intergalactic gases which can be observed and inferred, the amount of matter in the universe accounts for only a small fraction of one percent of the matter needed to give the universe its critical density. For several decades, teams of astronomers have scanned the heavens unsuccessfully in search of the missing *dark matter*. Even if we add supermassive black holes, large populations of *brown* dwarf stars, planetary bodies, neutrinos and other stuff, we still fall far short of the expected critical mass density. As we will see, this is not the only problem with the prevalent cosmology.

According to Big Bang theory, the universe first became transparent when it was 300,000 years old and the fireball had cooled to a modest 3,700 $^{\circ}K$. Below this temperature, it became possible for hydrogen atoms to form. This point in time signified the end of the radiation era, heralding the beginning of the stellar era. Previously, most of the energy in the universe was in the form of radiation. Thereafter the cosmos became dominated by the presence of matter. Since then the universe is assumed to have expanded by a scale factor of 1360. The left-over fireball radiation should also have expanded and cooled to approximately 3 $^{\circ}K$. This downgraded radiation would lie in the microwave frequency band and would appear to be coming to us from the edge of the observable universe.

In 1989 the Cosmic Background Explorer (COBE) satellite was launched to investigate the microwave background. Measurements confirmed the existence of a uniform radiation background corresponding to a temperature of 2.7 °K. The detection of this microwave background is now considered the strongest observational evidence in support of the Big Bang cosmology. The COBE data, however, conflicts with expectations in two ways. First, the microwave background is too uniform. It varies only by a thousandth of a percent and cannot explain how the presently observed lumpiness in the distribution of galaxies came into existence. Secondly, the COBE temperature data displays an unequivocal dipole anisotropy[26], believed to be due to the Earth's motion relative to a *comoving* reference space, which follows the general expansion of the universe. This nonconforming motion of the Earth amounts to 370 km/s. Compare this with a speed of 29.8 km/s for Earth in its orbit around the sun, and a speed of 250 km/s for the solar system circumnavigating the galactic center. This type of measurement, however, is strictly forbidden by the basic tenets of Einstein's Theory of Relativity. The measurement of the motion of the Earth relative to a cosmic background is in effect a modern-day MM experiment, but this time with a positive result, and with the background radiation defining a *stationary* ether. The idea of a space that can expand and stretch electromagnetic waves gives space all the attributes of a luminiferous ether. To be consistent then, we should logically conclude that the speed of light changed with the aging of the universe, as space expanded and became more tenuous.

Everywhere the Hubble space telescope looks[27] are millions of distant galaxies with large redshifts in their spectra, implying that they are moving towards the edge of the universe with high velocities. As we look far out into the cosmos, we also look far back into the past. For example, we see many galaxies now because they emitted light at a time when the universe was only one billion years old (according to the big bangers) and one sixth its present size. If the universe is now 15 billion years old, it has taken the light from these objects 14 billion years to reach us. They appear to be 14 billion ly away from us. But this is not where they are now. Using the cosmological equations of the Big Bang model for a universe of critical density ($\Omega = 1$), we can calculate[28] the present speed of recession of a galaxy and its present distance from us. According to this model, a universe with critical density expands at a rate proportional to the 2/3 power of time from the Big Bang. A galaxy which appears to be 14 billion ly from us is now actually 27 billion ly away and is receding from us at 1.19 times the speed of light. When it emitted the light we see, it was 4.4 billion ly away and was speeding away from us at nearly three times the speed of light.

Whoa! You say, I thought no two objects could have relative speeds exceeding the speed of light, c! The spectral Doppler shift of light from the galaxy indeed indicates an apparent speed of recession of less than c, but its actual speed is larger than c. This must be heresy , I hear you say. But modern scientists are trained to accept this kind of double-talk without question. Traditional logic no longer seems to apply, and persons who have not been initiated into the modern cult of physics are left out in the cold. The relativistic cosmologists have saved the day for now by cleverly declaring that velocities due to the cosmic expansion are not real and are different from normal velocities. They no longer refer to the galactic redshifts as *Doppler shifts* but as *cosmological redshifts* resulting from the expansion of space itself.

When the 300,000 year old primeval fireball became transparent, its size was less than one thousandth of our present universe. So why do we not see the redshifted microwave remnants of the fireball *in there* somewhere instead of all around us *out there* at a calculated distance of 44 billion light-years? The reason given is that we have always been well inside this fireball. But then, if the young universe was so much smaller, light from any point in it should have passed by us aeons ago. Yet we are apparently able to *see* back into the early universe by looking out at the edge of the cosmos. This is only possible, if the early universe was already almost infinite in extent and was expanding at many times the speed of light. The presently popular *Inflationary Model* of the Big Bang even proposes that the universe inflated instantaneously from the size of an atom to billions of light-years across in the first one trillionth of a second. Expansion velocities and accelerations had to be near-infinite. If you find this hard to accept, you should agree that not all is well with the Big Bang idea. Many troubling aspects of this hypothesis have come to light:

1   For light to be still reaching us from the early epochs of Creation, distant galaxies had to be receding from us at many times the speed of light. As explained above, this idea causes problems with the Theory of Relativity.

2   The interpretation of Hubble's redshift as a cosmological stretching of space and stretching of light waves also goes against relativistic principles.

3   As explained above, the observed nonsymmetry in the microwave background temperature defines a preferred reference frame, the existence of which is denied by the Special Theory of Relativity.

4   The COBE satellite data shows an extremely smooth microwave background. This is incompatible with the clustering of galaxies observed today.

5   Based on our knowledge of the thermodynamic and nuclear processes in stellar interiors, we believe to have an excellent understanding of stellar evolution. Some stars in our own galactic neighborhood, however, appear to be older than the 12 to 15 billion year old universe.

6   We see galaxies near the edge of the observable universe as they were 14 billion years ago. Yet these galaxies are fully evolved with normal stars ranging in age from 1 to 10 billion years, making these galaxies older than 24 billion years.

7   All heavy elements are manufactured in the hot interior of stars. Small amounts of helium and traces of other light elements could have been formed in the rapidly expanding primordial fireball, that is during the short radiation era lasting a few hundred thousand years. Cosmologists and nuclear physicists allege that the primordial fireball has seeded the early universe with as much as 20% helium. Traces of lithium, beryllium and boron might also have been produced. All other elements with mass numbers above eleven, however, could only have been produced in stellar interiors and in shockwaves associated with supernova explosions. This is at odds with the spectral lines seen in the light emitted by galaxies and quasars at the edge of the observable universe. Protogalaxies and quasars formed when the universe was less than a billion years old already show the unmistakable evidence of heavy elements. Hence, a

high percentage of stars must have lived out their lives and exploded as novae and supernovae already at this early age. Such an assertion is not compatible with our understanding of stellar evolution. Moreover, astronomers have never observed a so-called Population III star, containing no heavy elements, anywhere in the universe. Yet they should be plentiful, because all stars condensing out of the primordial fireball should have been Population III stars. They must all have completed their life span, making the universe much older than 15 billion years.

8   Number density counts of galaxies are compatible with a flat universe. Yet, the critical density required for a flat universe is more than a hundred times the actually observed mass density.

9   The Big Bang theory gives no satisfactory explanation for the apparent absence of antimatter in the universe.

10 New evidence[29] has been reported, which shows the cosmic expansion is accelerating rather than decelerating.

This last point suggests a nonzero cosmological constant, indicative of a cosmological pressure or repulsive force field, which continues to drive the galaxies apart. Such a universe has no need for a Big Bang. It could be much older and could have had a more gradual and less violent beginning.

The cosmic model proposed here is a quasi-steady-state universe, which has not necessarily existed forever, but rather is characterized by a slow evolutionary development. The galactic redshift is taken to indicate a recession of galaxies, driven by a repulsive force, which acts between galaxies but not on the stars within galaxies. As the space between galaxies increases, new hydrogen gas is created there, which condenses into new stars and galaxies, thus keeping the population density of galaxies approximately constant as the universe ages.

This is not a revival of the conventional *Steady State* hypothesis. Simple observation of nature makes it clear, there is no steady state of anything. Everything is seen to be in a state of flux and evolution. We believe in a dynamic universe that evolves but tends to maintain its overall form. There is continuous expansion, but ongoing creation serves to fill in the gaps to preserve the overall aspects of the universe.

We accept Hubble's interpretation of the redshift as a Doppler shift and assume galaxies recede from us with velocities that increase linearly and proportional to their distance. Hubble's proportionality constant is taken as H = 23 km/s per million light-years or H = 2.4 x 10^{-18} per second. We further assume the universe has existed for aeons of time in excess of hundreds of billions of years, perhaps trillions of years. No speculation is made as to how the universe came into being. A violent Big Bang is not needed. Rather, a continuous ongoing process of Creation, consistent with observation, is inferred.

Stellar systems are continuously being born, evolving into brilliant galaxies. Galaxies go through a life cycle lasting 20 to 100 billion years until they blink out, leaving behind supermassive black holes (SBHs), containing typically a hundred billion solar masses. Within each galaxy the dynamics are such that stars continually condense from gases and dust in the galactic disc, shining for periods of 1 to 10 billion years until their nuclear fuel is exhausted. During their relatively short life span, they slowly spiral towards the galactic center (see Sec. 5.7), where their material is eventually swallowed up by a monster SBH, to be recycled back into the universe by processes not understood at this time. Gravitational refraction and reflection of light around these SBHs (see Sec. 5.6), as well as violent plasma jet emissions from these SBHs, may account for the observed characteristics of quasars. According to our theory, quasars may be active SBHs at the centers of galaxies, and they may also be naked SBHs, that is burned-out cinders of extinct galaxies. We thus expect to find quasars at all distances in the cosmos, not just at the edge of the observable universe. This is consistent with spectral data from quasars, which often show the same redshift as nearby galaxies.

To explain the apparent expansion of the cosmos, we assume that SBHs at the galactic centers have a slight electric or magnetic monopole charge. The intergalactic fields from these charged galactic nuclei create the pressure that drives the galaxies apart. Stars within the galaxies are electrically neutral and are not affected by electric or magnetic fields. They remain gravitationally bound within their galaxy in the conventional manner.

Let us now look at the dynamics of this cosmological model. We will not use relativistic formulae in order to avoid unnecessary complexity, and also because we have doubts about the validity of some relativistic concepts. Let us assume a quasi-steady universe, uniformly populated with a number density of n galaxies per unit volume. As the universe expands, new galaxies form to keep n constant with time. Assume further that the universe is spherically symmetric around a center, which can be considered at rest. If the universe is infinite, we pick an arbitrary center to serve as reference point. Consider now a sample galaxy of mass M and inner charge q at a distance r from this reference point (see Figure 8). The sample galaxy is gravitationally attracted to all other galaxies and is electrically or magnetically repelled from all other galaxies. For analyzing the motion of this galaxy, we divide the universe into two regions by drawing a spherical boundary around the reference point, with the sample galaxy lying on the periphery as shown in Figure 8. We then label the volume enclosed by the spherical boundary as Region I, everything outside as Region II.

Because of symmetry and because gravitational and electric forces fall off inversely as the square of distance, we can make the following two simplifications:

♦   The resultant gravitational attraction of the sample galaxy to all galaxies in Region I within the spherical boundary is the same as if all these galaxies were concentrated at the center of the sphere. Similarly, the resultant electric repulsion caused by all galaxies in Region I is the same as if all galactic charges were concentrated at the center. Assuming the electric repulsion dominates over the gravitational attraction, the sample galaxy is subjected to a net force and acceleration directed away from the reference center. At time t, the net repulsive force is assumed to have imparted a velocity $v = dr/dt$ to the sample galaxy.

♦   The cumulative gravitational and electric forces on the sample galaxy due to all galaxies lying in Region II outside of the reference sphere cancel out to zero because of spherical symmetry.

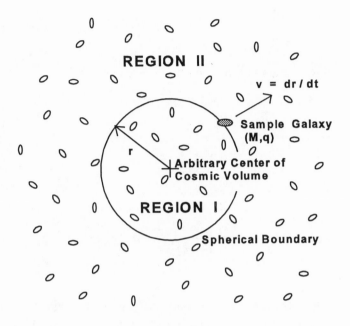

FIGURE 8.   Arbitrary Division of Universe into Regions I and II to Facilitate Analysis

Hence the net electric force on the sample galaxy is:

$$F_E = \frac{q}{4\pi\varepsilon_o r^2}\left[\frac{4}{3}\pi r^3 n q\right] = \frac{n q^2 r}{3\varepsilon_o} \tag{26}$$

The net gravitational force on the sample galaxy is:

$$F_G = -\frac{GM}{r^2}\left[\frac{4}{3}\pi r^3 n M\right] = -\frac{4\pi n G M^2 r}{3} \tag{27}$$

The total force per unit mass on the sample galaxy is then:

$$\frac{F}{M} = \frac{n}{3}\left[\frac{q^2}{\epsilon_o M} - 4\pi G M\right] r \qquad (28)$$

From Newton's second law of motion, we can write

$$\frac{F}{M} = \frac{d\upsilon}{dt} = \upsilon\frac{d\upsilon}{dr} = H^2 r \qquad (29)$$

where

$$H = \sqrt{\frac{n}{3}\left[\frac{q^2}{\epsilon_o M} - 4\pi G M\right]} \qquad (30)$$

Solving differential Equation (29) and applying the boundary condition, that v = 0 when we shrink the arbitrary reference spherical boundary to zero, we find

$$\upsilon = H r \qquad (31)$$

This is Hubble's Law, consistent with observation. The parameters contributing to Hubble's constant are given by Equation (30). Solving this equation for the galactic charge required to account for the observed cosmic expansion, we find:

$$q = \pm\sqrt{M\epsilon_o\left[\frac{3H^2}{n} + 4\pi G M\right]} \qquad (32)$$

Assuming 100 billion galaxies exist within a radius of 15 billion light-years, we derive an average galactic number density of $n = 7 \times 10^{-21}$

galaxies per cubic light-year, or $n = 8.3 \times 10^{-69}$ galaxies per m^3. Then, taking the average mass of a galaxy as $M = 2.4 \times 10^{41}$ kg and Hubble's constant as $H = 2.4 \times 10^{-18}$ s^{-1}, we obtain $q = \pm 7 \times 10^{31}$ coulombs per galaxy, which works out to one elementary charge (one extra proton or electron) for every 3.3×10^{17} (330 million times a billion) atomic mass units in the galaxy. The minimum electric charge necessary to balance gravitation is one elementary charge for every 10^{18} nucleons. We only need such a slight deviation from neutrality because electric repulsion between protons is over 10^{36} times stronger than gravitational attraction between nucleons.

The question arises as to how the SBHs in the galactic nuclei could become electrically charged. First, it is possible that charge may not be conserved in the *infinitely* compressed state of matter in the black hole singularity. Second, charges may become irretrievably separated during the accretion process onto a rapidly spinning SBH in the presence of strong magnetic fields. We only need a very small imbalance in charge, and hence only a minute preference for particles of different charge and mass to be captured. Suppose it is slightly more probable for protons to enter the SBH horizon than for electrons. Then a net positive charge would accumulate inside the event horizon and a net negative charge outside. It has been argued by astrophysicists[30] that a black hole's event horizon acts like an electrically conducting membrane with a resistivity of 377 ohms (or with unit impedance in the symmetric system of measurements - see Section 5.5). Perhaps the conductive event horizon shields the internal charge from outside view, so that from the outside the SBH appears to be negatively charged. In the laboratory, we know how to shield electric or magnetic fields, but we do not know any way of shielding gravitational fields. Evidently, charge can be concealed but energy cannot.

In summary, our cosmology avoids many of the inconsistencies that plague the Big Bang hypothesis. We do not need to search for large amounts of dark matter to make the universe flat. We do not have to invent unproven mechanisms to explain the initial phases of Creation, and we have no conflict with observational evidence.

GODS AND CREATION

«It happened then, as the most ungodly word
ever was uttered by a god himself,
— his proclamation:
"There is but one God! Thou shalt have
no other gods beside me!"
— a grim-bearded god, a jealous one,
who thus forgot himself —
And all the gods laughed and howled,
and tottered on their chairs, shouting:
"Is not the very essence of godhood
that there be gods and no God?"
If you have ears, listen — »
[Friedrich Nietzsche, 1844-1900;
translated from *Also sprach Zarathustra*[1]]

Many human societies have a belief in spirit forms dominating the physical and the *unseen* worlds. Primitive, tribal stone-age groups, who were dependent on the vagaries of nature, believed in nature spirits controlling their lives and destiny. Hence, it was important to live in harmony with nature, a concept we should still honor today. Culturally advanced societies established formal religious rites to honor and appease human-like gods, who were in charge of cosmic events and of human existence. These superhuman beings were both natural and supernatural, material and spiritual. The gods of the Maya, the Inca, the Aztecs, the Egyptians, the Babylonians, the Greek, the Romans, the Hindus, the Vikings, the Teutons, the African and Polynesian Societies and so on, were all real flesh and blood figures, but with superhuman powers. They lived separate from human society, but could enforce their desires upon humanity at will. Many of these gods were said to defy gravity. They were able to travel through the sky and live among the stars of the heavens. Many appeared to have access to highly advanced technology. Thor and Zeus threw lightning bolts (laser and particle beams). Others travelled in disc-shaped *vimanas*, as described in the Drona Parva [ancient Sanskrit text], in rocket-propelled thunderbirds [American Indian legends], or on fiery wheels as told by the prophet Ezekiel [Ezekiel 1: 4-28].

Because references to highly advanced human-like gods, coming here from the stars, are so numerous in ancient scriptures and folklore, we must give serious credence to Erich von Däniken[2,3,4], who claims our gods are extraterrestrial space beings. Many books, citing additional supporting evidence for this theory, have recently been written on the same subject, particularly in association with the UFO enigma. Most bookstores have recently set aside a special section for this topic.

Human contact with creatures and gods from other worlds is a recurring theme in religious scriptures and in the folklore and legends of almost all societies. Any reasonable person would concede that these people based their belief system on actually observed experiences. Physical contact with advanced extraterrestrial beings was evidently commonplace then. Frequent themes in ancient mythologies are:

♦   Earth is being visited by many god-like beings, who are spiritually and technologically superior to humans.

♦   Their abode is in the heavens. In many instances their origins are specified exactly. Stellar regions of origin commonly named are the Pleiades star cluster, the constellation Canis Major dominated by the *dog star* Sirius, the belt region of the constellation Orion and the constellation Lyra dominated by the bright star Vega. Planets of our own solar system, the mysterious *wandering stars*, have usually not been considered the home of gods. This is consistent with present-day knowledge of unfavorable living conditions on the surfaces of the planets in our backyard. None of our planets has been found suitable for the evolution of higher life forms. Our planets may, however, harbor space colonies, in which a life-supporting environment is artificially maintained. The ancient cultures somehow knew that the gods must have come from outside our solar system. This recognition could not have been logically deduced in a non-technical society, but must have been obtained through direct communication with the gods.

♦   The gods have human emotions and desires, such as jealousy, greed, ambition and lust for power and sex.

♦   The gods procreated the human races *in their image.* Conversely, if there were no real flesh and blood gods interacting with humanity, and if the human mind invented the gods, then the gods were created in our image. This latter point of view, however, ignores the evidence.

♦   The gods conducted warfare in the heavens, fighting for control over Earth.

The major deity in a typical polytheistic belief system might also have been credited with creating *the world*, a term applied to a portion of the Earth's topography then known to society. Seldom was such a personal god credited for creating the entire universe. Rather, the gods were thought to inhabit an already existing universe. The confusion of the eternal, infinite, all-powerful, supreme power of Creation with a personal *God* appears to be a relatively recent development and is confined to the so-called monotheistic religions: Judaism, Christianity and Islam. Strangely enough, when scrutinizing the sacred scriptures of these *monotheistic* world religions, we find ample evidence of many gods with ungodly traits. The principal deity, who has been given human attributes, has often been erroneously elevated to be the omnipotent Creator of the Universe. Yet, at the same time, he shares the heavens with a gathering of lesser gods and hordes of angels and other powerful spirits.

Let us take, for example, the God of the Torah and the Old Testament, who purportedly is the only deity recognized by the Jewish and Christian faiths. The biblical God of the Hebrews, who came from the heavens, was prone to jealousy [Exodus 20:5] and anger fits, typical human qualities, not befitting the omnipotent Creator. His name was YHWH, pronounced Yahweh or Jehovah. The Moslems later called him Allah. He was considered the procreator of several white human races. He demanded adoration, submissiveness and the sacrificial killing of animals [Leviticus 1,2,3]. On at least one occasion, he demanded the sacrificial slaughter of a person's child as proof of loyalty [Genesis 22:2-12]. He promoted the concept of vindictiveness by demanding *an eye for an eye*, and he endorsed bloody warfare against women and children. In the first book of Samuel [15:3], the Lord commanded Saul to «smite the Amalek and ... slay both man and woman, infant and suckling.» In Numbers 31, he exhorted Moses to rout the Midianites. In the ensuing battle, he approved of Moses telling his warriors to «kill every male among the little ones and kill every woman who has lain with a man, ...» [Verse 17], and he condoned the rape of 32,000 virgins captured as booty [Verse 35]. Thus, YHWH took quite a personal interest in human squabbles to smite and dishonor the enemies of his *chosen people*. He demanded to be obeyed, honored, loved and feared [see, for example, Genesis 22:12], not recognizing that love and fear are mutually irreconcilable. This behavior stands in stark contrast with the loving and forgiving *father* figure venerated by the Christian Church. Yet Christians insist their God is identical with the Hebrew god YHWH.

Considering the complete scenario portrayed in the Torah and the Old Testament, we must put YHWH into the same category with the ancient gods of India, Persia, Egypt, Greece, Rome, Northern Europe and Central America. That he was (is) not the sole omnipotent Creator of the Universe is evident from the wording in the scriptures. For example, he commanded Moses and his tribe that, «You shall have no other gods beside me, ... for I the Lord, your God am a jealous god» [Exodus 20:2-5]. This is an admission of the existence of other gods of comparable stature and power as YHWH. Many gods were also involved in the procreation of modern Earth humans: «... when the sons of *God* came in unto the daughters of men, and they bare children to them, the same became mighty men» [Genesis 6:4]. Note the expression, *sons of God*, indicative of YHWH having had many sons. This is in direct conflict with the New Testament statement, «God so

loved the world, that He gave His only begotten son, ... » [John 3:16].
Another reference to many gods is in Genesis 1:26, where we read:
«Let *us* make man in *our* image, after *our* likeness.» The biblical
scriptures also describe warfare in the heavens between gods, as the
Archangel Michael defeats the Bringer of Light, Lucifer [Isaiah 14:12;
Revelations 12:7-8]. Yes, YHWH was a powerful god, and he or his
successor may still hold dominion over planet Earth, but he is not the
omnipotent, eternal Power of Creation. Rather, he is part of Creation
and one of its many manifestations.

The omniverse (all that exists) cannot have been created by a person
or personal god, since a person cannot exist outside of the omniverse;
he/she has to be a part of it. A personal *creator god* can only exist
within space and time. Space and time are part of the energy structure
of this omniverse and were not present outside or before Creation.
Hence, the infrastructure must already have existed before the gods
came into being. Gods are second-generation, spiritual/material
entities, themselves created from the infinite spiritual energy of
Creation. Even though a *creator god* could not have created the
omniverse, he could well have aided in the creation of a sun, a planet,
the mountains and oceans on the planet. He could well have seeded
the planet with life, and he could have guided the evolution of life and
of human forms on the planet we call Earth.

Creation, however, is the conscious, living spiritual energy that
pervades every part of the cosmos. It is infinite, as it creates all space
in the first place. It is eternal, because it creates time, rather than
being subject to time. It is manifest in every star, galaxy and in every
subatomic particle. It is all-powerful, because it drives all processes
throughout the omniverse. It is all-knowing, because it is the source
of all knowledge and wisdom and is intimately connected with all
intelligent and thinking beings. It is alive, because it is the total of all
living entities in the omniverse. Creation created the omniverse out
of itself and keeps guiding it, constantly evolving towards greater
consciousness. Creation is the spiritual source of life-energy and
knowledge which rule all things. It is timeless, yet it contains all time.
It is ever present in the smallest and the largest manifestations of
existence. It can appear in any form, because it creates all form. It is

neither masculine nor feminine, but both. It is itself impersonal, yet all personal life forms, including animals, humans and gods, are representations of it. It rules the omniverse, including all conscious life, through its natural laws. Chinese Taoists strove to live in harmony with nature to achieve spiritual peace and enlightenment. This is not just a good idea. It is essential, because nature is where all life and consciousness resides. Those who think they can disconnect themselves from nature and Creation are choosing death, physically and spiritually.

When saying Creation is manifesting everything in the omniverse out of itself, we may be accused of subscribing to pantheism. But our spiritual perception about the truth of Creation is much more than pantheism. We also recognize the existence of gods within the grand scheme of Creation, but we do not equate any personal god with Creation. For this belief, we may be accused of polytheism. But our understanding of the multifold spiritual expressions of Creation is much more than polytheism. We also believe in only one omnipotent power of Creation, which is the source of everything. For this we may be accused of monotheism. As we see, none of the philosophical *theisms* are adequate for describing the real world. They are but descriptive labels without real meaning.

All living beings are endowed with the spirit of Creation, including gods and humans, who are but spiritual emanations of the all-soul of Creation. The idea of a universal *All-Soul* made up of all human spirits and other forms of consciousness, has already been expressed by early Hindu philosophers in the Brahmanas and the Upanishads over 2,600 years ago. They called this the Brahman-Atman principle. In later Hinduism, the triad of the great gods, Brahma, Vishnu and Shiva, was believed to consist of different incarnations (avatara), or separate physical expressions, of the Brahman-Atman All-Soul[5].

The omnipotent Creation Spirit does not need to be appeased by blood-sacrifices, nor does it need to be flattered by worship, nor does it need personal servants. According to the Old Testament, a face-to-face, personal intimacy existed between the god YHWH and his servant Moses [Deuteronomy 34:5; Exodus 33:20]. Similarly, the prophet Elijah served his god YHWH on a personal level [I Kings 18:36]. How the early Christian church fathers could take the god of the Old Testament and equate him with the infinitely greater power of Creation is difficult to understand.

As an even greater affront to credibility, the Christian Church found it advantageous to concoct a Holy Trinity to represent the sole, Omnipotent Power that created and rules all there is. The Trinity is thought to consist of the personal father-god YHWH, the Holy Ghost and Jesus the Christ. Jesus is the Greek translation of Y'shua, the New Testament prophet raised by Joseph, who acted as his Earthly father. *Y'shua bar Joseph* was also known by his given name Jmmanuel (Emmanuel), as had been predicted by the earlier prophet Isaiah [Isaiah 7:14; Matthew 1:13]. The designation of Y'shua (or Jmmanuel) as the Christ (Greek word for Redeemer) is almost certainly an idea edited into the scriptures by the compilers of the Gospels, who were greatly influenced by Paul's views on Christology[6]. We find no credible evidence in the scriptures for Jmmanuel having considered himself the *Redeemer*, or even the *Messiah*.

The Holy Ghost was invented by the framers of the Gospels and by the early church fathers to explain how the personal, physical god YHWH could wield such far-reaching power as to create the universe. And they needed the Holy Ghost to account for the immaculate impregnation of Maria, the virgin. With today's technology and scientific knowledge, we could easily effect a nonsexual conception through artificial insemination, gene splicing, cloning and the like. In the end, it is irrelevant to the mission of Jmmanuel and his words of wisdom, whether he was conceived naturally or otherwise. The process of natural conception is a greater miracle than conception by any other means and would not detract one iota from the greatness of the man, whom most of us admire as *Jesus*.

There is no specific reference to a Trinity in either the Old or New Testaments. For the *Unchangeable, All-Powerful God* to suddenly turn himself into a Trinity with the birth of Jmmanuel makes no sense. Jehovah's Witnesses, who make it their business to take every word in the biblical scriptures at face value, emphatically reject the concept of a Trinity. The Unitarian Universalist Church also rejects the Trinity, maintaining that, «*God* is not three persons in one, neither is he three separate persons. *God's* presence is manifest by his own Spirit, not by another being such as the Holy Ghost.» And according to Unitarian doctrine, it is sacrilegious to equate the enlightened prophet Jmmanuel (Jesus) with *God, the Almighty.*

Religious or spiritual truth has to be absolute and should be universal for all people. Christians, Moslems, Buddhists, or any other group do not have a monopoly on the truth. Since they all profess to different spiritual *truths*, they are most likely all deluded. And all truth must be compatible with observation and experience. The biblical texts are at odds with the spiritual *truths* expounded by other religions, and they are at odds with the physical world views of modern science. The disagreements go much deeper than the perpetual debates about biblical Creation versus Darwinian Evolution. We may argue at length whether the universe is 6,000 years or trillions of years old; whether the Earth is flat, whether it is at the center of the universe, whether it was created in a single act, or whether Creation is a continuing process. What we should be more concerned with are the basic questions important for our spiritual and physical well-being: «Who is in charge of planet Earth? Does spirit evolve? Is reincarnation a fact of life? What is my mission in this life? What do I need to learn here? ...»

We can send people to the moon. We can build satellite communication systems. We can build nuclear devices and can destroy Earth, if we choose. Yet our science and research communities have nothing to say about where we go after death, or where our consciousness was focused before birth. Our modern science establishment denies even the existence of spirit. There are no Federal Commissions or State Departments of Spiritual Science. Ancient civilizations were significantly more advanced in this area.

Modern Western societies are spiritually impoverished. Christianity, as we know it from Church doctrine, has little to offer, neither does Islam or Judaism. Their priests are still trying to sell us resurrection of the body and a heaven filled with harp-playing angels. And for sinners of the flesh and those who do not comply with their dogma, they have a fiery hell populated by horny devils with pitchforks, ready to torture the transgressors with physical pain till the end of time. Because of this intellectual and spiritual dearth in their doctrines, the organized religions offer little opportunity for real spiritual growth.

People who search for truth and spiritual guidance are all too eager to follow anyone who promises to provide them with a spiritual anchor point. Many New Thought groups have arisen, who try to fill this spiritual vacuum with positive values. But just as many New Age charlatans, swindlers and just plain deluded characters are eager to take advantage of the situation and profit from the craze. And then we have the dark, sinister side, exemplified by charismatic, egocentric cult leaders, who lure their followers into disaster and death. Death cults, whose tragic finales gained worldwide attention, have become all too commonplace in recent memory: The People's Temple of Jim Jones, who committed mass suicide with his congregation in Guayana in 1978; the Solar Temple of Luc Jouret, whose members took their own lives in Switzerland and Canada in 1994; the Heaven's Gate followers of Marshall Applewhite who left their Earthly containers in California in 1997, so as to *graduate to an advanced spiritual level.*

The storming and destruction of the Branch Davidian church and compound by U.S. Government agents in Texas in 1993 is a different story. Not all the Branch Davidians, who died in the conflagration, laid down their lives willingly. Army tanks and heavily armed helicopter gunships waged war against women and children. Military power won. Maintaining that U.S. Attorney General Janet Reno was not responsible for the wanton killing of this religious sect is like saying that Hitler was not responsible for the killing of European Jews. After all, they chose not to save their own lives. If only the Branch Davidians had been willing to leave their homestead, denounce their faith, co-operate with Government police, betray their brothers and sisters, let themselves be imprisoned on drummed-up charges and let themselves be deported to a foreign country, they would have been saved.

It was not the first time the U.S. Government had tried this approach. The country, which prides itself for its freedom of speech and religious tolerance, has traditionally stepped in when a religious group was on the verge of becoming too independent and economically powerful. A case in point was the peaceful Oregon community of Rajneeshpuram, founded by Osho, who was then known as the Bhagwan Shree Rajneesh. The highly successful, ecological farming commune grew to a city of over 5,000 permanent residents and up to 10,000 visiting *Sannyasins*, who shared the work and communal life. In 1984, Osho was arrested on charges of alleged immigration fraud and racketeering. While in prison, he was purportedly poisoned, and was then deported to India with some of his followers in 1985. By 1986, nearly all residents of Rajneeshpuram had been evicted or forced from their homes by the U.S. Government through heavy taxation and persecution — but enough of that.

Our discussion has been unwittingly diverted into the political arena, which dominates modern life. Let us return to the subject of gods and Creation, and let us refocus on the grand scheme of things. We have a living, spiritual omniverse. The all-powerful Spirit of Creation is the prime cause and is continually unfolding into new patterns of form. It is dividing itself into separately evolving spirit forms, which we call living beings. The purpose and goal of this evolving omniverse is for the Supreme Spirit to raise its level of consciousness and to expand its experience. Growing consciousness expresses itself in the evolution of higher life forms. Their raised level of consciousness contributes to the growth of the Creation Spirit. All that the individual spirits experience, the Creation Spirit also experiences. As the runner in the movie *Chariots of Fire* expressed it, «The Almighty enjoys running (or any other experience) by means of me.»

Individual spirit forms exist at many levels. We may group these into evolutionary categories, such as *plants, animals, humans, gods*, although the dividing lines are not sharp. This makes the distinction between animals and humans, or between humans and gods, for example, somewhat arbitrary. Within each of these groups, we find a hierarchy of different beings; so also among the gods. Gods at the higher evolutionary levels are able to wield enormous physical and spiritual power, and they may have been entrusted by Creation with assisting in the evolution of life and consciousness throughout entire stellar regions. These are the ones worshipped by Earth humans as their creator gods.

They may seed planets with life and may periodically accelerate the development of higher life forms on these planets. The lesser gods and the more highly evolved humanoid races may also aid in this noble task. The activities of the latter probably account for many UFO phenomena and for the superhuman beings described in ancient folklore. We should be forewarned, however, that some of these beings may have selfish interests and may not be here for our welfare.

On Earth, the gods came and created humankind in their image by donating their genetic material and by genetic engineering of the indigenous prehuman species.   Many mysterious gaps in our anthropological, archaeological and historical records can easily be explained, if extraterrestrial gods have been interfering with human evolution and history. We can find ample evidence for human evolution having been mysteriously accelerated on several occasions. For example, Cro-Magnon Man, who appeared suddenly 35,000 years ago could easily have been such an extraterrestrial implant. The indigenous Neanderthal Man had a small brain, made only primitive stone tools and displayed no artistic talents. Then arrived the Cro-Magnon race with skulls and brains as large as those of modern humans. They created highly artistic, polychromatic paintings on cave walls (and probably elsewhere), which can put most modern art to shame. They arrived with a ready-made, sophisticated toolmaking technology, allowing them to manufacture spears, bows and arrows, bone knives and sewing needles.

Other aspects of the human biology and psyche also support the idea of modern humanity having roots in the cosmos, in addition to its obvious terrestrial evolutionary connections.   One such evidence comes from recent research into the structure and functioning of the human brain. Underlying our thinking, rational brain are several more primitive animal brain structures.   These are physically separate brains, which testify to our reptilian and mammalian roots in Earth's evolutionary chain. Our *sensorimotor* brain consists of the spinal cord and the brain stem and is almost identical to the ancient brains of Triassic and Jurassic reptiles. Modern reptiles and mammals have developed additional structures in the midbrain region, including the cerebellum, a separate brain believed to control movement and balance. With increasing complexity in the evolutionary family tree, mammals also developed a distinct forebrain, the cerebrum, which then took over most of the behavioral functions. Human brains also have all these sub-brains, evolved over the last 300 million years or so. What makes the human brain different from the neurological systems of lower animals is the neocortex, an intricate outer layer surrounding the cerebrum, which gives us the power of rational thought.

The human cortex contains tens of billions of neurons, each one interconnected with up to a thousand other neurons. The total number of neural interconnections tally in the tens of trillions. The extraordinarily complex neocortex with its interconnections takes up more than eighty percent of the mass of the human brain, yet is supposed to have evolved in just a few million years. This accelerated evolution of human intelligence is severely out of line, when compared with the slow evolution of the primitive brain structures, which took half a billion years to develop. We may suspect the human species to be much older than the three or four million years quoted by anthropologists. The mystery goes away, if we assume that many of our human traits were implanted from an extraterrestrial gene pool.

If you think the theory of an ET origin of humanity is an unwarranted inference, consider this: Neurobiologists have determined that the adult human brain utilizes only five percent of its thinking capacity. In other words, we have twenty times more neural connectors than are needed by even the most intellectually active human. Moreover, by age six, the brain of a child has five times more neural connections and a five times higher learning capacity than the adult brain. By age twelve, however, eighty percent of this brain mass dissolves,[7] because it remains unstimulated and thus excessive. Hence, a child has a brain that is a hundred times more sophisticated than required for human life on Earth. Darwinian evolution cannot account for this. No competitive advantage, no natural selection is at work to evolve a brain that is a hundred times more powerful than we can utilize. Only one logical deduction can be drawn: Some of our forebears had a higher intelligence and lived in a more sophisticated society than we. We have inherited a complex, anachronistic brain structure, which is inexplicably advanced beyond our biological, sociological and spiritual stage of development. Again, extraterrestrial meddling with Earth human's evolution could easily explain this anachronism.

But why would the gods be interested in creating higher life forms on Earth? The answer lies in the spiritual nature and purpose of the evolving omniverse. Human life forms can only grow in wisdom and evolve in consciousness through the material life's experiences. Hence, spirits need to incarnate in material bodies in order to evolve. Evidently, planet Earth has been carefully nurtured for many millions of years to produce the biological infrastructure necessary for supporting human life. Human life needs the ecologically balanced, self-sustaining multiplicity of plants and animals. They are our natural support system, both materially and spiritually. Extraterrestrial, god-like humans have made a major investment in planet Earth and do not want to see it destroyed through the greed of Earth humans. This may explain the recent rash of extraterrestrial visitors observing human activity and warning contactees of dire consequences, if Earth humans do not change their destructive ways. Billions of planets may have formed in the Galaxy, many of them inhabitable; but Earth is very precious for the local spirits who call it their home. The destruction of the fauna and flora on Earth would leave billions of spirits without a chance for a material life for thousands, or perhaps millions of years.

Yet, the gods may still have another reason for hanging around the vicinity of planet Earth, both benevolent and sinister in nature. Gods in the upper echelons of development are highly advanced spiritual entities and may be able to experience life without the need for a material vehicle. Although they would have sufficient power and knowledge to materialize in any form they wish to suit the occasion. Their spiritual life's functions may be sustained by telepathic communication of thoughts and emotions (see previous Chapter entitled *Life is Communication*). Human emotions are naturally communicated much more easily than words, thoughts and ideas. The possibility of gods feasting on a diet of human emotions may not be such an absurd concept as it appears at first glance. The concept has been explored further by Alan Watts[8] in his book *UFO Visitation*. The subject has also been extensively discussed in the alleged teachings from the Pleiades, channeled through Barbara Marciniak and published in her book, *Bringers of the Dawn*[9].

Our strongest emotions are love and fear, but other emotions such as anger, joy and sadness are also continuously broadcast by our spirit-mind (see Figure 1). The benevolent gods, including our creator gods, are nourished by our emanations of love, which also feeds the Spirit of Creation. The resulting expansion of consciousness in the omniverse then filters back to all living entities for their well-being. Some of the more sinister gods (demons, devils, Satan, perhaps the *Grays* of UFO abduction lore) feed on our more negative emotions of fear, anger and sadness. These entities have a vested interest in destroying harmony and in keeping the turmoil going by instigating drama, conflict, war, greed and envy in human affairs. Looking at the sad state of our social interactions on Earth, we may conclude that these malevolent gods are in control of Earth's politics and its religious institutions, working behind the scenes to keep conflict alive. The sacrificial slaughter of animals and humans to appease the gods, falls into the same category. The sun and war god, Tezcatlipoco, of the Toltecs and Aztecs, for example, was offered the beating hearts torn out of the chests of sacrificial victims. The human life force was believed to be his favorite food [10,11].

SPIRITVAL EVOLVTION
AND REINCARNATION

«At the end of the way
The master finds freedom
From desire and sorrow,
— Freedom without bounds.

...

He has come to the end of the way
Over the rivers of many lives,
His many deaths.
— And now he is one.»
[Siddharta Gautama, 563-483 BC;
translated from the *Dhammapada*[1]]

Reincarnation, also known as *transmigration of souls* and as *re-embodiment*, has been a fact of existence in Eastern philosophy and religion for many millennia. Reincarnation and the *law of karma* are central to the belief systems of the Hindu, the Buddhists, the Jains and the Sikhs. The belief is based on the conviction that the essence of a person is his spirit, or his soul, which is indestructible; that all living beings are manifestations of the same spiritual essence. As an individual soul passes through cycles of birth and death, it may return many times in human or animal form. What a person does in one life will determine his or her fate in the next, and so on. Such is the doctrine of karma, the spiritual law of cause and effect. The goal of the individual spirit (*atman*) is to perfect itself through many life cycles, until it becomes indistinguishable from the Universal Creation Spirit (*Brahman*) and merges with It.

Many classic Greek philosophers also believed in reincarnation. But Western thought on this subject was subsequently influenced strongly by the triad of world religions originating in the Mideast: Judaism, Christianity and Islam, respectively built upon the teachings of the prophets Moses, Jesus and Muhammad. Official doctrines developed within these religious movements have turned away from reincarnation in favor of *resurrection*, a conditional one-time revival of a person's spiritual and physical existence. We must reasonably doubt, however, whether the unadulterated teachings of the religious founders and prophets actually attested to such a viewpoint.

The belief in reincarnation was newly introduced into European and North American philosophy during the idealistic countermovements of the 18th and 19th Centuries, in reaction to the *Age of Reason* of 17th Century Europe. The Romanticist and Transcendentalist poets and philosophers of that period discovered a renewed interest in Eastern philosophy and religion. Eastern thought also found its way into the Rosicrucian society and the Freemasonic Lodges, which had a profound influence on the founding of the United States of America. During the 19th Century, the Russian spiritualist Madame Blavatsky [1831-1891] founded the *Theosophical Society*, based on the teachings of the Egyptian Neo-Platonist and mystic Plotinus [205-270]. The Theosophical doctrine accepts karma and reincarnation as natural processes, which further the evolution of the spirit. Each spirit progresses along its own path at its own pace, putting each person at a distinctly different level of spiritual growth. In modern American thought, such an idea meets with a great deal of resistance. The concept runs counter to the American ideal that *all men* (and women) *are created* (born) *equal*. Similarly, the idea of a child destined to live a hard life to atone for a transgression in a previous life is hard to accept by a Christian. The law of karma makes a mockery out of the *forgiveness of sins through the grace of God*. Today, many New Age groups have incorporated reincarnation and karma into their belief systems, while avoiding the negative Buddhist interpretation of the burdensome *wheel of rebirth and death*. Many New Agers believe a person's karmic debt can be overcome and transcended in a single lifetime.

Has Jmmanuel, alias Jesus, taught reincarnation? We can expect the Christian churches to deny such an assertion. Yet the original biblical scriptures probably contained many references to re-embodiment.[2,3,4] The editors and compilers of the gospels were strongly inspired by the views of Paul,[5] however, who was obsessed with making the historical figure of Jmmanuel into Jesus, the Christ, the redeemer of humankind. And so, almost all references to reincarnation may have been redacted out of the scriptures.   After all, the concepts of karma and reincarnation were incompatible with the convictions of Paul and later church authorities. According to church doctrine, an erring soul could only be saved by the grace of God through the intervention of Christ, the Savior.   The law of karma, on the other hand, puts the responsibility on the individual to correct his or her own erring ways. Through rebirth in a new body, the spirit gains the physical opportunity to learn and redeem itself, to extinguish any karmic debts incurred in a previous life.   Divine grace and forgiveness are comforting, but are not needed for the spirit on its evolutionary path to perfection.

Even though the topic of reincarnation may have been carefully edited out of the Proto-Matthew and the Proto-Mark texts, the New Testament still contains clues[2] to a belief in reincarnation. In Matthew 11:14 Jesus says to the multitudes: «And if you are willing to accept it, (John the Baptist) is Elijah, who was to come (again).» In Matthew 16:13-15 Jesus asks his disciples who the people say he is. They respond: «Some say you are John the Baptist, some Elijah; others, Jeremiah or one of the other prophets.» Evidently, the people believed that prophets, and others with a mission, could after their death be reborn into a new physical body to complete their objective.

Other, non-biblical texts written at the time of Jesus, or shortly thereafter, also contain references to reincarnation. One such ancient text, written in Aramaic, was allegedly found in 1963 in a tomb near Jerusalem. It largely parallels the gospel of Matthew, but affords a better insight into the teachings of Jmmanuel (Jesus) and portrays the character of the prophet in a different light (see Chapter 8). James Deardorff,[2] after studying it for six years, has come to the conclusion that the controversial document is most likely an unedited Proto-

Matthew. The ancient chronicle has become known as the Talmud of Jmmanuel. In it, Jmmanuel freely discusses the fine points of spiritual evolution and reincarnation.

Evidence of the belief in reincarnation can also be found in the Old Testament. In the early third century, the Christian theologian Origen[6] [185-254] had already pointed out the strange case of Jacob and Esau, of whom God (JHWH) said, «Jacob have I loved, but Esau have I hated,» before they were even born.[7] Origen, who was a firm believer in reincarnation, thought JHWH must have referred to deeds in prior existences of Jacob and Esau. Alternatively, JHWH could be accused of bigotry. Such a view, however, would be considered blasphemy by the church and would be judged unacceptable.

But, if we are seriously looking for confirmation of re-embodiment, we do not have to rely on ancient philosophy alone. In today's society, the idea of reincarnation is no longer considered a strange oriental misbelief. Thanks to many *new thought* movements, more and more independently thinking Westerners are willing to accept reincarnation as fact, and for good reasons. Every so often, we read or hear of accounts, in which people recall events from a prior existence. In some cases, these memories were brought to light through hypnotic regression into past lives, a technique popularized by America's *sleeping prophet*, Edgar Cayce[8] [1877-1945]. We justifiably eye past life memories recalled by adults with suspicion, since delusion, wishful thinking and people's tendency to make themselves important cannot easily be sifted out from the real thing. The situation is different, however, when young children under the age of four have knowledge, wisdom, memories and unusual abilities that they could not possibly have learned or invented in their short lifetime. Child prodigies fall into this category. When a three-year old plays beautiful tunes on a piano without having been musically trained, this person probably acquired the knowledge and ability through a real prenatal experience. I have personally observed such unusual and inexplicable behavior in one of my sons. When he was two years old, he was able to eat gracefully with a knife and a fork in perfect conformance with Central European etiquette. By age three and a half, he lost this ability and began to hold his spoon or fork clumsily in his fist, like most other youngsters.

Accounts from all over the world have been and continue to be reported, wherein children remember specific details of their previous lives. They remember their former parents, their siblings and where they have lived. They have knowledge of closely kept family secrets, of hidden treasure, and so on. Many of these memories have been corroborated with actual people, living and deceased, with actual buildings and places, and with historical events. Such physical and circumstantial evidence for reincarnation has not gone unnoticed by Western psychologists,[9] who have investigated this phenomenon and have presented their positive conclusions in the scientific literature.

But reincarnation only makes sense if we believe in the independent existence of the spirit or soul, the true self; not the false self, which is the ego created by our erroneous identification with the body and the material mind (see Chapter 4). When I was young, I mentally struggled to find proof for the existence of an independent soul. Oddly enough, what eventually convinced me of its reality were its delimitations. My arguments went somewhat like this: «I am aware of being conscious. My consciousness is uniquely associated with my self, my being, which includes my body, my brain and my thinking mind. If my consciousness were just a byproduct of my brain activities, then there should be nothing unique about it. Another person with essentially the same brain would have a consciousness indistinguishable from mine. Hence, I should be able to refocus my consciousness so as to view the world through his eyes and live his life. This possibility does not seem to exist, except in rare cases of possession. Therefore, my unique consciousness must be independent of any brain functioning.» Through introspection and analysis of my experiences, I later learned to make a clear distinction between mind and spirit. I recognized my conscious self as the essence of my being and as my independent spirit. I found my spirit to be uniquely individual, but mysteriously connected to conscious life around me.

A person's spirit is larger and wiser than the mind and body. We do not know how or when anybody's spirit was created, only that it is imperishable and that it will exist for all time. Our existence would be without meaning, if it were confined to a short period of time and to a mortal body. The idea of our consciousness lighting up only once, as we pass through Earthly life before entering *oblivion*, makes no sense. Only the continued existence of a person's spirit makes his or her existence meaningful.

Corroborative evidence for the independent existence of a person's spirit can be gleaned from out-of-body experiences (OBE) and near-death experiences (NDE). Such incidents are common and are accepted as real experiences by the persons encountering these phenomena. OBE events, also known as *astral travel* and *etheric projection*, have been reported throughout recorded history. They have been as frequent among North Americans as among Tibetans, Egyptians, Greeks or Australian aborigines. Shamans in indigenous American Indian cultures have made regular use of astral projection techniques to gain esoteric knowledge from the spirit world, often through identification with their totem animal spirits. Well-known authors have written about their OB experiences, among them J. W. von Goethe, D. H. Lawrence, Aldous Huxley, Jack London and Emily Brontë. Charles Lindbergh experienced a vivid OBE while on his celebrated transatlantic flight. In more ancient literature, we find descriptions of astral travel experienced by a sixth century Greek mystic, Hermotimus of Clazomene, by the Old Testament prophet Elisha, and by several Catholic monks and saints.

Astral projection can occur spontaneously during periods of extreme mental or emotional fatigue. Alternatively, some people can produce it at will by entering an altered state of consciousness induced through meditative mind control. In a typical OBE event, a person feels his or her conscious self separating from and rising above the physical body. The separated self is discerned as a tenuous form having the same outline as the physical body but none of its imperfections. This tenuous, translucent and radiant manifestation of the conscious spirit appears to be a nonmaterial energy form akin to a holographic image. New Age groups refer to it as our astral or etheric body, or as the body of light. The ancient Egyptians called it *ka*, a mirror image of the body, but constructed of finer matter. It may be equivalent to the

German *Doppelgänger*, the Norwegian *vardger*, the Celtic *caslach* and the Old English *fetch*.

Once the spirit consciousness, or astral body, is released from the flesh, it can apparently travel unencumbered wherever it will, its only connection with the physical body being a tenuous *silver cord*, the spiritual umbilical, which can stretch indefinitely. In this separated state, the surroundings are perceived from the new perspective of the etheric body (spirit) and not through the eyes and ears of the physical body left behind. The astral body seems to have no limitations as to where it can go. Some spiritual voyagers have, however, reported difficulties around strong electric and magnetic fields. Such fields may be found around high-voltage transmission lines, for example. Besides causing disorientation, these fields are sometimes perceived as a barrier, preventing the spirit from penetrating that region of space.

There may also be a connection between astral travel and dreaming. In primitive, indigenous societies around the world, people believed their spirits escaped from their bodies during sleep, leaving the physical bodies unconscious. Dreams were regarded as the actual experiences of the traveling spirit. Common dreams associated with the sensation of flying or floating were assumed to be caused by the flight of the spirit. I have repeatedly dreamed of floating up and down flights of stairs in an upright posture, but without touching the ground. If not a direct OB experience, it could perhaps be a memory of how a I traveled as a spirit between lifetimes.

According to investigators, more than ten percent of the population have had some kind of OB experience. Many believe it is a natural state of being, which can be induced consciously with the appropriate training. Local libraries and bookstores have some excellent books to assist a prospective astral traveler.

A special case of OBE is the near-death experience (NDE). A person faced with certain death undergoes a spontaneous OBE, but has no opportunity to communicate this experience to the living. Only if actual death is miraculously avoided does the spirit return to the body, leaving the person with a memory of the NDE and enabling him or her to communicate this incident. Ernest Hemingway had such an experience in WWI, and he retold it in one of his novels.[10] Near-death events were rare occurrences until the late twentieth century, when medical advances often made it possible to revive people from imminent physical death. During the 1970s and 80s, many ND experiences were brought to the public's attention by such investigators as Elisabeth Kübler-Ross[11], Raymond A. Moody[12] and Kenneth Ring.[13]

First-hand accounts from people having gone through ND experiences tell about observing their own bodies on the operating table, or at the scene of an accident, and recall in minute detail the activities taking place while their mind was *unconscious*. The particulars of their NDE memories usually check out accurately with accounts of witnesses at the scene. Typically, NDE memories appear to have been obtained from a viewpoint different from the ground-level perspective of the witnesses. This is only possible if the center of consciousness has disassociated itself from the body and has made it own observations. Similarly, many memories arising from OBE events could not possibly have been obtained by ordinary means. If such reports and observations are factual, then the spirit is able to experience its surroundings and remember the experiences without the aid of a brain or the senses of the physical body. The mechanism is not understood. But then neither do we understand the structure of the energy form we call spirit. It must have structure in order to have individuality and the capability to retain information.

To gain a deeper understanding of our spiritual existence, we must be able to discuss the relevant concepts intelligently. As mentioned earlier, much confusion exists about our understanding of consciousness, spirit, soul, self, psyche, mind, life force and personality, because their meanings are colored by different ethnic, cultural and linguistic backgrounds. Moreover, these expressions cannot easily be translated from language to language for lack of a simple one-for-one correspondence between words in different tongues. I feel it is important here to distinguish between things and qualities. Things, in this context, are primary phenomena which have a separate existence. Qualities, characteristics and properties cannot exist by themselves, but are attributes. For example, matter, radiation, force are *things*; whereas mass, color, frequency are *qualities*. Similarly, I will consider spirit, self, life force and mind[*] as things, but consciousness and personality as qualities. Life itself is a *process*. Consciousness is a quality of the spirit. It is like the brightness of a candle flame. Consciousness can be transferred in the process of reincarnation like a candle flame can be transferred to another candle. The energy pattern of the flame is transferred and recreated in the candle being lit, but no primary substance is actually transferred. Whereas consciousness is without substance, the incarnating spirit is a distinct energy form.

My concept of the individual spirit is analogous to the soul in Christian and Buddhist theology and as defined by the Greek philosopher Plato. I am avoiding the word *soul*, however, because it is emotionally entangled in many different ways among people of differing backgrounds. The individual spirit has a primary existence of its own; but it is the sum total of all its qualities, imprinted upon it, that makes it unique and significant. Metaphorically, it may be illuminating to compare the spirit with a well-cut and polished diamond. The sparkling gem has been shaped, refined and perfected through a long process, starting with its crystallization in the hellfire of the Earth's interior. It was then brought to the surface by tectonic processes, washed out of the rock by the clear waters of a mountain stream, then joyously discovered by a prospector. Its beauty was brought to life by the utmost care and attention of a master gem cutter, who cut and polished its facets to perfection. A goldsmith then mounted it in a wedding band for a happy bride to enjoy as a symbol of love and permanency. Just as many processes have shaped and perfected the diamond, so many life experiences have shaped and perfected a human spirit.

To describe a diamond as a mass of crystalline carbon gives no clue to its essence and its value. Similarly, saying that the spirit is made from the fine stuff of the universe cannot even begin to define it. The value and essence of a diamond lies in its many inherent and acquired

---

[*]   The independent existence of the mind is in doubt.

qualities, such as clarity, color, size, cut and accuracy of its facets, the perfection of its polish, the beauty with which light refracts and sparkles in all colors of the rainbow. Correspondingly, the significance and individuality of a spirit resides in its qualities.

> **A spirit's beauty is its capacity for love**
> **and how brightly it sparkles with joy.**
> **Its greatness lies in its consciousness,**
> **its zest for experiencing and appreciating**
> **the magnificence of all Creation.**
> **Its value is judged by how well it**
> **illuminates the path for others.**

The spirit imparts the life force, which makes an organism conscious and alive. Yet the spirit can neither be identified with the process of life, nor with the life force, which is impersonal. Each individual spirit is unique and personal. But how much of an individual's personality is imprinted on his or her spirit? What traits are transferred to the new being into which the spirit incarnates? These are difficult questions, which do not have a simple answer.

Just what do we mean, when we say an individual spirit evolves towards perfection through many physical life experiences? What learned and acquired characteristics become a permanent part of this spirit? What qualities are lost when a person dies? What knowledge can the spirit recover from the Akashic records? I do not profess to know the answers. We get no help from our sciences, since they study only the material manifestations and ignore the spiritual aspects. It is indeed a sad state of affairs, when our celebrated sciences cannot answer the most rudimentary questions relating to the immortality of the spirit.

In spite of the dearth of reliable knowledge about these matters, we can draw reasonable conclusions and make logical extrapolations consistent with the spiritual models presented. We can be certain that not all personality traits are preserved as a person's spirit goes from life to life. Genetically inherited talents, character traits and physical characteristics will die with the body. As well, all knowledge and memories held by the material mind-brain system will be lost, unless they are retrieved again in the new life from the Akashic records or by means of a superconscious group memory. But emotionally charged passions and habits, having become second nature, probably imprint themselves on the spirit and become a permanent part of it. A person's capacity to love, for example, expands the spirit permanently. Other qualities affecting the spirit directly are a person's integrity, sense of justice, moral values, fearlessness, compassion and sense of truth and freedom.

Other questions connected with the evolution of human spirits through successive life cycles remain unanswered. One such enigma arises from the present exponential growth of Earth's population. Today, we have six billion humans on Earth, more than the cumulative total of all humans ever living before in recorded history. We may legitimately inquire about the source of all these newly incarnated spirits. Is the supply infinite, or are we scraping the bottom of the barrel to find new souls? Judging by the moral decay in the modern world, we may suspect the latter. In Jewish mythology, a storehouse of souls in heaven allots spirits for newly born infants. Eventually, as the story goes, this depository will become empty, and a child will be born without a soul, an event believed to herald the end of the world. As reincarnation is not an established belief within the Jewish community, the story does not tell whether the spiritual depository on the *other side* is replenished by the souls of the dead or not.

Can new spirits be created? Are there spiritual conservation laws analogous to the physical conservation of energy and electric charge? We do not know. But we can logically discuss alternative possibilities. To supply the exploding human population with spirits, one or more of the following four hypotheses must be true:

♦   The Universal Spirit of Creation creates new human spirits all the time as needed. Newly created spirits would be spiritually naive and inexperienced. They would compete with older spirits for chances of a material life. This hypothesis goes against the idea of a long evolution of spirit. We also find no evidence of primitive new human spirits, who are innocently devoid of love, fear and other human emotions, and who lack a sense of ethics.

♦ We have a backlog of spirits on the *other side* awaiting their chance to reincarnate in a human body. Prehistoric civilizations may have existed, perhaps tens of thousands or even millions of years ago, with high populations of many billions of souls. In this scenario, the rest period between death and rebirth would have to be indefinite; that is it could be short or it could last thirty millennia. This possibility does not entirely solve the problem, because we would still have to ask, «Where did the billions of souls come from thirty thousand years ago?» Space travel, perhaps? By contrast, Tibetan Buddhists believe the rebirth of a human spirit takes place immediately. After the death of their Dalai Lama, who is considered a reincarnation of Chenregi, the search goes on for the living Buddha in a child born at the exact moment of death of their prior religious leader.

♦ The evolution of individual spirits runs parallel with the biological evolution of the species. A primitive spirit starts out in a primitive life form, then evolves through the animal kingdom before graduating to the human realm. According to this view, human spirits are not categorically different from the spirits of animals. Any shortage of human spirits could be filled with spirits from the animal kingdom. From personal experience, I have known animals with more spiritual strength and capacity for love than many humans. We should note here that the word *animal* is derived from the Latin word *anima*, the soul.

♦ Human spirits can reincarnate here from other parts of the universe, and vice versa. In this hypothetical scenario, spirits would travel freely through the universe at many times the speed of light and would not be subject to the limitations of physical space travelers. One authority on this subject says, «Not so.» Esoteric information obtained by Eduard *Billy* Meier[14] from alleged extraterrestrial sources denies human spirits the ability to leave our planetary neighborhood.

Extraterrestrial spirits would have to be transported here in their physical embodiments by means of material spacecraft. Could this explain the recent rash of UFOs in our skies as spiritual supply ships? We will report more about the spiritual wisdom disseminated by Meier's missionary study group in the next chapters. Billy Meier has accumulated a large body of spiritual wisdom and prophecies, which in my opinion are of higher consistency and wider scope than the spiritual legacies of Edgar Cayce.[15]

An important aspect of spiritual evolution requires our acceptance of brother and sister spirits at all levels of non-enlightenment. We often wish everybody on Earth would be at the same level of spiritual, emotional and intellectual growth. But this is not realistic. For us to learn and grow, we must seek out those who are more advanced. Their help is needed for our spiritual progress. And we must help those of less enlightenment, if by nothing else than by being a shining example of integrity and love. We must have tolerance for the intolerant, love for the fearful, compassion for the insensitive; we must educate the ignorant, console the suffering, and we must speak out against corruption, greed and envy. Moreover, we must be willing to learn, to accept guidance and love from more advanced spirits. This brings to mind a fable. In this story, a group of individuals, whose spiritual growth was found lacking, were reborn into a land of plenty with the most delicious food decked out for them to enjoy; except for one problem. Their forearms were five feet long, making it impossible for them to feed themselves. They soon learned they had to feed each other to survive.

Spiritual evolution and the law of karma can provide answers to a question frequently asked by Christians: «Why does *God* allow war, strife, tragedy and suffering to exist?» We must look at conflict and tragedy with different eyes. These challenges may be necessary for our growth. Often we are unwittingly guided into such situations. Synchronicities[16,17] are proof of the Universal Spirit guiding and supporting our growth by creating situations from which we can learn, and by supporting our positive ventures in life with unexpected help. Sometimes, the Creation Spirit acts through an angelic envoy to work miracles for saving us from untimely disaster and death. None of us is ever alone. We each have a caring spiritual support group, which derives its powers from the Infinite.

THE STORY OF JMMANUEL

«Truly, I have not come to bring peace,
but the sword of knowledge about the power of the spirit,
which dwells within humans.
And so I have come to bring wisdom and knowledge
and to provoke son against father, ...
servant against master,
citizen against government, and
believer against preacher and priest.»
[TJ 10:44,45; compare Matthew 10:34-38]

«Blessed are those who are rich in spirit
and recognize the truth, for life is theirs.»
[TJ 5:3; compare Matthew 5:3]

He did not know it then, but he was subconsciously guided to an old
forgotten tomb buried in the hillsides just outside of Jerusalem. The
year was 1963, and the name of the amateur archaeologist was Isa
Rashid,[*] a Lebanese priest of the Greek Orthodox church. The cave,
then filled with sand and rubble, was a tomb belonging to Joseph of
Arimathea, into which the body of Jmmanuel, alias Jesus of Nazareth,
was placed after his crucifixion. On several occasions, shortly after
the discovery, Rashid returned with his friend, Billy Meier, in the
darkness of night to excavate the tomb. Underneath a flat rock, they
found a set of scrolls embedded in tree resin, which had been used to
preserve them. Meier had been prompted to look for this document by
extraterrestrial intelligences from the region of the Pleiades. The

---

[*] Following Rashid's wish, his real name has not been publicly disclosed to
protect his family from attacks by right-wing Christian and Jewish radicals.

document, written in Aramaic, contained an historic account of the life and teachings of Jmmanuel.

The unearthing of these scrolls and the subsequent intrigues and machinations to destroy and discredit this manuscript provide enough material for a suspense novel. The plot is reminiscent of an Indiana Jones script. It vaguely parallels the finding of the golden tablets, containing the Book of Mormon, by the latter-day prophet Joseph Smith, the subsequent elimination of evidence and the persecution of the key figures involved.

Rashid, who was schooled in Aramaic writings (the Hebrew language spoken by Jmmanuel and his disciples), and who also had a rudimentary command of German, spent the next eleven years translating the *Talmud Jmmanuel* (TJ), the title given to the document, into German. We can surmise that Rashid consulted other biblical scholars for help in translating difficult portions of the text and for affirming the scroll's authenticity. The contents of the TJ are heretic, to say the least, to the Christian as well as the Jewish faiths and establishments. News of the document's existence apparently reached influential authorities in the Christian and Jewish clergy, who regarded the document with fear and considered it a threat to their religious dominance. So they set out to obliterate the scrolls and destroy and discredit the people knowing of its existence. Rashid justifiably became afraid for his life and the safety of his family and started to move from place to place to evade his persecutors. In August of 1974, a refugee camp, where he stayed with his family, was bombed and destroyed by Israeli commandos; officially in retaliation against Palestinian guerrillas, but actually in an effort to capture Rashid and his heretical scrolls. Rashid and his family escaped, but the scrolls were lost. They were either destroyed by fire or fell into Israeli hands. Fortunately, Rashid had already translated 36 chapters of the TJ and had sent the translated text to Billy Meier. Unfortunately, these 36 chapters accounted for only a quarter of the writings in the Aramaic scrolls. Along with the loss of three fourth of the writings, any proof of the existence of the original scrolls also vanished. In March 1976, Rashid was murdered by unknown assailants in Baghdad. Billy Meier meanwhile edited the German text for grammatical consistency and clarity and started distributing a German version of the TJ. In 1992 an English translation[1] of the TJ was published by Wild Flower Press. Clandestine persecution continues against Billy Meier, who has so far survived more than 16 alleged assassination attempts by undercover agents of different political and religious groups and by the mysterious *Men in Black*, associated with hostile extraterrestrial factions.

What makes the TJ so controversial and offensive to many is its contradiction of some of the most holy and cherished tenets of Roman Catholicism, such as the immaculate conception, the holy Trinity and Jmmanuel's sacrificial death as the *Lamb of God*. Even though, Jmmanuel is portrayed as a wiser and greater prophet in the TJ than in the New Testament. The TJ describes him as an extraordinary teacher of the power of the spirit and of reincarnation. Most controversially, the TJ shows him surviving near-death on the cross, a viewpoint shared by the Moslem world.

Jmmanuel's life story and his teachings were first written down by his faithful disciple and scribe, Judas Iscariot. According to the TJ, Jmmanuel was not betrayed by his disciple Judas, but by Juda Ihariot, the son of Simeon, a Pharisee. The mixup was facilitated by the similarity in the two names, and was endorsed by Simeon to hide his son's guilt and to protect his family name.

So far, only one serious study of the TJ text has been performed by Dr. James W. Deardorff[2], who took early retirement from his position as professor at the Oregon State University in order to investigate the validity of this extraordinary document. After more than six years of intense scrutiny and analysis, he convinced himself that the TJ is most likely a genuine, unedited Proto-Matthew, because of its resemblance to the New Testament gospel of Matthew. In his opinion, the TJ removes all inconsistencies from the biblical story. It naturally resolves all contradictory and illogical statements that had previously been pointed out and criticized by biblical scholars. Even minor inconsistencies, not obvious to a layman intent on creating a fake document, are absent in the TJ. Because of this high consistency of the TJ text, and because of its spiritual relevance and wisdom, this document cannot easily be brushed aside as a cruel hoax perpetrated by Billy Meier, who does not appear to be a sophisticated biblical scholar.

As Deardorff has pointed out, the theological establishment shies away from a serious study of the TJ, not so much because of its heretical nature, but because of the total lack of physical evidence supporting the archaeological find, and because of the many references in the TJ to extraterrestrial guidance. Apparently, Jmmanuel had been educated, guided and protected throughout his life by extraterrestrial intelligences from the celestial region of the Pleiades star cluster. Jmmanuel's teachers of wisdom were from the same advanced civilization that continues to monitor Earth's society, and which is allegedly in contact with Billy Meier. Their mission is to disseminate spiritual truths, so as to turn people away from the delusionary *truths* spread by the cult religions of Earth.

As in the book of St. Matthew, the TJ story starts by listing the genealogical lineage of Joseph all the way back to Adam. «Adam, the father of one of Earth's human races, ... was begotten by Semjasa, the leader of the celestial sons, who were the guardian angels of god, the great ruler of the voyagers, who ... traveled here through vast expanses of the universe.» Jmmanuel's birth was prearranged by his Pleiaran spiritual leaders. They decided to bring a highly evolved spirit to Earth as a prophet, who would teach the story of Creation and the spiritual lessons of life. Jmmanuel's spirit was too highly evolved to be born to normal Earth parents. So they chose the celestial son Gabriel (not the archangel) to be the father and an Earth woman Mary to carry Gabriel's child. The virgin birth problem is a non-issue in the TJ. The *star of Bethlehem* at Jmmanuel's birth, the light guiding the holy family to Egypt, the *spirit descending like a dove* at Jmmanuel's baptism, and the *ascension* into the light after his recovery from the crucifixion are explained by the actions of Gabriel's vimana-like spacecraft. Similarly, the *angel* appearing at Jmmanuel's tomb was an extraterrestrial apparition who immobilized the guards.

Efforts by astronomers and historians to identify the guiding star of Bethlehem with a comet or a supernova have failed to come up with a plausible candidate. No bright supernovae or comets have been recorded anywhere else on Earth during that period. Presently, the most widely accepted scientific explanation for the star of Bethlehem points to a close conjunction of the planets Jupiter and Saturn in the summer of the year 7 BC. This suggestion, however, is absurd and does not give recognition to the wisdom of the Magi. Surely, the wise kings from the East must have been well versed in astronomy and aware of the planetary cycles. They would not have mistaken such a predictable conjunction as a bright new star heralding the birth of a heavenly king or messiah. Being educated magi, they surely were also familiar with the diurnal motions of stars from east to west. This regular daily celestial motion could not have been guiding them to Bethlehem. A *star*, which truly led them to such a precise location as a stable in a particular town, must have displayed a nonconforming motion of its own and must have been much closer than any celestial object. A light beam emanating from an intelligently controlled atmospheric craft affords a much more plausible explanation. Earth people did not have flying machines in those days. But an extraterrestrial vimana would perfectly account for all documented characteristics of the biblical *star of nativity*.

By the time Jmmanuel reached adulthood, he was also aware of his extraterrestrial legacy. After his baptism by John, Jmmanuel was taken off the Earth for forty days and nights and was educated in the spiritual wisdom and mastery of life by his Pleiaran mentors. Jmmanuel then taught this wisdom in turn to the people during his mission on Earth, both before and after his crucifixion. He admonished humans to strive for knowledge of the power of the spirit and for wisdom to follow the directives of Creation. He discussed reincarnation and the evolution of an individual's spirit. He elucidated life's learning experience as an error and correction process. Accordingly, a person can only learn through his or her mistakes while living a material life. Moreover, honest errors made in the pursuit of spiritual wisdom incur no spiritual, karmic consequences. He preached against the hypocrisy and greed of the scribes and Pharisees, against suicide and male homosexuality. He differentiated between the commandments of god (the creator of several human races), the laws of nature and the directives of Creation, the omnipotent, infinite and eternal power, which lovingly guides the evolution of the omniverse. He promoted personal integrity, fearlessness and love for Creation and all its creatures. He predicted great wars and natural disasters. For Simon Peter, his disciple, he prophesied: «Owing to your lack of understanding, the world will shed much blood, because you will falsify my teachings and spread it erroneously among the people. You will be guilty of the death of many people, as well as for the origin of a false name for me and for the evil insult of calling me the son of god, and calling god Creation itself» [TJ 18:33,34].

After Jmmanuel's betrayal by Juda Ihariot and his crucifixion, he was laid to rest in a grotto belonging to Joseph of Arimathea. There he was nursed back to health by friends from India, who came and went through a secret second entrance to the tomb. After three days, he miraculously reappeared in the flesh and was taken up into the sky by his true father Gabriel, whose spacecraft appeared to the witnesses as a metallic light. In the following years, the Pharisees and Sadducees started to persecute the disciples and followers of Jmmanuel. The fiercest among them was a man from Tarsus named Saul. Jmmanuel, who had lived under cover in Damascus for two years, decided to frighten Saul into abandoning the persecution of Jmmanuel's followers. He waylaid Saul and his gang as they traveled to Damascus to arrest Jmmanuel's brother Thomas and Judas Iscariot. During the night, as the group came close to his hiding place, Jmmanuel startled them with a bright display of pyrotechnics and pretended to be the ghost of Jmmanuel, ordering Saul to stop persecuting his disciples. Saul was frightened out of his wits. He truly believed Jmmanuel to be a supernatural apparition with supernatural powers, and he agreed henceforth to pursue knowledge instead of people. In this way Saul was converted to become the apostle Paul. Jmmanuel then moved on towards the north and east, spreading his spiritual teachings wherever he went. — The salvaged part of the TJ ends here.

Billy Meier, who had some knowledge of the story told in the remaining parts of the scrolls, gives the following account of the later events in Jmmanuel's life. Jmmanuel kept teaching the people about Creation and spiritual truth. He had to flee frequently because of the revolutionary nature of his teachings. With his mother Mary, his brother Thomas and his disciple Judas Iscariot, he then traveled east to India, a difficult journey of several years filled with hardship. High in the foothills of the western Himalayas, his mother became ill and died when Jmmanuel was 38 years old. During the next six or seven years, Jmmanuel migrated through vast areas of Afghanistan, Pakistan and India. At age 45, he married a young woman and settled down in Kashmir in a town now known as Srinagar. He lived a normal family life and had many children. After a busy life of preaching to people throughout that region, he died of natural causes at an age between 110 and 115 years. He was buried in Srinagar. Jmmanuel's story and teachings were first written down by Judas Iscariot. After Judas died around age ninety, Jmmanuel's son Joseph continued writing his father's story. Then, some time after Jmmanuel's death, Joseph returned to the land of his father, taking with him the original scrolls. He hid them in the tomb where his father had lain and where Rashid and Meier were prompted to rediscover these scrolls. Joseph remained in Jerusalem for the rest of his life.

Ample historical evidence exists for the claim of Jmmanuel (later called Jesus) having lived in India[2,3,4]. Moslems and Hindus in that part of the world have known him as Yuz Asaf, and a tomb in Srinagar is identified as his burial site. Kersten[3] enumerates more than 21 historical documents, which confirm Jesus having lived in Kashmir, India. Other historical evidence can be found at a site in Kashmir named Murree, where locals can direct inquisitive visitors to the Tomb of *Mother Mary*.

But critical questions remain. Is the TJ the actual testament of Jesus, the true account of the biblical story that changed history, and does it accurately represent his teachings? James Deardorff makes a compelling case for its genuineness. As well, many examiners, including myself, who seriously studied this document, find the TJ more acceptable than the heavily redacted versions in the Christian bible. The ultimate judgement on this issue must be left to the reader who examines the TJ with an open mind. Moslems, Buddhists and Jews have less of a problem than Christians when it comes to accepting Jmmanuel as a normal, but highly evolved, human being. An impartial scholar can find no shred of evidence for Jmmanuel having been a god, the God, or the Creator of the universe.

Could Billy Meier have concocted the whole story of the TJ scrolls and their contents? Possibly, but not likely. Critics may point out that Meier may have invented the story of Isa Rashid and the Aramaic scrolls to account for the lack of physical evidence for their existence. Under such a scenario, Rashid had to die, his real name had to be withheld and the tomb of discovery had to be destroyed by a hill slide to foil any attempts of a serious inquiry into the purported facts. The mysterious disappearance of evidence is not unique, however. We have mentioned earlier the disappearance of the tablets containing the book of Mormon. Sources of esoteric knowledge have historically been either destroyed or been discredited. This is particularly common in the field of ufology. A cosmic conspiracy[5,6] may truly be at work to keep the general population in the dark. Extraterrestrial intelligences probably believe that Earth humans are not ready mentally, spiritually or ethically to accept the universal truth. A recurring theme transmitted through UFO contactees, including Billy Meier, is that Earth humans have a genetic defect, making them cruel, aggressive and dangerous; that humans have to grow spiritually first, before they can be entrusted with the secrets of the omniverse.

If the TJ is not genuine and Billy Meier is its real author, then he must be considered a philosopher and wise person in his own right, greater than the compilers of the biblical gospels and wiser than many classic philosophers. I have studied the TJ in great detail and have helped in the production of a more accurate English version of this controversial script. Following are my own thoughts and observations regarding some of the obvious discrepancies between the TJ and the New Testament. Many more arguments supporting the TJ as an authentic ancient document can be found in Deardorff's[2] critical analysis.

<u>Resurrection versus Recovery:</u>

The belief in Jesus' resurrection from the dead constitutes the core of Christian doctrine. Without it, Jesus is not God but entirely human. In the TJ, Jmmanuel denies he is the son of god. Throughout the entire document, the TJ stresses Jmmanuel's spiritual teachings, not his divinity. His life's mission was to teach humanity about the power of the spirit, not to redeem humanity by being the sacrificial *lamb of God*.

Is it possible that Jesus was only seemingly dead, as claimed in the TJ, when he was taken off the cross? Jesus' alleged death was confirmed only by the word of a Roman centurion, hardly a medical expert. Such weak evidence would not stand up in today's courts. Even Pilate expressed his astonishment that Jesus should have expired so soon [Mark 15:44]. Subsequent events in the biblical story can be explained by recovery from near-death as easily as by resurrection from irreversible physical death. Even today, our medical experts are vague in their definition of clinical death; and many a person declared dead by a doctor has miraculously returned to life. When Jesus said to the Jews: «Destroy this temple and in three days I will raise it up,» [John 2:19] he referred to the healing of his tortured body through the power of his spirit. Even with his physical body declared dead, he was able to revive it through his spiritual power. He was living up to his teachings. It was a natural act consistent with Creation. No magical shift in the universal order needed to take place.

After Jesus arose from his deathbed and appeared before his disciples and the people, all perceived him as a material person. Even the disbelieving disciple Thomas convinced himself of Jesus' materiality by touching his body and his wounds. The reappearance of Jesus in his normal, material body does not prove resurrection in the biblical sense. On the contrary, a resurrected, reconstituted body should have been perfect and without wounds. The reported facts are more consistent with medical recovery. Nothing supernatural was needed. Over 500 people witnessed the living Jesus in his physical body after his crucifixion. Paul wrote in his first Epistle to the Corinthians:

> « ... and that he was seen by Cephas, then by the *twelve*; after that was seen by more than 500 brothers at one time; ... After that, he was seen by James, then by *all the apostles*. And last of all, he was seen by me also...» [I Corinthians 15:5-8]

In his own words, Paul states Jesus was seen by the original *twelve* disciples, not eleven; then later by *all* the apostles. This is confirmation of the TJ claim that Paul was aware of the identity of the real betrayer, Juda, the son of a Pharisee who hanged himself out of guilt. Paul, alias Saul, may have been hunting down Judas, the disciple in order to eliminate the person who could disprove the official version of Jmmanuel's betrayal, so as to protect Simeon and his family from shame. The TJ portrays Saul as being one of the conspirators, who plotted Immanuel's capture with the help of Juda, the son of Simeon [TJ 26:45].

Among the eye witnesses of the revived Jesus, Paul was the only one who believed Jesus to have arisen in a spiritual body, rather than a physical one. To wit:

> «It is so with the resurrection of the dead; ... it is the spiritual body that is raised.» [I Corinthians 15:42-44]

Besides being at odds with other eye witnesses, Paul's view is contradicted by later church authorities proclaiming the resurrection of Jesus' physical body. But consistent with his later views, Saul firmly believed he was seeing a spirit, when he encountered Jmmanuel on the road to Damascus [Acts 9:3-9]. The TJ solves this anomaly by explaining how the physical Jmmanuel deceived Saul into believing he saw a ghost [TJ 33:13-30]. Many other New Testament anomalies are similarly resolved in a natural way by the TJ.

The Celestial Connection:

Why is it so easy for people to believe in a heaven as the abode of God with his host of angels, but so difficult to accept the presence of extraterrestrial intelligences in the cosmos? Is it because they are afraid to make the obvious connection between the two topics? One of the major stumbling blocks preventing the TJ from being accepted is its intricate entanglement with extraterrestrial lore. The TJ encompasses a cosmic perspective, as opposed to the biblical scriptures, which view the world as a Mediterranean playground. What the biblical Genesis describes as the creation of the world would from a wider perspective be seen as the terraforming of planet Earth, the transformation of a dense, vaporous cover into a transparent, breathable atmosphere, the separation of continents from the oceans, the seeding of the planet with plant and animal life, and the biogenetic engineering of human races suitably adapted for Earth's environment.

The TJ is clear about the cosmic origins of Earth humans. Emissaries from extraterrestrial civilizations have repeatedly visited Earth to establish colonies millions of years ago, hundreds of thousands of years ago, and most recently thirteen thousand years before the present. Adam, the father of one of Earth's human races, was created then.

> «Semjasa, the celestial son and guardian angel of god, the great ruler of the voyagers who traveled here through vast expanses of the universe, took a terrestrial woman and begot Adam, the father of the white human race.»
> [TJ 1:2]

According to cosmic lore[7], various human races have started colonies on Earth at different times, going back as far as 400,000 years ago. Early settlers came from star systems in the vicinity of Sirius and Lyra. Later influxes came from regions in Orion, the Hyades, the Pleiades and from Vega, all of which had previously been colonized by the ancient Lyrans. The Pleiaran societies occupy several planets in the general region of the Pleiades star cluster, but their worlds are alleged to be dimensionally displaced from the visible Pleiades by a time shift of a fraction of a second. The Pleiarans have an advanced technology and a raised spiritual consciousness, and they have lived in peace for the last 50,000 years. They have had a longstanding interest in Earth's societies, because their genetic material exists in many Earth humans. We are their wayward brothers and sisters.

The Pleiarans, who created Adam, have been fostering our spiritual development by paving the way for a string of prophets, who were commissioned to lead humanity back onto the right path and away from self-destruction. Through the efforts of the Pleiarans, a wise, ancient spirit form has been repeatedly reincarnated as the prophets Elijah, Isaiah, Jeremiah, Jmmanuel, Muhammad and possibly many others. Even though the spirit was highly developed and wise, the reincarnated prophet needed to be reeducated every time by the Pleiarans with essential knowledge required for his mission. Thus, Jmmanuel was educated by the Pleiarans in the secret spirit lessons and was prepared for his mission during forty days and nights following his baptism by John the Baptist [TJ 4:1-5]. Billy Meier believes himself to be such a reincarnated ancient spirit. He has been schooled since childhood by his Pleiaran mentors (his UFO contacts) to prepare him for his mission as the New Age prophet. His tutoring parallels the tutoring of Jmmanuel.

Like the gospels, the TJ contains many prophesies of future events. Upon first reading the TJ, the reader is confronted with prophesies that are entirely too accurate and appear to be written in hindsight. Because Meier had total control over the TJ as its editor, we may suspect Meier of having inserted these prophesies into the text. Even more disconcerting, we may be suspicious of Meier inventing the entire text in the first place.

We are used to the vague prophesies in the cryptic book of Revelations, in the obscure verses of Nostradamus and in the nebulous predictions made by many self-proclaimed prophets. In contrast, the TJ is precise. We read about the coming of the prophet Muhammed in five hundred years, followed by many centuries of persecution of the Jews by the Arab world [TJ 30:10-14]. In two thousand years, there would be a terrestrial population of five billion [TJ 25:34], there would be wars and natural disasters [TJ 25:9-11], false prophets [TJ 25:8], military aircraft, ships and tanks [TJ 25:29], projectiles and missiles [TJ 25:30] with nuclear warheads [TJ 25:31], and space travel by Earth people [TJ 3:19; 4:49]. Our present period was predicted to be critically significant. Jmmanuel foretold the Jews would never find peace for two thousand years [TJ 25:7], and that Jmmanuel's true teachings would be taught anew at that time [TJ 3:17; 4:48; 15:75; 32:44]. But most disturbingly for many readers, the TJ gives two thinly disguised allusions to the coming of the New Age prophet Billy Meier, who would live in a peace-loving country in the North [TJ 14:18; 15:75-81]. Moreover, in two thousand years, the celestial sons (ufonauts) would reveal themselves to Earth people [4:50].

A critical person has difficulties accepting the TJ as genuine, unless he or she also accepts the continued guidance and monitoring of our activities by a clandestine Pleiaran presence. On the other side of the coin, the philosophy expressed by the teachings of Jmmanuel is more self-consistent and closer to reality than many parts of the New Testament. And the teachings are consistent with the mission assumed by Billy Meier.

If we acknowledge life as a natural aspect of Creation, then we must concede that we Earth humans are not alone in the universe. And considering the universe is billions, perhaps trillions of years old, the existence of untold highly developed civilizations among its quadrillions of star systems is certain. Moreover, humans must learn and progress through their own experiences by making their own errors. It is a universal aspect of reality. It explains the cosmic policy of noninterference with developing civilizations. Hence, advanced intelligences like the Pleiarans can be expected to monitor, but not interfere with our affairs. A limited amount of guidance is afforded only to avert disaster. Such benevolent interest in their space brothers would naturally extend over periods of millennia. Therefore, if the Pleiarans supported Jmmanuel in his mission two thousand years ago, they should be even more concerned with our modern-day civilization. They should try to warn and educate us through a new prophet. This new prophet may just be Billy Meier. What is his mission? Simply put, it is to help in saving humanity from itself. Because this is too immense a task for one man, we must not be surprised to find others who have been enrolled to spread the truth. But there are also many who spread disinformation, disguised as truth, for their own gain. It is up to each one of us to recognize the difference. This is part of our learning experience as an individual and as a society.

Personally, I believe Billy Meier's intentions to be sincere. His photographic evidence of Pleiaran beamships is unchallenged, in spite of his detractors. He is risking his life and his reputation for the spiritual welfare of humanity. He says all the right things. He preaches for population control and the protection of the environment, and he warns against violence and war. His teachings and warnings, like those of Jmmanuel, are desperately needed at this time to turn around the crazy mentality of the masses. The spiritual teachings of the Pleiarans, a la Meier, are close to my own thoughts about the meaning of life. Similarly, I find the physical universe, as described by the Pleiaran sources, more plausible than the schemes dreamed up by our cosmologists.

Is the TJ an Authentic Archaeological Find?

This is the question which prompted Deardorff to spend many years perusing the TJ and comparing it with the New Testament scriptures. After carefully analyzing the written text, he has not found any evidence to support the hoax theory. Rather, he has uncovered persuasive proof for the TJ being a genuine Proto-Matthew. Except for some reservations noted above, I have reached the same conclusion.

As an example, when we carefully compare the text in Matthew 24:27 with the words in TJ 25:42, the TJ verse appears to be older and closer to the Aramaic source, hence contradicting the hoax theory. This verse has not been specifically treated by Deardorff, but has puzzled me during my translation efforts. Compare the following verses prophesying the second coming of Jesus. All four references clearly have a common origin:

> [TJ 25:42]
> «Denn wie der Blitz ausgeht und leuchtet vom Aufgang bis zum Niedergang, so wird auch sein mein Kommen ... »
> («For as lightning flashes and radiates from rise to setting, so will be my coming ... »)
>
> [Matthew 24:27]
> «For as lightning cometh out of the east and shineth even unto the west, so shall also the coming of the Son of man be.»

[Luke 17:24]
«For as the lightning, that lighteneth out of one part under heaven, shineth unto the other part under heaven, so shall also the Son of man be in his day.»

[Quelle - another unofficial prototext, often referred to as Q]
«For just as when lightning flashes, it shines from one part of the sky to the other; that will be the way with the son of man ...»

The German version of the TJ interprets the interval between *Aufgang* (rising) and *Niedergang* (setting) temporally as the time between onset of the lightning flash and its termination. In contrast, Matthew, Luke and Q interpret the phrase spatially as the region between the places where the sun rises and where it sets; i.e. from east to west or from one end of the sky to the other.

When we think about the two different interpretations rationally, there is only one logical explanation: The original Aramaic source must have been ambiguous in its context, allowing the Aramaic words for *Aufgang* and *Niedergang* to be associated with either the lightning flash or the diurnal path of the sun through the sky. The German version in the TJ is similarly ambiguous, but contains no implied reference to the sun. Its literal meaning would be temporal, referring to the duration of the lightning flash. Private consultation with Billy Meier, who is acquainted with Aramaic writings, has confirmed this notion. He favors the temporal interpretation.

If either Rashid or Meier were the originator of the TJ, why would he try to be less precise than the accepted versions of Matthew, Luke or Q, from which he would have copied the verse in the absence of the Aramaic TJ scrolls? There would have been no reason for him to even think of a temporal interpretation when the spatial representation was the only reference; specially when the spatial picture makes more sense geographically.

Literally hundreds of verses in the TJ appear to be older and more original than the corresponding verses in Matthew or the other gospels. If the TJ were the product of a hoaxer, he would have to be extremely creative and well versed in biblical history, theology and ancient languages. In my judgement, the TJ is a genuine, old document; but certain verses may have been edited in by Meier.

A SELF-CONSISTENT WORLD VIEW

The *Second Law of Thermodynamics* is often quoted as being the governing principle that defines the evolution of the universe. We disagree with that notion. But to make our point we have to digress, so as to clarify what is meant by the *Second Law* and by the obscure concept of *entropy*.

Thermodynamics was an important field of study during the 19th century. It was at the forefront of the physical sciences then, and scientists and engineers forged new concepts and acquired new insights. New knowledge about the utilization of heat energy for producing mechanical work and motion was the catalyst for sparking the industrial revolution. It facilitated the development of steam engines and internal combustion engines, leading to new modes of transportation, which opened up previously remote areas of the globe for exploration, travel and commerce.

Many of the new insights came from the study of gases. Earlier investigations had shown that an ideal gas, when heated, would expand in volume in direct proportion to its absolute temperature. If the gas was constrained from expanding by placing it in a vessel, its pressure would increase in direct proportion to its absolute temperature. Subsequent 19th century contributions to modern thermodynamics were threefold:

1.   A kinetic theory of gases was put forward by Rudolf Clausius [1822-1888], which explained the behavior of gases from a microscopic point of view. The theory treated the gas as an assemblage of billions upon trillions of freely flying molecules, undergoing elastic collisions with each other and with the walls enclosing the gas. It assumed the molecules move in random

directions with different velocities, distributed among the molecules in a random but statistically predictable way. Pressure is exerted on the walls by the impulses imparted by the continuous molecular bombardment. The theory relates the temperature of a gas directly to a statistical average of the kinetic energies carried by the gas molecules.

2.   Heat was recognized as an energy form that could be converted to other forms of energy and vice versa. Mechanical, electrical and chemical energy, for example, could be converted to equivalent amounts of heat energy. Robert Mayer [1814-1878] determined the mechanical energy equivalent of heat. According to his measurements and calculations, 4.18 joules of mechanical energy could always be converted to one calorie of heat. Mayer proposed that the total amount of energy is conserved in any process; that energy can neither be created nor destroyed, but that it can be converted to other forms. This energy conservation principle is known as the *First Law of Thermodynamics*.

3.   Whereas mechanical energy could always be completely converted to heat, investigators found the reverse not to be true. Sadi Carnot [1796-1832], who studied the possibilities of using heat energy for the production of work and motion, found that heat energy could only be extracted from a hot substance, if the heat engine was able to reject waste heat into an environment of lower temperature. Heat energy only flowed from a region of high temperature to a region of low temperature, never in reverse. All heat engines had to operate between heat reservoirs having different temperatures. Only the temperature difference ΔT could be exploited, not the total heat content of a substance at temperature T. Thus, the efficiency of heat energy conversion in an engine is limited to $\Delta T/T$.

The recognition that thermodynamic processes are often irreversible led Clausius and Ludwig Boltzmann [1844-1906] to the generalization that all natural processes proceed towards a state of greater *disorder*. From a statistical point of view, heat was considered to be of greater disorder, due to its randomness of molecular motion, than mechanical, electromagnetic or chemical energy. When energy became degraded into low-grade heat at uniform temperature, it could no longer be recovered for useful work.

As an example, consider an insulated box filled with a substance (gas, liquid or solid), and let one half of the substance initially be at a high temperature and the other half at a low temperature. By itself, heat flows from the high-temperature side to the low-temperature side until everything in the box is at a uniform temperature. The substance is now in thermodynamic equilibrium and remains stable in this state. To reestablish the original temperature difference is not possible without external intervention, without applying an energy form of a higher order. Thermodynamically, the uniform end state has a higher disorder than the initial state of high and low temperatures. In thermodynamic language, the final state has a higher *entropy* than the initial state. This tendency for the entropy of an isolated system to increase, that is for the disorder to increase, or (as I like to put it) for the energy contrast in the system to decrease, is known as the *Second Law of Thermodynamics*. The formal expression of the Second Law is: «In a closed system, all processes occur in such a way as to increase the entropy of the system.» A more whimsical version of the Second Law is Murphy's Seventh Law of Engineering: «Left to themselves, things go from bad to worse.»

In all real processes, some energy is irretrievably degraded to heat. All machines have therefore a practical efficiency of less than unity, and a *perpetuum mobile* becomes an impossibility. In a mechanistic world, all natural processes go towards a state of equilibrium. Unstable situations spontaneously move towards greater stability. Energy peaks and valleys erode to a state of low energy contrast.

Considering the physical universe as a closed system and applying the Second Law, the universe should degrade towards a state of ever increasing disorder, or decreasing contrast. It should end up in an *entropy death*, where everything in the universe is at the same low temperature, slightly above the present cosmic background temperature of 3 °K, or lower if the universe keeps expanding. Many philosophers and scientists believe that the irreversible dissipation of cosmic energies defines a unique arrow of time. An egg once scrambled cannot be reconstituted by spontaneous processes, and hence time cannot go backwards. But is the universe really running down in a continuous process of energy degradation?

Even a casual observer must admit that the universe is not following the thermodynamic predictions. Stars and galaxies form and light up from previously dissipated material. New mountain chains form out of previously eroded hills and valleys. New life forms unfold into ever increasing complexity and beauty. The universe evolves towards higher organization and multisplendored expressions of form. We observe an increase in contrast, rather than the decrease expected, if the universal entropy increased as proclaimed. How is this possible?

The Second Law of Thermodynamics only applies to unguided physical processes left to themselves. If we have a guiding agent, another force besides the laws of inanimate physics, the workings of the omniverse explain themselves. That force is the Spirit of Creation and its desire to evolve to higher levels of complexity, consciousness and beauty.

The universe is alive. Life is ever-present throughout it. Yet our scientists keep asking whether there is life elsewhere in the universe, or whether we are alone. Enlightened people must consider such questions foolish. Our intuition and our wisdom tell us that *life is*, that life is the only reason for the universe to exist. An intuitive writer, Richard Bach,[1] comes to this insight in his novel, *Running from Safety*, as the hero of the story struggles to validate and revitalize his *inner child*. The universe is full of life, even if most people are not aware of it. From the extraordinary viewpoint of the poet or the artist, the world is inherently mysterious, exciting, full of wonder and life. For a dull and materialistic person, the world seems boring, petty and without purpose.

The material and spiritual worlds are not separate. They form one world, in which the spiritual processes control the material processes. We often refer to everything there is as the universe. But this word is most commonly used to denote the physical universe alone. For that reason, I prefer the use of the term *omniverse*, which I define to include the spiritual, as well as the physical nature of everything. And I consider it to include the possibilities of past and future universes, as well as parallel universes. The latter may exist in a different dimensional framework, of which we are not aware.

Originally, Creation was pure spirit. Then the Creation Spirit brought forth the physical universe in a burst of energy as a material expression of itself. Only by unfolding its material aspects can Creation and the omniverse evolve towards higher levels of being and expression. All physical life, as we know it, is both spiritual and material. But the spiritual substructure in all things guides the evolution of all things.

The spirit of Creation pervades everything and gives the omniverse a cosmic consciousness. The rocks, the trees, the atoms, the stars and galaxies are all in the consciousness of Creation and are maintained by it, thus ensuring their continued existence. This cosmic consciousness is analogous to the group consciousness, the common subconscious or the superconscious contemplated by various psychologists, except that the cosmic consciousness of Creation embraces everything, not just the human realm. The cosmic consciousness is focused at a multitude of individual points, thereby creating the conscious spirits of individual life forms. The seemingly separate existence of many focal points of awareness resembles the sparkling reflections of sunlight on the many wavelets of the ocean's surface. And just as the sun's reflection can shift from one wavelet to another, so a person's consciousness can translocate from one material life form to another in the process of reincarnation.

As the cosmic Spirit Power controls the material world, so does a person's spirit control his or her mind and body (see Chapter 4). When we say *mind over matter* we really mean *spirit over matter*. We have ample proof of the spirit's dominance in the many aspects of faith-healing, psychic surgery, telekinesis, and the like. Spirit power can give a person superhuman strength and endurance. Many miraculous survival stories have their origin in spiritual strength and willpower.

Willpower is rooted in the spirit, but it manifests through the material part of the mind. In moments of acute emotional crisis, a person can draw an almost impossible amount of energy from the spirit realm. We have all read of heroic tales in which a frail woman, involved in a car wreck, manages to lift a two ton automobile to free her trapped child. But spirit power is not confined to humans and gods. Animals can call it forth also. As a case in point, I can give the following account of a dog's spirit overcoming impossible physical odds. Animals, in contrast to human behavior, do not have a sophisticated mind capable of deliberate deception. I therefore believe this story to be most relevant.

Several years ago we rescued an abandoned dog and nursed her back to health. Once cleaned up and physically well, she transformed into a beautiful white Samoyed. She was a high-spirited being with almost human behavior and feelings, and she soon became a member of the family. A favorite activity of hers was to greet visitors at the door. When she heard the doorbell ring, she would run to the gate and howl with excitement to greet the new arrival. She displayed her affection by happily jumping around the guest, not always to the visitor's liking. After three years, during which she brought much happiness into our lives, she developed an inoperable tumor in her brain stem. She rapidly lost control of all her motor functions on her left side. If she tried to stand up, her left legs would buckle and she would fall over. Eventually she could no longer hold her body or her head off the floor. I had to physically lift her up, carry her outside and prop her up, so she could relieve herself. All day, she lay motionless on her side, unable to get up and unable to eat. Several times during those sad last days, visitors came and rang the doorbell. Through the power of her spirit, she gathered the necessary strength to jump up and run to the door to perform her usual greeting ceremony, overcoming all her physical dysfunctions, only to collapse onto the floor at the doorstep, unable to move. As inspirational as these sudden spurts of life energy were, the end results were heartbreaking. Within a few days, we had to end her suffering and set her spirit free. Whenever we witness such a display of spiritual willpower, we are reminded that ultimately all power is derived from the omnipotent spirit power of Creation. This cosmic spiritual energy can be directed to perform miracles on the physical level. At some stage in our spiritual evolution, we will be able to control our physical surroundings with our spirit power alone and create material objects and events out of *nothing*.

The Spirit of Creation keeps creating and perfecting the omniverse all the time. It is an ongoing process of material and spiritual growth. Figure 9 illustrates the evolution of the omniverse schematically. It is not strictly a time-line chart, but is more akin to an organization chart, showing the interrelationships among different aspects and manifestations of Creation. At the end of the evolutionary cycle, everything returns to its origin, so that there may be no real beginning or end in time. Everything evolves, with Creation in charge of the process. Creation and evolution are not mutually exclusive. The theories of biblical creationism and Darwinian evolution are both severely lacking in understanding.

**Evolution is the process
by which Creation perfects itself,
on a cosmic scale as well as in each individual being.**

Within the greater picture of the evolving omniverse, the evolution of the species is only a small part of the action.

The boxes in the graph are not meant to separate the various items and concepts, but are used only for the sake of organizing our thoughts. In reality, everything is interrelated and imbued with spirit. Spirit constitutes the high-energy infrastructure of the omniverse, out of which all physical manifestations crystalize. The graph similarly shows the evolution of spirit, matter, life and culture as separate lines of development. Again, this separateness is illusionary. The living Spirit expresses itself in all spheres of reality, and it creates all physical aspects of nature.

**The physical universe co-evolves with the evolution of life
to facilitate ever higher expressions of the spirit.**

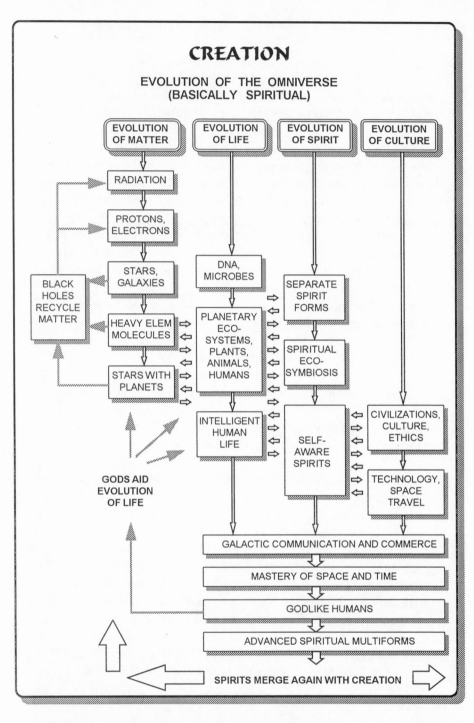

FIGURE 9. Schematic of Living Omniverse

The physical existence of many life forms provides the opportunity for a multifaceted unfolding of nature. On the physical plane, the evolution is towards greater beauty and diversity, diversity in form, function and process to enable a rich and harmonious interaction between living entities. The basic process of life lies in communion (see Chapter 4). Interactions and communications eventually take on evolutionary aspects of their own, bringing forth civilizations, culture and technology. On the spiritual plane, the evolutionary trend is towards more acute and expanded consciousness. An expanded consciousness means a greater capacity for beauty and for ethical values.

With greater awareness and physical life experiences come higher spiritual understanding and wisdom. A consciousness aware of the splendor of Creation is permanently changed. Wisdom is a higher-order form of knowledge. It is the art of knowing how to utilize knowledge for the benefit of spiritual growth. Wisdom is accumulated only through conscious analysis of personal experiences. You cannot learn or teach wisdom in school. A good teacher can, however, plant the seeds of wisdom in a person's mind, opening it up to the desire for learning the most from life's experiences.

When we look at Earth's society, we may become dismayed by the widespread lack of wisdom. Humans have much to learn and are far removed from being the *Crown of Creation*. Surely, no person with a trace of wisdom can seriously consider Earth's humanity as the highest form of intelligence the infinitely vast omniverse can produce. There must of necessity be higher intelligences inhabiting the omniverse. Otherwise, all of Creation would seem like a joke.

This takes us to the inescapable realization of an omniverse inhabited by countless intelligent civilizations, including highly advanced godlike creatures; gods, who are masters of space and time and who have conquered the vast chasms of space between star systems and galaxies. Perhaps they can even bridge parallel worlds separated by different time dimensions. Gods have learned how to tap into the vast spiritual energies contained in the cosmic substructure, and they are able to wield enormous physical power. They could readily destroy whole planets and civilizations. To do so would not be in their interest, however, because such actions would be a regression in their own spiritual evolution. All life forms are part of a cosmic ecology, and even gods depend on the ecological and spiritual infrastructure being there. Thus, gods nurture the physical evolution of life forms and the spiritual and cultural development of human societies. At the highest evolutionary levels, before merging again with Creation, spirits have no need for material bodies. Their joy of existence may lie in the sharing of their life energies with other pure spirit forms in what is labeled in Figure 9 as *advanced spiritual multiforms*.

Another curious entry in this chart is the box marked *spiritual ecosymbiosis*. In the course of this last half century, we have become aware of the great importance of planetary ecosystems, in which the geology, climate, oceans, atmosphere, minerals, plants and animals, including humans, all form a complex interdependent support system referred to as the web of life. Our society is just now beginning to grasp the significance of this. Namely, that damage done to any part in the ecosystem will inevitably have dire consequences for human life. We cannot continue to pollute the resources of nature and drive living species into extinction without severely damaging our own quality of life and without threatening our own survival. As discussed earlier, the differentiation between the physical and spiritual aspects of life is arbitrary. Just as we are an integral part of a physical ecosystem of life, we are also a part of a spiritual ecosystem of interdependence. Whether we like it or not, we are spiritually connected to every plant, animal, raindrop, rock and everything else on this Earth.

The ideology presented here, of a living, spiritual omniverse evolving towards higher consciousness, provides a backdrop for all observable physical events. It also affords a logical explanation for phenomena that the scientific establishment does not want to acknowledge, because it does not understand them. Psychic, spiritual and other strange phenomena, however, fit logically into an omniverse dominated by continuous spiritual evolution. They are natural aspects of a reality, in which physical objects are high-energy perturbations of the omnipresent Spirit of Creation longing for self-expression.

Paranormal, metaphysical phenomena, such as ESP, telepathy, telekinesis, spiritual healing, auras, and so on, as well as reincarnation, angels, gods, extraterrestrial intelligences and UFOs all fit rationally into this world view. Spiritual and material life is naturally abundant in a living omniverse. And the nonmaterial nature of elementary particles, the strange behavior of quantum phenomena, and the presence of a *pregnant* energy continuum underlying all space, are not just expected but are essential.

THE ROAD TO FREEDOM

**The path from darkness to light,
from ignorance to wisdom,
from fear to love, is also
the road from bondage to freedom.**

The concept of freedom is possibly the most controversial subject among abstract ideas. The common understanding of freedom, of being able to do anything a person desires, preferably without consequences, is naive. The notion is also unworkable, since society can only exist within a framework of laws that curtail such unbridled freedom, in order to protect its citizens from hurt and damage and to prevent society from becoming chaotic. In this naive sense of the word, absolute freedom cannot be allowed to exist.

When nationalist leaders speak of liberty, they refer to freedom from physical oppression and from domination by power-hungry tyrants, dictators and manipulators. Even though many bloody wars have been fought to oppose such oppression, political freedom from domination and persecution is only a superficial freedom, although an important one for those liberated from a totalitarian regime.

Socialist politicians and economists often define freedom as being free from hunger, danger, disease, wants and worries. From a humanitarian standpoint, such freedom is highly desirable and commendable, but it remains an unattainable, ideal state in a real world. Only the illusionary concepts of *paradise* and *heaven* in our cult religions come close to this ideal situation. Life in such a paradise would probably not be conducive to spiritual growth and would lead to moral and spiritual stagnation.

Wise men have said that freedom is not so much concerned with being *free from* something, but rather with being *free for* something. This idea delineates yet another dimension of freedom. As much as we want to be free from all the negative influences in life, free from external and internal bondage, we also want to be free for creating positive values, such as a joyful state of mind and a harmonious environment.

Curiously though, not everyone in our society wants to be free. Many want to be told what to think and what to do. Such a phlegmatic attitude results from not wanting to accept responsibility, because increased freedom comes at the price of more responsibility. People often find it more comfortable and less confronting to follow the herd. Not to strive for truth and freedom, however, is to miss the purpose of living.

True freedom is a mental and spiritual state, rather than a physical one. As such, it cannot be forced onto the population. Neither can it be bestowed. We do not need kings, politicians and their armies, or the Pope to guarantee us freedom.

Freedom must be won through conscious personal effort.

In our quest to gain freedom, we must generate the necessary willpower and make the commitment to embark on the voyage leading to emotional and spiritual growth. And spiritual growth cannot take place without serious efforts of conquering fear and overcoming negative habits and attitudes. The task is not easy, but is rather a hard row to hoe. True freedom is achieved through victory over fear and the dark miscarriages of the mind, and through the expansion of our consciousness and wisdom. And to make our newly won freedom permanent, we need to banish ignorance and unconsciousness. The ignorant mind creates its own hell and bondage. Hell is not a physical place, nor a spiritual one, but a psychological state in a person's mind.

As we pointed out in the Introduction, happiness cannot be pursued. The idea was an unfortunate misconception in the minds of our founding fathers. We can, however, pursue the endeavor towards greater freedom, leading to a better life of joy and happiness.

10.1 Point of Departure

Any journey must have a beginning and a destination. We may never reach the end of the journey, and our goals may change as we go along. But we cannot embark on a meaningful endeavor unless we can plot a course; and we cannot decide on a course unless we know where we are on the map. To get from here to there we must recognize our point of departure. Similarly, if we are trapped in a hole and want to get out, we first need to recognize that we are in a hole. Then we need to determine the size and depth of the hole and survey our resources, so we can plot a strategy for getting out and away.

So, as with any predicament, we must first recognize and define the problem, before we can find a solution. Defining the problem is often more difficult than finding the solution. The same is true in our pursuit of freedom. We must define what keeps us from being all that we can be. We must recognize how we are enslaved by ignorance and by lack of consciousness. We must investigate the causes of our negative personality traits that bind us and restrict our freedom. Freedom means not being impeded by negative emotions, not being controlled and consumed by *evil* passions and not being hooked to needs. Rising above our evil passions and letting go of our needs to control, to worry, to be right, to look good, and so forth will liberate us.

In this Section, we are concentrating on the negative aspects of human behavior, so as to define where we are and what has to be healed to allow us to grow. Not everyone is afflicted with the same character faults, but each one of us will recognize and hopefully own up to some of these traits. Whom the shoe fits, should wear it. Then in the following Sections, we will plot the course for correcting these errors, for turning negative traits into positive ones. In our analysis of mental and pathological maladies, we will be avoiding the word *psyche*, because its meaning is not well defined. Often the word is taken to refer to the spirit, at other times to the mind, or the consciousness, or the subconscious, or the emotions, or the personality. All these concepts are separate and different.

Figure 10 attempts to define the roots of our negative personality traits that enslave us. Here we have divided human shortcomings into three categories: negative mental attitudes caused by ignorance, negative emotions having their roots in lack of consciousness, and evil passions caused by ignorance and by spiritual unconsciousness. We should recognize that all mental states, passions and emotions are self-induced. A person cannot make someone else responsible for his or her thoughts, feelings or actions.

The mind, which gives us a material kind of awareness, can be dysfunctional and can have negative states. Wrong thinking causes us to have wrong attitudes, leading us into negative interactions. The spirit, however, is always positive. Only the lack of spiritual consciousness contributes to negative emotions and evil passions. Spirit controls our primary emotions, which are love and fear. But spirit by itself is not responsible for our passions. The thinking mind has to enroll our emotional participation to become passionately involved. For evil passions to develop and prevail, the thinking, conniving mind must take advantage of a lack of spiritual consciousness. It takes intelligence to be wicked and evil. Pure spirit is innocent and cannot be evil. So-called *evil spirits* must have a physical component, since they require a conniving mind. Poltergeists and evil-minded ghosts are emanations of a deranged living mind, often belonging to a person residing in the haunted house.

Needs, Attachments and Attitudes:

Our negative mental states are the minor sins. A partial list of the most important ones is presented in Figure 11. They can be corrected by introspection, self-analysis, interactive psychoanalysis, and through plain experience of what is good for us in the long run. Most of them are brought forth by imagined needs or attachments, some are caused

ROOTS OF NEGATIVE PERSONALITY TRAITS

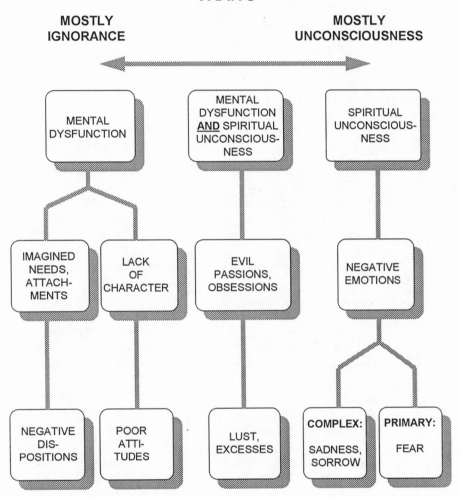

FIGURE 10

NEEDS, ATTACHMENTS AND ATTITUDES

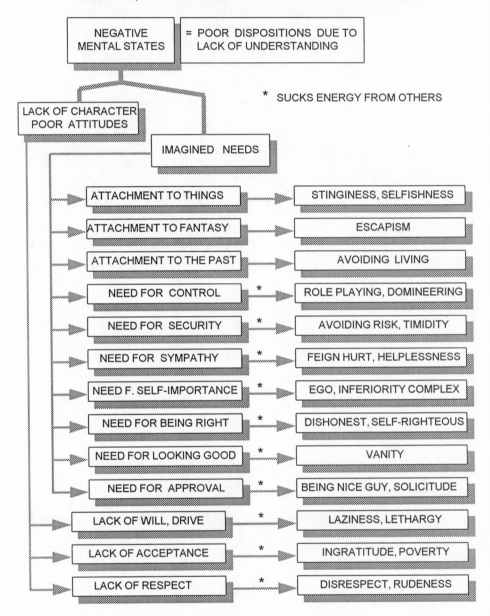

FIGURE 11

by a real lack of positive character traits. For example, misers and pack-rats are attached to things, and this attachment gives rise to stinginess and selfishness. By investing their material and spiritual resources in things and by not sharing them, they limit their freedom of choice for the best use of such resources. Their experience of life becomes restricted. Similarly, people who live in the past fail to grasp the joys of the moment and miss many opportunities for living the happy life and many opportunities for learning and expanding their consciousness. The need for security also severely restricts freedom of choice, resulting in missed opportunities for enriching a person's life. Avoiding risk is giving in to fear, which is the strongest inhibitor of freedom.

The needs for control, sympathy, self-importance, being right, looking good, approval, and so forth, also enslave a person. They control a person's behavior and limit his or her options for living, learning and growing. Some people crave for sympathy and feign being ill or helpless to get the attention they think they need. But by doing so, they avoid responsibility and miss the opportunity for making themselves stronger through self-control. Other people have to be right all the time. When they make a mistake, they lie to cover it up, thereby closing the door to the opportunity for correcting the error and learning from it.

In everyday life, the most freedom is available to a person when he or she has a maximum number of choices, options and opportunities. Attachments and needs always limit a person's power of choice. A big obstacle to my personal growth was my need for approval. I was trying to be the nice guy, never disagreeing openly with people, even when I knew they were wrong; often trying to help and rescue people from their own follies, even though I knew I was preventing them from learning their lessons in life. Outwardly grand gestures were made for the wrong reasons. As a result, my own choices were limited and my own development was postponed.

Negative mental states can also develop by default, when positive character traits are lacking. Lack of willpower creates laziness. Lack of respect and consideration produces rudeness. Lack of acceptance results in ingratitude. A chronic lack of acceptance causes poverty. Poverty is a state of mind, not an economic condition. Frequently, several maladies combine to produce poverty, such as attachment to things (stinginess), need for security (risk avoidance), lack of acceptance and lack of willpower.

In varying degrees, every person has a whole assortment of illusory needs. A widespread affliction among people is the need for control. It results in different kinds of role-playing in everyday life. James Redfield has made a thorough study of this in his best-selling novel, *The Celestine Prophecy*.[1] The motivation for such role-playing is the competition for spiritual energy, because taking it away from somebody makes a person feel superior. And feeling superior is important for those who have no joy in their hearts. People resort to at least four different control dramas to suck energy from others. But when they fulfill their needs by playing their favorite control dramas, they reinforce their dependence on satisfying their cravings, until these dramas become a chronic pattern of behavior. Those who have a need for self-importance, as well as control, will use intimidation for exalting themselves over others. People with a need for security and control will play being aloof to induce others to direct their energies towards them. Those who have a need for being right will control their victims with interrogation. People who thrive on sympathy will control willing suckers with a *poor me* routine. Usually the victims do not realize their energy is being sucked out.

Human drama in everyday life is filled with degenerate mental behavior falling into the categories of Figure 11. Needs, attachments and wants marked with an asterisk suck spiritual energy from those who enable such conduct by being willing collaborators. Both, the person trying to fulfill his or her imagined need and the person who plays along with it, lose freedom in the interaction. These manipulative games, which we call social interactions, will continue as long as the processes described here are not consciously recognized and corrected. Many *drama queens* and *drama kings* play their games with such perfection that the game itself becomes their essence and purpose in life.

Negative Emotions:

The primary emotions* are love and fear. Spiritual consciousness allows love to exist. Fear thrives in the absence of spiritual consciousness. Fear takes over wherever love is not. The more we fill our spiritual being with love, the less space we have for fear to exist. Fear is the only primary emotion which keeps a person from advancing spiritually.

**The greatest victory in the fight for freedom
is the conquest over fear.**

When we ask mountaineers and rock climbers why they risk their lives for such a seemingly trivial pursuit, they answer: «We climb the mountain because it is there.» Yet this is not their true motivation, whether they acknowledge it or not. In truth, they climb the mountain to confront and conquer their fears, because overcoming their fears leaves them with a wonderful and exhilarating feeling of newly found freedom.

Aside from fear, Figure 12 tabulates a number of complex emotions. These are not true spiritual emotions by our definition and should be listed with the passions in the table of Figure 13. They are included here only for convenience, because they are customarily called emotions. Typical complex emotions are joy and happiness on the upside and sadness, sorrow and emotional pain on the downside. Both the mind and the spirit are responsible for creating complex emotions. Happiness is both a state of mind, as well as an emotional state rooted in the spirit. Similarly, the negative complex emotions are mental and spiritual. Sadness, sorrow and emotional pain are only possible when a person suffers from a lack of understanding as well as a lack of consciousness. They are reactions to perceived personal loss or disappointment; but they are ultimately caused by

---

* Note, what we call primary emotions or spiritual emotions here are akin to the German notion of *Gemüt*. What are commonly called emotions, are not strictly spiritual.

NEGATIVE EMOTIONS

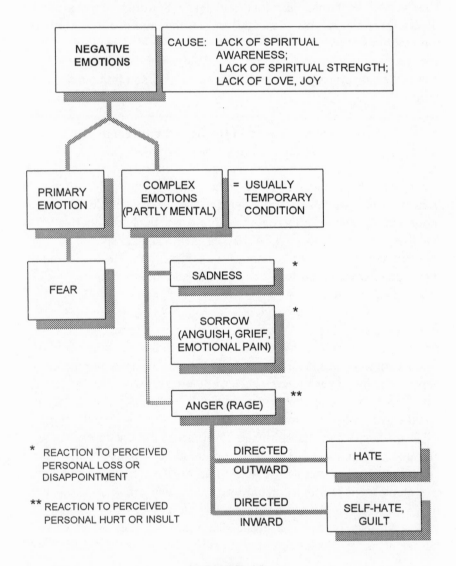

FIGURE 12

EVIL PASSIONS

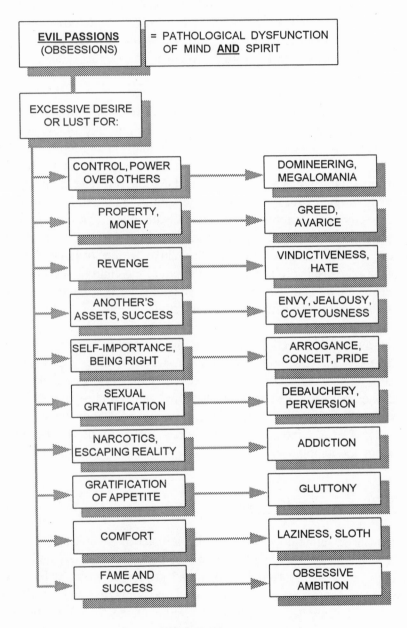

FIGURE 13

self-pity, which is an advanced pathological form of the need for sympathy. These negative passions can eventually slide down all the way to despondency, depression and *Weltschmerz*. We need both intellectual learning and spiritual growth to overcome sadness and sorrow.

Anger, listed here as a complex emotion, is a reaction to a perceived personal hurt or insult. It does not quite fit into any of our three categories of negative personality traits. It belongs in a group by itself. Self-help literature often considers anger to be a positive behavior when used correctly. Expression of anger can be good, if it releases pent-up rage and internal stress; if it is only a temporary outburst, followed by introspective recognition of the cause of the anger. Frequently, the problem is resolved at this point, and the angered person realizes the futility of the outburst and the triviality of the original cause. Sometimes, a display of anger is used to educate a child or subordinate about an unacceptably bad or insensitive behavior. But it should never be used to frighten a person into submission.

When anger is allowed to go beyond the temporary stage and is not resolved, it can become a severely destructive force. If directed towards another person or group, it gives rise to hate and vindictiveness. If directed inward, it results in self-hate and guilt. A chronic condition of vindictiveness, hate or guilt is like acid that consumes the spiritual well-being of a person. It then becomes most harmful to a person's freedom and happiness.

Evil Passions and Obsessions:

Judeo-Christian theology has compiled a roster of *Seven Capital Sins*, for which a person's soul will somehow be punished in a fiery hell with real physical pain. Hell is considered an actual place, where the unrepenting souls are tortured in unbelievably creative ways. These tortures in hell are described in great detail in Dante Alighieri's *Inferno* and are depicted in Hieronymus Bosch's *Allegorical Triptych Paintings*. Here the depraved, guilty souls are shown as they are being mutilated by vindictive devils. The possibility that evil passions (called sins by the church) already harm the spirit by themselves, without external punishment, seems to have escaped our learned theologians.

The *Seven Deadly Sins* are stated to be pride, covetousness, sexual lust, anger, gluttony, envy and sloth. I disagree with this list on several accounts. First, anger does not fit into the category of deadly sins. Second, covetousness and envy stem from the same depravity and are not separate obsessions. Third, the list leaves out the three most destructive evil passions: the lust for power, the lust for property and money, generally called greed, and the lust for revenge, known as vindictiveness. Consequently, I have put together my own list of evil passions and obsessions in Figure 13. The evil passions result from a pathological lack of understanding in both the mental and spiritual realms. They retard the evolution of the spirit, because they prevent love from flowering.

The list of evil passions includes many of the same tendencies previously discussed under negative mental states. The difference lies in the degree of depravity and whether the evil habits have penetrated to the core of a person's being. Innocent needs and attachments may in time become habitual negative character traits. Eventually, they may become obsessive, turning into pathological passions, which affect the health and growth of the spirit. Evil passions are much harder to heal than needs, attachments and attitudes. Greed is more pernicious than stinginess.   Arrogance is more difficult to cure than immodesty, dishonesty or vanity. Just as lack of knowledge and understanding limit our freedom, so negative emotional passions imprison and enslave us.

Entire novels can and have been written about any one of these evil passions, describing how they enslave by controlling a person's thinking and actions. The four gravest ones affect our human society most adversely. They are lust for power, greed, vindictiveness and envy. Our politics of capitalism and socialism are based on greed and envy, respectively. No wonder that Earth's societies are in moral decay. But the worst of the evil passions, overshadowing all others, is the lust for power and control. It results not only in manipulation, domineering, subjugation and megalomania, but can degenerate further into homicide and genocide. Examples from recent history are the evil manias of Stalin and Hitler, which fit into this most destructive category. Compared with these extreme evil obsessions, some of our church's deadly sins, such as sloth, anger and gluttony seem tame and harmless.

10.2 Healing of Sin

«Free from desire, free from possessions,
Free from the dark places of the heart,
Free from attachment and appetite, ...
The wise man becomes himself a light,
Pure, shining, free.»
[Siddharta Gautama, translated from the *Dhammapada*[2]]

After elaborating on the negative aspects of our needs, attachments and passions, we may be left depressed and angry about human behavior overall and about ours in particular. The need for change is evident, and the prospects for salvation are good, because the universal Power of Creation supports positive change. But first we must recognize our errant behavior patterns and take responsibility for them. Anger about our own shortcomings is a strong motivator for change, yet we must not let anger turn to guilt. Guilt is a useless and destructive *emotion*, unless it is immediately transformed into a resolve for correcting the errors in our thinking and behavior.

The above words of the Buddha suggest that freedom and enlightenment can be achieved by disowning all our desires, attachments and passions. And this may well be the most direct way for a holy man seeking release from Earthly burdens and the *wheel of rebirth*. However, most of us strive to enjoy our physical existence, as we value it for advancing our spiritual growth. As such, we may see two flaws in the advice of the Enlightened One. First, a well-established spiritual law holds that what we simply disown, without first working through it, will come back to haunt us. Second, getting rid of all desires, attachments and passions, whether good or bad, is like throwing the baby out with the bath water. Here we advocate converting negative aspects into positive ones, because we still want to enjoy the rewarding experiences in life. We do not just want to be free *from* those desires that bind us; we also want to be free *for* following the dreams that enrich us.

Willful changes for the better require knowledge; and only the mind can accumulate knowledge by learning through life's experiences. Knowledge erases ignorance, inspiring positive thinking and action. The resulting positive circumstances allow the spirit to expand and grow into raised levels of consciousness. This is how we become wiser. If we have to atone for an *original sin*, ignorance is surely it. Ignorance and lack of consciousness are what we need to overcome. Ignorance is vanquished by knowledge and understanding. New knowledge is gained by making a conscious effort for positive change. This takes willpower, which derives from the strength of our character. Character is built with knowledge and moral conviction gained from life's experiences. The process is circular and is akin to lifting ourselves up by the bootstraps. Supportive spiritual energies, however, are available for allowing us to do just that.

As in any other endeavor, a good plan is to identify the resources, outline the method most likely to succeed, specify the tools needed, and establish milestones and goals. For the quest towards freedom, the resources are both spiritual and mental, with the mental energies being cultivated by our spiritual strengths. These resources are love, faith and willpower. Willpower is needed to generate the courage for setting out on the difficult journey to conquer fear. First we need to have faith in ourselves and in the process of life. Initially, faith must be scooped up out of the spiritual realm. *A priori* faith is not the result of something else, but requires having faith in faith itself. Then with faith, love and willpower, we can generate the courage to enter new experiences of living. As we steadfastly keep on the course of pursuing meaningful experiences, overcoming setbacks and discouragements in the process, we will in the end be rewarded by positive results. From these, we gain confidence and increased faith for proceeding to the next level. Having now less fear, more faith and courage, a whole new vista of life's experiences opens up for us.

Just as with many vicious circles that keep people entrapped in their needs, dependencies, attachments, passions, addictions and poverty, we can put ourselves on the uplifting spiral of ever increasing faith, willpower, courage and confidence (see Figure 14). This is what we mean by lifting ourselves up by the bootstraps. It is a process of will, drawing on our spiritual resources. Integrity and love are needed as a foundation in this process to ensure that we proceed in a positive direction.

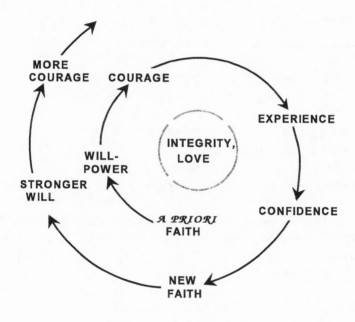

FIGURE 14. Resource Spiral

Having outlined our replenishable resources, let us now outline a method for success. The following steps are necessary for any endeavor, whether we want to fix the kitchen sink, climb a mountain, or embark on the path to a better life.

PLAN OF ATTACK

Stage (Step)	Action	Qualities (Tools) Needed
1. Recognition	Define Problem or Status Quo	Knowledge, Clarity, Truthfulness
2. Vision	Define Goals and Options	Clarity, Focus
3. Choices and Intention	Choose to Proceed	Faith, Willpower, Courage, Forgiveness
4. Actualization	Work towards Goal	Enthusiasm, Action
5. Perseverance	Complete Mission	Perseverance, Tenacity

We have dealt with Stage 1 extensively in Section 10.1. In Stage 2, we use our mind's eye to see beyond our present condition. We are not going to get any more in life than what we can visualize ourselves to be. We need to define goals and plot a course to achieve them. This requires clarity and focus, so we can see our options clearly. Our overall, long-term goal is a raised consciousness level, which will open our experience up to more freedom and happiness. Our specific goals are different for each of us and depend on what needs, attachments or passions need to be transformed. In every case, it is important to give up the negative trait in favor of a corresponding positive alternative.

In Stage 3, we lay away our insecurities, considerations and doubts. Here we need to make the commitment to ourselves to remain focused on working towards the goal. Most of all, we need to stop dwelling on what does not work and what we no longer want. We need to effect a shift in consciousness. Otherwise we cannot escape from the way it used to be and from our former nature. By a single act of will, we choose to proceed along the selected path.

In Stage 4, we actively put our visions into reality. This is a most important step. Here we convert self-realization into actualization, a process often neglected by many New Age seekers on the spiritual path.   To make progress, we need to proceed with intention, enthusiasm and joyous passion. We need to put our heart into it. Enthusiasm and virtuous passion do not just capture the attention of others, they are essential for us to advance spiritually. But all efforts can fail, if we do not have the perseverance to complete the mission. This fifth stage is as important as the fourth and can be a long, continuous journey. Progress is made in a series of small steps, and we must not give up. Many individual steps will eventually lead us to the goal. It is profitable to remember the little rhyme:

Perseverance prevails
When all else fails!

To plot a path for taking us from darkness to light, from evil to the benign, from bondage to freedom, we have to know the opposite, positive characteristics for a given negative trait. Often there is not a clearly defined exact opposite to every negative need or passion. I have made an attempt to arrange positive aspects with their corresponding negative sides in Figures 15 through 21. For that purpose, I have chosen seven facets, or arenas, of everyday experience, so as to associate and group corresponding patterns of behavior.   These facets have been arbitrarily chosen.   Other groupings are possible. The reader and seeker may want to define a different area of concern and construct his or her own chart. I have selected the following seven facets of experience:

FIGURE	FACET OF EXPERIENCE
15	Control and Power
16	Worth and Ownership
17	Action and Interaction
18	Integrity and Justice
19	Security and Risk
20	Sensory Experience (Sight, Hearing)
21	Sensory Experience (Taste, Smell, Touch)

CONTROL AND POWER

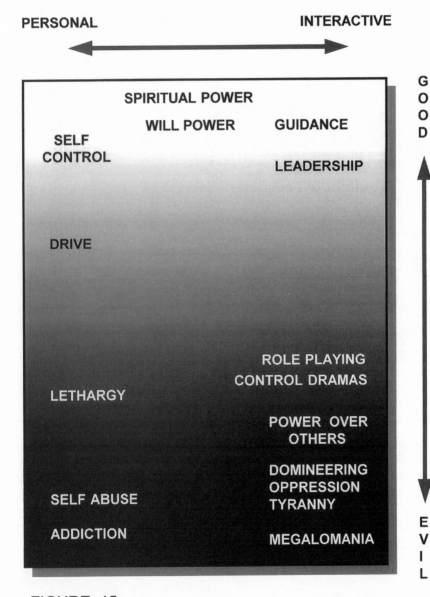

FIGURE 15

WORTH AND OWNERSHIP

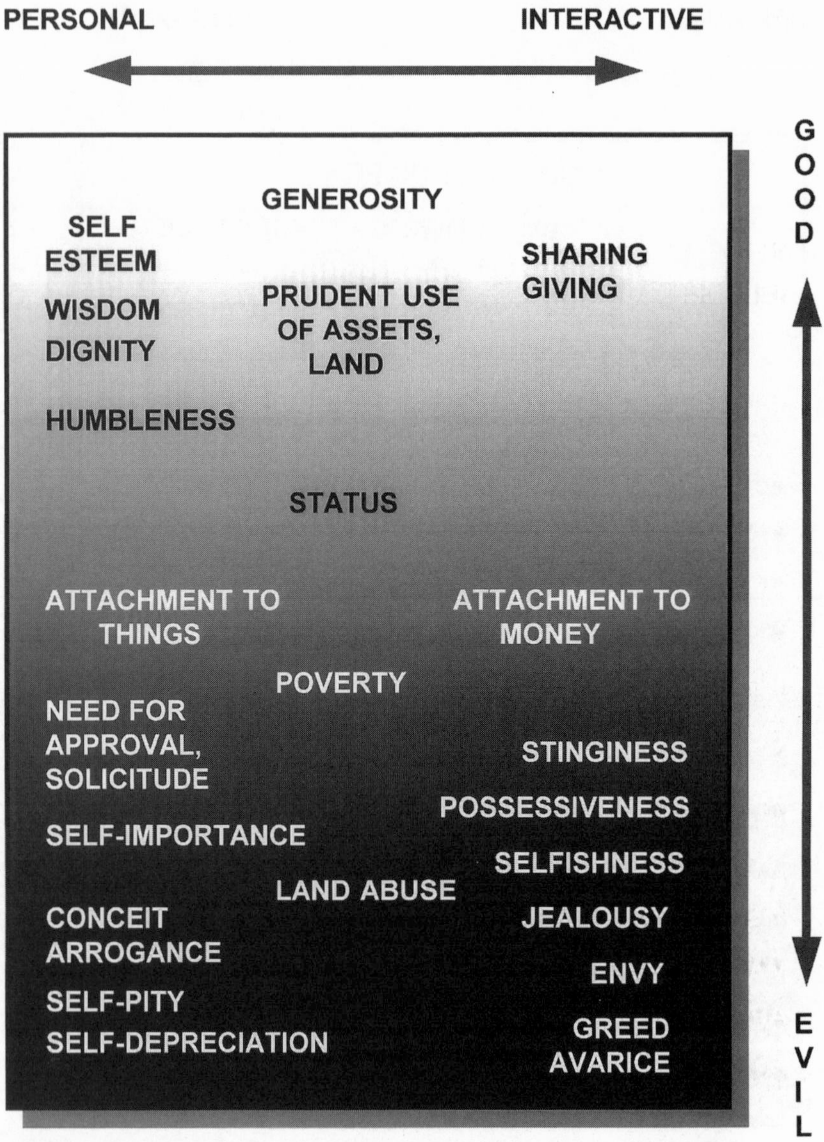

PERSONAL

INTERACTIVE

G
O
O
D

GENEROSITY

SELF
ESTEEM

SHARING
GIVING

WISDOM
DIGNITY

PRUDENT USE
OF ASSETS,
LAND

HUMBLENESS

STATUS

ATTACHMENT TO
THINGS

ATTACHMENT TO
MONEY

POVERTY

NEED FOR
APPROVAL,
SOLICITUDE

STINGINESS

POSSESSIVENESS

SELF-IMPORTANCE

SELFISHNESS

LAND ABUSE

CONCEIT
ARROGANCE

JEALOUSY

ENVY

SELF-PITY

SELF-DEPRECIATION

GREED
AVARICE

E
V
I
L

FIGURE 16

ACTION AND INTERACTION

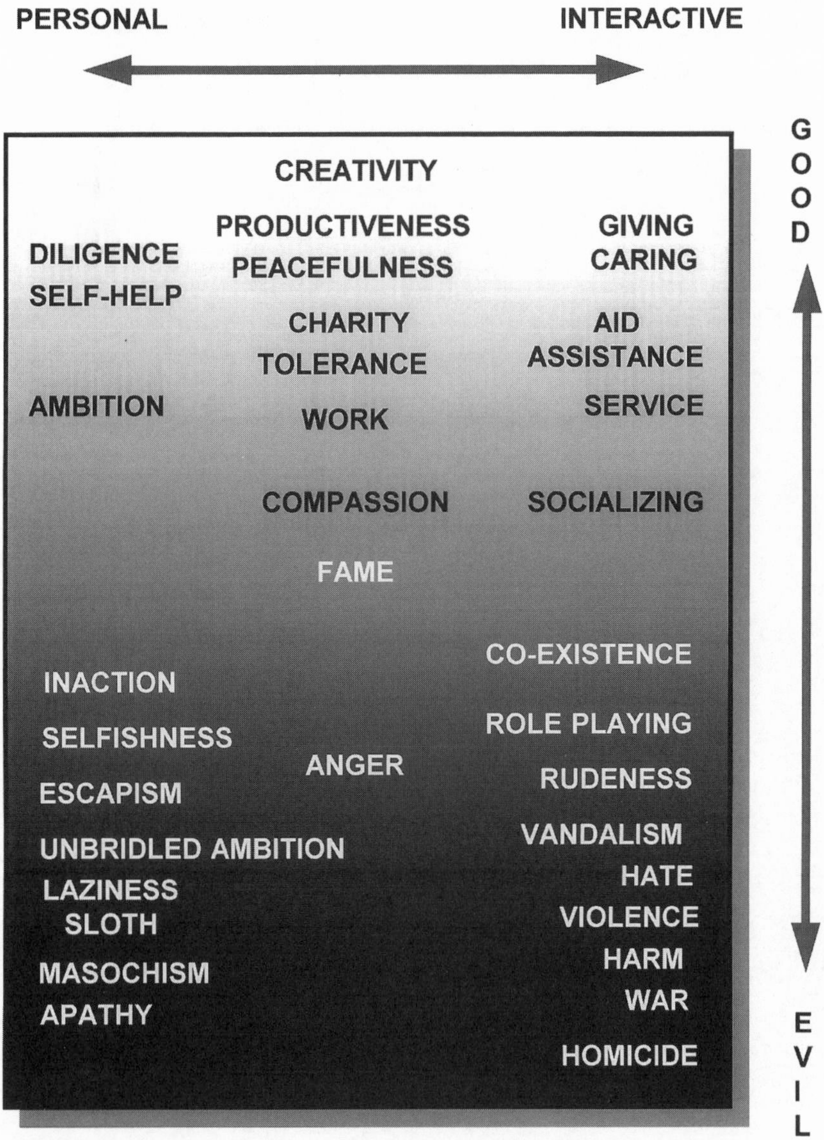

PERSONAL   INTERACTIVE

```
                    CREATIVITY                                    G
                                                                 O
              PRODUCTIVENESS              GIVING                 O
DILIGENCE     PEACEFULNESS                CARING                 D
SELF-HELP
                  CHARITY                   AID
                  TOLERANCE              ASSISTANCE

AMBITION            WORK                   SERVICE


               COMPASSION               SOCIALIZING

                   FAME


                                      CO-EXISTENCE
INACTION

SELFISHNESS                           ROLE PLAYING
                   ANGER
ESCAPISM                                RUDENESS

UNBRIDLED AMBITION                     VANDALISM
LAZINESS                                  HATE
  SLOTH                                 VIOLENCE
MASOCHISM                                HARM
APATHY                                    WAR                    E
                                                                V
                                       HOMICIDE                 I
                                                                L
```

FIGURE 17

INTEGRITY AND JUSTICE

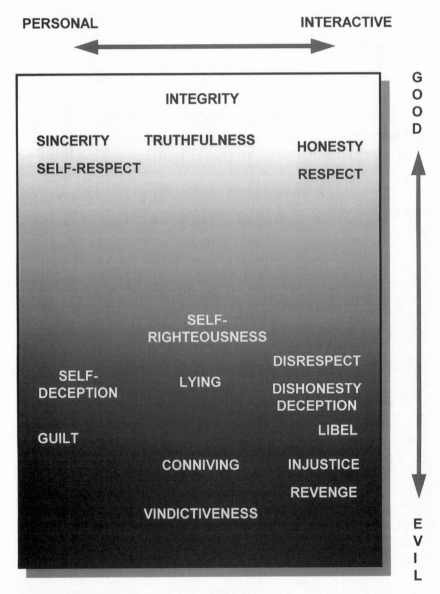

FIGURE 18

SECURITY AND RISK

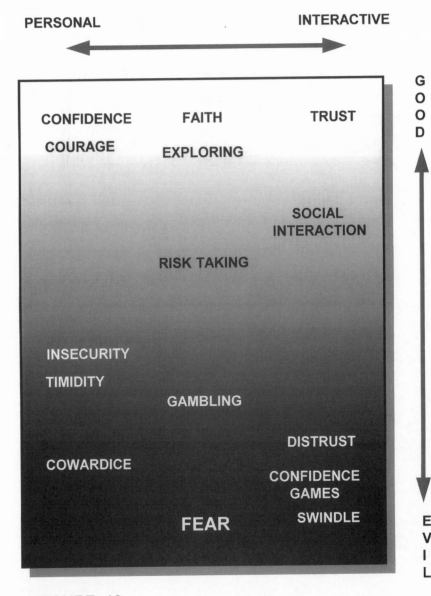

FIGURE 19

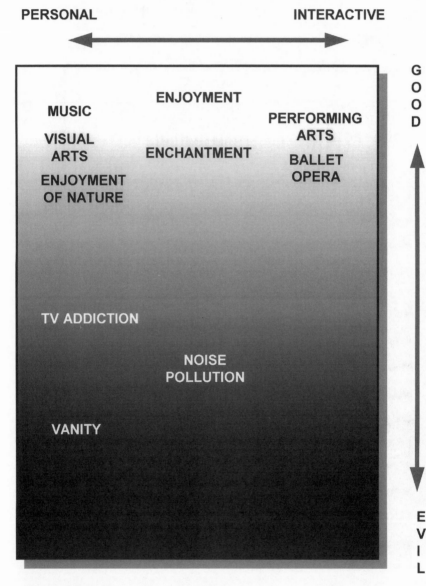

FIGURE 20

SENSORY EXPERIENCE 2
[TASTE, SMELL, TOUCH]

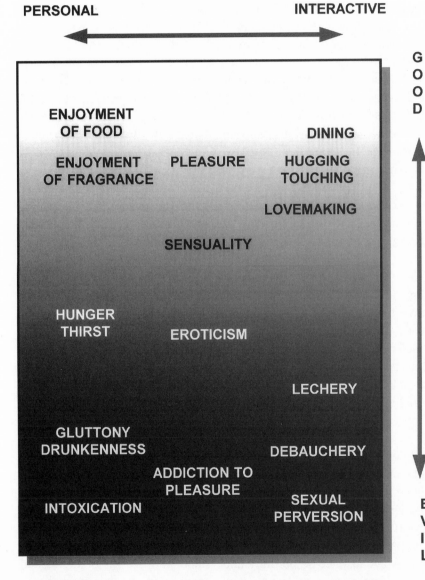

PERSONAL ←——————→ INTERACTIVE

GOOD ↑ EVIL ↓

ENJOYMENT OF FOOD

DINING

ENJOYMENT OF FRAGRANCE   PLEASURE   HUGGING TOUCHING

LOVEMAKING

SENSUALITY

HUNGER THIRST   EROTICISM

LECHERY

GLUTTONY DRUNKENNESS   DEBAUCHERY

ADDICTION TO PLEASURE

INTOXICATION   SEXUAL PERVERSION

FIGURE 21

In each chart, the negative, evil aspects are positioned at the bottom and the corresponding positive, desirable traits at the top. Note that for each arena of experience there is a personal facet and an interactive one. For example, in the chart labeled *Control and Power,* the personal aspects deal with self-control, whereas the interactive aspects deal with power and control over others. A close study of these charts may afford the reader with more clarity and focus in the wilderness of human weaknesses and strengths, of human folly and sapience. With the help of the charts, it is easy to select the positive personal goals to strive for, such as: self-control and willpower to overcome addiction, self-esteem to overcome self-pity, wisdom and dignity to overcome arrogance, generosity to overcome poverty, diligence to overcome laziness, tolerance and compassion to overcome anger, self-respect to overcome guilt, integrity to overcome conniving and vindictiveness, courage to overcome timidity. On the interactive level, we need to turn domineering into guidance, envy and greed into sharing, violence into caring, deception into respect and honesty, distrust into trust.

Note that we have separated sensory experience into two categories. Sight and hearing are more in tune with spiritual qualities and appear to have few negative aspects. Abuses of sight and hearing are rare, yet many ways of enjoying these sensory inputs are available to us. Taste, smell and touch, however, give us physical pleasure, and many ways of abusing and overindulging in such pleasures are possible. We must not let palatal pleasure turn into gluttony, and we must not let affectionate touching and conjugal bliss turn into sexual debauchery and exploitation.

Whereas the charts designate positive alternatives to our needs, attachments and evil passions, they do not help much for pairing up negative and positive emotions. As pointed out earlier, the only two primary emotions are love and fear. Fear takes hold in the absence of spiritual love. Complex emotions are sadness, sorrow, anger, joy and compassion. With emotions, it is often difficult to cite exact opposites, simply because we do not fully understand emotions on an intellectual level. Hate, apathy and fear have all been quoted as being opposites of love; yet hate, apathy and fear appear to have nothing in common. The opposite of fear is fearlessness, but love and wisdom may also qualify in many situations. We need spiritual growth to overcome fear and make room for love. Fear has been programmed into us genetically for the preservation of our physical bodies to ensure the survival of the species. It plays its proper role in the material world to protect us from harm. It has no place, however, in our spiritual, social and cultural development. When we use fear to hold us back from spiritual and emotional growth, it becomes a harmful roadblock and keeps us from living.

Courage, often quoted as the opposite of fear, is not an emotion. Courage does not overcome fear, it just bypasses it. It is a sheer act of willpower, called up from inner strength and faith. We keep being afraid, but we do what needs to be done anyway. Courage is a very desirable tool for circumventing fear. Yet courage without wisdom can be foolish, when it needlessly puts a person in mortal danger. A safe way of practicing courage is through generosity. Generosity enlarges the soul and displaces timidity. In my youth, I had a kind and wise geometry teacher. I still remember his advice, offered while I was timidly trying to solve a geometrical construction problem on the blackboard: «Be generous and take bolder steps.» In other words: «Do not hold back, go ahead and live. Be what you want to be, do what you want to do. Be generous towards yourselves and others in all your actions. Take risks to learn something new, to experience life more intensely.» Often we have to take risks in our emotional and social lives. Generosity and courage are invaluable tools in our personal quest.

Our complex emotions of sadness, sorrow and sentimental pain need some elucidation here. Pain, grief and disappointment have all the appearances of being real. But upon reflection, we find they do not exist in the outside world. They are illusions in our mind, going around in short-circuit fashion. Emotional pain and sorrow are manifestations of self-pity, of feeling sorry for ourselves. Hence, emotional pain is conquered by letting go of the need to feel sorry for ourselves. Also, the opposite of anguish is not necessarily peace. Peace could mean emotional deadness. The well-meant wish of *peace be with you*, uttered during the Catholic church mass may often be counterproductive. A more uplifting wish would be: «May you find the strength to live in love and joy.»

Our primary emotion of fear cannot easily be overcome by any single effort. Freeing ourselves from negative emotions comes through spiritual growth and wisdom. And we have no simple, itemized to-do list for spiritual growth. Spiritual growth arises naturally out of our conquest of addictions and negative passions. The most effective tools for overcoming the latter are *letting go* and *forgiving*, which are discussed further in the following section. The pathways for healing our addictions and evil passions follow the resource spiral advanced previously in Figure 14. In the diagram shown below, we have expanded this spiral to give a more detailed illustration of the actions required and the tools available to us:

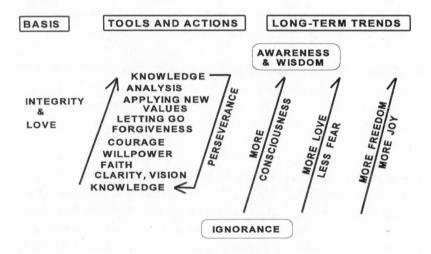

FIGURE 22. Process of Healing *Sin*

In this schematic, note how love, freedom, joy and consciousness are treated as evolutionary processes, rather than absolute qualities a person owns or lacks. The trend is towards more consciousness, more love, more wisdom, more joy and more freedom. The process does not automatically take place, however. We have to help it along by actively participating. Prerequisites for pursuing this evolutionary path are integrity and a love for ourselves, for our fellow humans and for Creation. The milestones and touchstones along the road are our levels of awareness, wisdom, fearlessness and joy. When we are more joyful, less fearful and more aware of the grand design of Creation, our consciousness has expanded. Although many pitfalls imperil the traveler along this road, there are no failures, only experiences from which we learn. Engineers familiar with feedback control know that a mechanism or process has to deviate from the ideal state before corrective action can be taken. In a home heating system, for example, the temperature has to drop below a preset value by a measurable amount before a signal is generated that turns the furnace on to correct the temperature deficiency. Similarly, we must err before we can make a correction. This is how we learn. Life's experiences are like that. Errors, or sins, are not evil or bad, as long as we learn from our mistakes and make corresponding corrections. Negative behavior becomes evil only, when we persist in it, despite better knowledge of how others may be harmed by that behavior. The road to freedom may have many switchbacks. So we must not be discouraged by obstacles, caused by unwise decisions, in our quest. They are opportunities by which we can re-evaluate our path. They are the error signals needed by the autopilot to keep us on course.

The error and correction process does not only apply to human development. Creation learns and perfects itself in the same manner. Nature continuously experiments with new forms and beauty, exploring their merits and modifying them to fit the overall harmony of the omniverse. Inconsistent forms are ephemeral and decay, if they do not conform to the laws of nature and the overall plan of Creation.

10.3   The Liberating Power of Forgiveness

Let go, my friend, release it fast,
That heavy load! Let bygones be.
Forget pain, vengeance and the past.
Live here and now; and you are free.

Once we acknowledge and accept how we suffer from hate, anger, guilt, arrogance, laziness, envy, greed, or any of the other addictions or passions, and once we choose the path to freedom, we can take two giant steps forward by forgiving and by letting go. First, we need to have enough love and compassion to forgive ourselves for the negative character traits. As well, we need to forgive those who we believe have wronged us; not for the sake of the alleged offenders, but for our own benefit. Others do not need our forgiveness. We need not even tell them. They will be able to recognize the change in us by our new attitude and actions. The second step is to simply let go of our needs for possession of things, for clinging to the past, for feeling hurt or being sick, for revenge, for competition, for approval or for status. Letting go is tantamount to forgiving ourselves, society and the world. The two steps are not independent, but are parts of the same process.

We can gain a great amount of personal freedom instantaneously by the simple act of forgiving. Forgiving and letting go, however, are not always easy. These actions require faith and courage. We need to trust ourselves and the spiritual power of Creation for supporting our quest toward freedom. Such faith, or trust, gives us the confidence to proceed.

After Jmmanuel, alias Jesus, had been nailed to the cross, he was presumed to have said: «Father, forgive them; for they know not what they do.» [Luke 23:34] He showed no hate or vengeance toward his executioners. This made him free, even though he was hung on the cross and left to die. Such spiritual strength, wisdom and compassion were unheard of in the biblical lands and could not be comprehended by either the Romans or the Jews. Even unto this very day, some Jewish people fail to understand how their policy of *an eye for an eye, a tooth for a tooth* is a recipe for bondage and eternal persecution.

Physical, spiritual and cultural differences between Arabs and Jews cannot provide any rational excuse for not being able to live harmoniously side by side in the same country. Only the refusal to forgive past injustices and hurts by either side keeps the animosities and atrocities going. The *never forget, nor forgive* attitude regarding the holocaust also keeps many modern-day Jews enslaved.

The liberating power of forgiveness, versus the chains of vengeance and hate, apply to all living organisms and organizations: humans, animals, nations and the entire human society. A tiger, who bears a grudge against hostile humans and becomes a man-killer, is no longer free. Peace between nations could easily be achieved, if people could put aside their differences and historical grudges, if generosity, forgiveness and wisdom could triumph over greed, envy, vindictiveness and ignorance. Many disadvantaged people on Earth, who feel society has given them a rotten deal, could lead a freer and happier life, if they could only forgive themselves and the world and let go of their need to blame someone else for their misfortune. The need to blame others shows a lack of integrity and a failure to take responsibility for one's own life. A positive person sees adversities as challenges and opportunities to learn, not as misfortunes.

PERSONAL POWER

What do we mean by *personal power*? As a prelude to answering this question, let us contemplate the following quotes, some from classic literature and some from contemporary sources, including my own.

«The Creator has not given us the spirit of fear,
but of power and of love and of sound mind.»
[II Timothy 1:7]

«Be larger than your fear! Do it now.»
[Stewart Emery, Actualizations Workshop, 1981]

Your power begins where your fear ends,
and your power ends where your fear begins. [D.R.]

«They can because they think they can.»
[Virgil, 70-19 BC]

«Your greatest power is the power of choice.»
[Ralph Waldo Emerson, 1803-1882]

Real power does not rule with an iron fist,
but with guidance and restraint. [D.R.]

«Whatever you can do or dream you can, begin it!
Boldness has genius, magic and power in it.»
[Johann Wolfgang von Goethe, 1749-1832]

All dreams come true if you have the courage to pursue them.
[Anonymous]

All power ultimately derives from the spiritual realm. [D.R.]

Personal power — some seem to have it, others do not. People often associate personal power with charisma, with self-assurance and confidence. Yet not all people with charisma are highly evolved spiritually or work for the welfare of humankind. Hitler had enough charisma to seduce an entire nation. The Kennedys are said to have charisma, even Bill Clinton. The Pope does not have it, neither does Ronald Reagan or George Bush, but most successful actors have it. How do we explain this enigma? Charisma has to do with *perceived power*, not real power. In order to be perceived as a powerful person, it helps to be taller than six foot two, to be good looking, to be a little ruthless, and to exude sensuality and self-assurance. If such a person is also a man in a position of high political influence, this combination of attributes proves utterly irresistible to a large section of our female population, who vote with their feelings, their sensuality and their need for security and protection. Real spiritual power or wisdom has nothing to do with it. Charisma and personal power are not the same. And as we know from history, even thoroughly evil persons can have charisma.

Personal power has more to do with being in charge of our own life than it has to do with power over others. Many personal attributes and behavior patterns affect our relationship with power, some positively, others negatively. The more important associations are:

Spirit and power,	knowledge (wisdom) and power,
fear and power,	faith (trust) and power,
freedom and power,	courage and power,
choice and power,	money and power.

Some of these relationships are intertwined. We will explore the above associations further within the rest of this chapter. We will elucidate and depose the last of these relationships first. Materialistic people associate power with money. Beliefs and misconceptions about the influence of money on human behavior abound, such as: «The love of money is the root of all evil,»[1] or «the lack of money is the root of all evil.»[2] Neither is accurate. By common arrangement, money is a token receipt for value contributed to another person or the community at large. The holder of the note can later trade it in return for goods and services. As a piece of metal or paper, it has little intrinsic value. Since the production of goods and services requires energy, however, money can be considered as representing a specific number of energy units. In this context, money does symbolize economic power and can be used to accumulate material wealth.

Money is neutral and is neither good nor evil. Our relationship with money and what we do with it, however, have ethical implications. Our correct relationship with money should be, «to enjoy and use money, but never be used by money.»[2] It is a master and slave relationship. Money can serve us well in our constructive pursuits, but we must never become enslaved by money interests through greed for material things, and we must never use money to buy or enslave others. When used correctly, money can augment our power of choice and thus our material freedom. Money, however, cannot buy wisdom, courage, fearlessness, love or happiness. It cannot buy personal power, because such power can only be achieved through personal effort.

Often, people with great personal power also have a positive attraction for money, because they can easily influence the flow of wealth. Just as with money, however, personal power must never be used to exploit others, because forced exploitation is evil and violates the spiritual laws of Creation. But the worst manner in which to control and subjugate others is through fear; by making subjects afraid of being harmed, if they do not submit. Such abuse of power is contemptible and evil. A god who must be praised and feared is more of an evil dictator than a guiding light. Gods who resort to instilling fear have not conquered their own fears, but try to exalt themselves by making others more fearful than they are.

Fear is the greatest inhibitor to personal power. A master knows not fear. Power and fear cannot co-exist. Our power ends where our fear begins. The fear of living full out robs us of our power. Our imaginary need for security and comfort holds us back. The more we give in to our fears, the less freedom we have and the less opportunity for enjoying love and ecstasy. Fear is primarily caused by our identification with the ego, the false self. We are afraid, because we do not know who we are; because we do not accept ourselves as spiritual beings whose essence cannot be hurt by material threats.

We have to rely on our internal resources to outmaneuver and diminish our fears. The gradual conquest of fear is won by strengthening our faith, willpower and courage, as discussed in the previous chapter (see resource spiral in Chapter 10). With enough inner strength, we can be larger than our fear, and our personal power can grow in direct proportion with our conquest over fear.

11.1   Power of Alignment

> «The fates lead him who will,
> Him who won't, they drag.»
> [Seneca, 4 BC-65 AD]

Alignment with a higher will, goal or purpose creates a powerful entity to be reckoned with. When the magnetic domains in a piece of iron align themselves, a powerful magnetic field is created. When all members of a rowing team pull their oars in perfect unison, they win the race. When light waves are emitted in a single direction and in synchronism, they create a powerful laser beam. A 100 watt light bulb gives enough light to read by, but a 100 watt laser beam is powerful enough to burn a hole through half inch of solid material in seconds. When two electromagnetic waves are superimposed coherently (i.e. in phase and moving in the same direction), the electric and magnetic fields in the wave double, but the power in the combined wave is quadrupled. Thus, great power augmentation is possible and available through alignment.

We know from history, whenever a group of people is aligned with a common purpose, they become a world-shaping force. This is true for ideological, national, social and religious movements. The process works whether the purpose is good or evil. Inevitably, the evil movements will die out or be defeated, however, because they are not aligned with the higher power of Creation. What we call good and evil is based on arbitrary value judgments. Absolute values are determined by the laws of Creation. Through trial and error experience, we have found that whatever is in harmony with the laws of nature and Creation empowers us. So we conclude that these actions are good. Whatever works against nature and its laws destroys itself, because it is not supported by the power of Creation.

The universal Spirit of Creation provides us with an endless resource of power, and we can tap into this power by the simple act of aligning with it. By conscious choice, we can grow in harmony with nature, or we can ignore the laws of nature and degenerate. It is our choice. When we align with the spiritual forces of nature, the Universal Power can flow freely through us, enabling us to create our lives in harmony with it. When Obi-Wan Kenobi in the moving picture *Star Wars* says: «May the Force be with you!», he should have meant: «May you choose to align with the Force, so its power can materialize through you.» The Force is there all the time and is easily accessible. It is up to us to align with it to gain access to its power. Our life force comes from the power of Creation. Successful living is not possible without aligning with it. When we are fully aligned with Creation, we can direct its unlimited spiritual powers to create the life we want, to work miracles and to heal others. Jmmanuel and other miracle workers have demonstrated this to be so.

Before we can gain access to the forces of Creation, we must first recognize the truth about our spiritual nature. Then we must intentionally exercise our freedom of choice to align with the truth. Through personal power, we can change the material world only so much, depending on how many other minds use their spiritual power for similar or different ambitions. But we can influence society by guiding the thought patterns of other members in the community towards positive change. We cannot change the natural laws which shape reality, but we can help bring society towards a realization of these laws and towards more harmonious living within these laws. By being aligned with the spirit of Creation, we can magnify and direct its power to produce the physical effects we project through our intentions. This works best when many like-minded individuals harmoniously and simultaneously project their thoughts for positive change into the world. Large groups praying for peace can expect positive results. If all Earth humans prayed for peace, it would immediately become a reality.

To affect the conduct of human society at large is difficult and time-consuming. But we can make immediate progress in our own relationship with reality by improving our perception of it, so that our experience of it becomes a fulfilling and happy series of events. After all, our experiences are our only interaction with the material world, and our quality of living depends on these experiences.

Being comes before doing and having. Being has to do with self-realization, with knowing that the infinite power of Creation is available to us for transforming our ideas and dreams into reality. But ideas and dreams are cheap and plentiful. Making them happen is where the power is. To become a master of living, we have to actualize our dreams and visions. We have to confirm just how we want our life to be and then imagine it into reality. We need to be a creative generator. We need to shine, not just reflect. When our ideals are in alignment with the Almighty, the universe always says *yes*. The *no*s are our own. When our *being* and *doing* are in harmony, the *having* follows automatically.

We affirm our commitment to a fulfilling life by accepting who we are and who we want to be. It is not an accident, that all affirmations start with *I* and *I am*. Here is a sample of affirmations, which can assist us on the road to better living:

I   take responsibility for being the cause of my life, for waking up and experiencing life to the fullest in accordance with the will of Creation.

I   accept that life is simple and that it is to be lived with maximum participation and enjoyment.

I   realize that love and faith are the only spiritual qualities I need to overcome my fears.

I   acknowledge that my fears are caused by my lack of acceptance of my spiritual power and magnificence.

I   will not let fear keep me from fully living and from being all I can be.

I   have confidence in myself to become a happier and more loving person.

I am human,	I am healthy,
I am spirit,	I am prosperous,
I am divine,	I am open,
I am whole.	I am wise.
I am creative,	I am fearless,
I am strong,	I am loving,
I am choosing,	I am joyful,
I am free.	I am alive!

Affirmations can be used by themselves or in conjunction with meditation. Meditation is a powerful method for becoming aware of the spirit within us. The purpose of meditation is to let the spirit gain full control over mind and body. First, the mind has to be silenced, however, because it does not readily give up control. Valuable techniques can be gleaned from numerous books on the subject. Some may work better than others for a person. It is an individual matter, depending on how much the material mind and body are in control of a person's existence. The reader is encouraged to experiment with several methods until he or she finds the most expedient way to quiet the incessant chatter of the mind. When used correctly, meditation can have a healing effect on a person's psyche and body, and can diminish, even eliminate, emotional and physical pain and afflictions.

11.2 Freedom and Empowerment

Creation gave us the freedom to exercise our power of choice, to choose between liberty and bondage, between good and evil, between heaven and hell. Our freedom of choice is restricted only by self-imposed limitations. We must take back the power we have transferred and given away to objects, people, places, experiences, beliefs, decisions, emotions; to imaginary needs, attachments, afflictions, passions and addictions. To regain our full spiritual potential, we must first wake up to the truth and to the realization of who we are. We must become aware of our spiritual resources. To actualize and realize the self is to live freely, not confined by the self-imposed limitations in our mind. It means taking responsibility for our lives. We must not wait for somebody else to take us by the hand, but must motivate ourselves by an act of will and step out into the light. By drawing upon our inner resources, talents and abilities, we can live a life of total participation, fulfillment and love. As a first step into the light, a person should heed the following advice:

Trust in yourself! Trusting yourself is having faith in Creation; it is knowing that you are one with the unlimited power of Creation, which governs all life and nature. Reaffirm your commitment to life that you have already made before birth. Affirm life and life will affirm you. By trusting in yourself and by committing to the great experience of living, you start repossessing your power. And forget about security and comfort.

The security in the familiar is a figment of the mind.

Live life with intensity, but do not be consumed by it. Stay in control of your destiny. Do not get caught up in life's external dramas, but concentrate on the process of truly living, which occurs internally. Through the experience of living, the spirit expands to higher levels of awareness and power. When working on our own spiritual development, our freedom of choice is unlimited. Similarly, our personal power is also potentially unlimited, even though it may take countless lifetimes to ascend to limitless godlike status.

When exercising our freedom to augment our personal power, we must not violate the rights of others. An essential condition of liberty is our willingness to let others make their own choices. To live together compromises freedom. Harmonious life in a community requires civil laws and regulations which restrict an individual's freedom of choice. In community living, it is important to safeguard everybody's quality of life. The welfare of the community must be placed above personal whims and material gains. All malevolent and destructive behavior must be curtailed. Nowhere is the conflict between community values and personal greed more pronounced than with the property rights guaranteed by the US Constitution. The conflict is most evident in semirural areas, which are being devoured by suburban sprawl at an alarming rate. The notion of people being able to do anything they want with their property is a naive concept. The American Civil War was fought to curtail the *property rights* of slave owners. We must now look at land ownership in the same way. To exploit the land and destroy all living creatures on it is against the laws of nature and against the moral cornerstones of life and Creation. Being confronted by overpopulation, an unsustainable economy, the wholesale destruction of Earth's resources, runaway crime and pollution, we must as a society redefine our *god-given*, Constitutional rights to unrestricted land ownership, to the use of firearms and to profligate reproduction. The survival of our society, if not the human species, depends on it.

Ideally, when the goals and wishes of the individuals are in alignment with those of society, the conflict of choice does not arise. In that ideal state, the delimitation of a few individual liberties is a small price to pay for a better life for all. In such an environment, our personal power would be positively enhanced by the greater power of the community. Can we ever achieve such ideal, closely knit community living on a societal level? Only time will tell.

CREATIVITY, BEAUTY
AND HAPPINESS

**Love, joy and creation
Make life a celebration.**

Love is essential for living. It is literally *love or die*. Love is the purpose, the goal and the path to its own fulfillment. We should love ourselves enough to follow our natural inclination to express, to create and to assert ourselves into life. To master living, we need to be open and willing to explore and discover what works and what enriches us. Happy living depends on celebrating life and living our visions. Refusing to experience and to know is to be asleep. It takes great courage to wake up, because it means acknowledging the truth. This is scary for many people. Yet we must remember, learning and growing are primary functions of living. Without them, decay and regression take over, which are the chief characteristics of death.

Creativity, beauty and joy have their origins in the spirit. They are the emblems of a happy life. All three spiritual values have to be present for the experience of complete happiness. The much-sought-after, elusive emotional state of happiness is often mistakenly identified with physical pleasure, contentment, thrills and entertainment. This is not what we mean by happiness here. We aim for a higher goal of spiritual bliss, consisting of joy, ecstasy and enlightenment, which are on an entirely different plateau from pleasure. Creativity, beauty and joy are different facets of happiness and are not easily separated. Nevertheless, we will try to bring out their most characteristic qualities and relationships by discussing them one at a time.

Creativity:

The *modus operandi* of the all-encompassing Eternal Spirit is continuous creation. True creation brings forth substance and form out of nothing. This is how the Creation Spirit brought the universe into being. Creation keeps maintaining and perfecting the universe by unfolding itself into ever greater multiplicity and beauty of form and frequency. We are part of the universal scheme of things, and we can play an important role in the material and spiritual evolution in our sphere of influence. For the human spirit to express itself through creativity is natural. Creative self-expression enriches our experience of life. The physical world provides the means and the arena for such creative expression.

Because we think and operate on the physical level, we find it difficult to create from nothing. Human experience of physical creativity is limited to recreating new forms from existing ones. We have learned with our science, technology and industry to manipulate energy forms at will for our purposes. On the material level, we take minerals out of the ground, refine and process them. Some of these we mold and shape into functional parts, which we then assemble into an airplane, an automobile, a piano or a computer. Industry takes a natural resource, reworks it into a new form and assigns a function to it to make it useful. On the mental level, scientists and philosophers create new thought forms, or ideas. Engineers, designers and architects use ideas to create plans, which in turn permit the transformation of raw materials into complex structures.

On the aesthetic level, artists transform their perception of reality into physical form, portraying the essence of a thing or phenomenon. True art always has an intangible quality to it that touches the soul. It has to speak to us on a spiritual level. The spiritual content of creative art is easily recognized in music. The freedom of expression of an artist is greater than that of a scientist or engineer, whose mind is preoccupied with logical thinking. Being trained as a scientist and engineer, I have to relax my mind, when I want to pursue my artistic talents and create freely from within. Often, a little wine and inspirational music work wonders to free the mind from the straightjacket of linear thinking and to get in touch with my creative side.

The painter, the sculptor, the composer, the writer, the philosopher, the scientist, the engineer, the architect, the machinist are all creative in their respective areas of expertise. The artist is a master of perception and expression. The technologist is a master of form and function. Most magicians, conjurers, politicians, lawyers, marketeers, salesmen and priests have historically been masters of deception. Their type of creativity is not in keeping with the spirit of Creation.

The reader may rightfully point out the existence of many happy members of society who are not engaged in highly artistic pursuits and who nevertheless lead fulfilling lives. This group includes dedicated people in service oriented professions, such as teachers, physicians, nurses, welfare workers, naturalists, even some politicians and priests. Mother Teresa and Albert Schweitzer, for example, considered their lives richly fulfilling and rewarding. When service people work from love and compassion, and when they dedicate themselves to creating a better life for others, they are creative in their own way. They create joy and value in themselves and others. They create new opportunities for fellow humans by developing people's capabilities and by helping them overcome their limitations. But many public servants in today's society act from ego and greed for power, control and material gain. Consequently, these people are seldom happy, yet they may still learn from their life experiences. A person need not be happy to learn and evolve spiritually. Often we learn more from negative experiences than from positive ones.

Enjoyment of life manifests itself through self-expression, which is made possible in a most direct way by artistic creativity. A life filled with joyful creativity is a happy life. It is a life well spent. The art of living does not get much better than that. We create from within by calling forth that which is unlimited and without form. Through our imagination, we give it form and bring it into existence. When we consciously create what we want in this manner, we are empowered.

Our mind is a powerful tool for projecting creative thoughts into the world, where they may effect physical change. Whereas such activities of the mind create an illusion of a separate ego consciousness, the truly creative source in us is not the mind but the spirit, which is naturally connected to the infinite power of Creation by being part of it. The mind is creative only in a limited sense for maintaining order in the world of thought and for self-preservation. It is diligently at work interpreting sensory data and sorting information into orderly patterns consistent with our belief system. The associated chatter often interferes with creativity. To get in touch with our inner creative self, we have to still our mind. Only then can we play with our spiritual energies. We can attain this quiet state through the practice of meditation.

Beauty:

The Universal Spirit keeps creating ever new forms of beauty and symmetry in nature in the process of mineral, floral and faunal evolution. So it is also intuitively natural for humans to create beauty and to appreciate beauty in nature and art. Appreciation of beauty takes place in a quiet and serene atmosphere, when we have freed ourselves from all baggage of human drama. Beauty is the touchstone of the spirit. It is not just external, but is mainly an internal quality or experience. Appreciating beauty leads to a feeling of inner joy. Surrounding ourselves with natural and manmade beauty makes for a happy home and environment.

In my youth, I had only a limited understanding of spiritual values. When in my late teens, a young lady asked me if I had a personal philosophy. In my ignorance, I associated philosophy with dry, circular arguments like Descartes' *I think, therefore I am*, and I had no good answer. She told me her philosophy was to never destroy anything beautiful. This shows that girls mature faster than boys. I now recognize that beauty is truly a bridge to experiencing happiness. Sincere appreciation of beauty allows us to recharge our spiritual energies. *The Celestine Prophecy*[1] explains how we can tap into the energy fields of nature by contemplating beauty, wherever we find it.

Happiness:

Happiness is not a thing that can be pursued and captured. It is an emotion we must consciously call forth. Happiness does not depend on somebody else *making us happy*. When movie stars marry for the fifth or eighth time, hoping to find happiness at last, they are deluding themselves. They need to make a personal effort to beautify their attitude towards life. Happiness is not given. It is a joyous state of being and is created from within. It follows naturally, once we have created a state of mind and a personal environment which are aligned with Creation. The glow of happiness envelops us when we remember our divine, spiritual nature and origin. A person who has liberated him- or herself from attachments, needs and the dark places of the heart is able to generate and maintain the glow of happiness more often and at will.

Happiness is not possible without spiritual awareness. The previously quoted English translation of Verse 5:3 from the *Talmud Jmmanuel*[2] says: «Blessed are those who are rich in spirit and recognize the truth, for life is theirs.» I prefer to translate it more freely as: «Happy are those who are aware of their spiritual heritage.»

Happiness can be experienced on a number of different levels. The state of being happy is a process that needs to be cultivated, allowing us to progress towards a more joyful and fulfilling life. The ancients recognized seven spheres of heaven and associated them with the seven more readily observable celestial orbs of the solar system. By analogy with the seven layers of heaven, we may define seven levels of happiness. From the lowest state to the highest, these are:

1. Physical pleasure, entertainment.
2. Physical and emotional security, prosperity, contentment.
3. Absorption in pleasant activity, play, work.
4. Communion of love, conjugal bliss.
5. Joyful creativity, appreciation of beauty in art, music, nature.
6. State of timelessness, living in the moment, ecstasy.
7. Experience of oneness with Creation, enlightenment.

The first two levels involve our physical feelings and thoughts. In Levels 3, 4 and 5 the feeling of joy and well-being takes on an emotional quality. Levels 6 and 7 are the purely spiritual states, which meditating members of the Buddhist faith aspire to attain. Buddhists believe emotions and passions are hindrances to the experience of ultimate bliss. But I believe that a state of emotional happiness, properly refined, can be carried over and integrated into levels 6 and 7. We do not need to renounce all passionate behavior; rather we should shed our evil passions, but nurture our good ones. Passion is our vital energy enlisting the support of the *Gemüt* (heart and soul). So, while on Earth:

Choose aliveness,
Joyful passion.
Give it all your might.
Add commitment,
Perseverance
And your world is bright.

SOVRCES AND REFERENCES

CHAPTER 1

1. American *Declaration of Independence*, Continental Congress (Philadelphia, 4 July 1776). The sentiments expressed in the Declaration were taken from the writings of the English philosopher John Locke (1632-1704).
2. Stated goals of *The Constitution of the United States of America* (first ratified on 17 September 1787).
3. Lao Tzu, *Tao Te Ching, A New Translation*, by Gia-Fu Feng and Jane English, Viking Press (1972).
4. *Talmud Jmmanuel; Die Lehren Jmmanuels*, transl. into German by Isa Rashid, Wild Flower Press;
   The Talmud of Jmmanuel, transl. into English by Julie H. Ziegler and B. L. Greene, Wild Flower Press (Newberg, Oregon 1992).
5. H. P. Blavatsky, *The Secret Doctrine*, Theosophical Publishing House (Madras, India 1888).
6. *Kant, Gesammelte Schriften*, Prussian Academy of Sciences, Critical Edition, 22 Volumes (Berlin 1902-1944).
   H. Allison, *Kant's Transcendental Idealism: An Interpretation and Defense* (New Haven, Conn. 1983).
7. Friedrich Schelling, *System of Transcendental Idealism*, transl. by Peter Heath (Charlottesville, Virginia 1978).
8. Henry David Thoreau, *Walden*, Modern Library Edition.
9. *The Collected Works of C. G. Jung*, Bollingen Ser., No. 20, transl. by R. F. C. Hull, Vol. II, Psychology and Religion: West and East, Princeton University Press (1969).
   C. G. Jung, *Aion: Researches into the Phenomenology of Self*, Bollingen, Princeton University Press (1959).
   C. G. Jung, *On Synchronicity*, Bollingen, Princeton University Press (1960).
10. Khalil Gibran, *The Prophet*, Alfred A. Knopf, Inc., Random House (NY 1951).
11. Ernest Holmes, *The Science of Mind*, Dodd, Mead & Co. (NY 1938).

12. B. S. Rajneesh, *The Silent Explosion*, Ananda-Shila (Bombay, India 1973).
    B. S. Rajneesh, *The New Man: The Only Hope for the Future*, Rebel Publishing House (Cologne 1987).
    B. S. Rajneesh, *The Golden Future*, Rebel Publ. House (Cologne 1987).
    B. S. Rajneesh, *Beyond Psychology*, Rebel Publ. House (Cologne 1987).

13. Werner Erhard, *Erhard Seminar Training, Inc. (EST)*, Intensive experiential seminars conducted in 1980s, sometimes referred to as Self-Help Psychotherapy or Primal Scream Therapy. Author of Audiotapes entitled: *Creation: A Matter of Distinction*; also *Parents: The Fundamental Relationship*; also *Celebrating Your Relationships*; also *A World that Works for Everyone; About You Making a Difference*, (San Francisco, Calif. 1982).

14. Stewart Emery, *The Owner's Manual of Your Life*, Doubleday & Co. (Garden City, NY 1982). Author of Actualizations, book and psychotherapy workshops conducted in 1980s.

15. Terry Cole-Whittaker, *What You Think of Me is None of My Business*, Oak Tree Publications (LaJolla, Calif. 1979). Dynamic minister of LaJolla Church of Religious Science and Terry Cole-Whittaker Television Ministries.

16. New Age Literature spans a wide range of subjects, such as: Self-Improvement, Self-Realization, New Psychology, Spiritualism, Meditation, Channeling, Visualization Techniques, Communication with Nature Spirits, ESP, Astrology, Belief in Ancient Mysteries and Prophecies, Belief in Atlantis and Mu, UFOlogy, Wisdom from Extraterrestrial Sources, Spiritual Poetry, etc. Some examples are:
    M. S. Peck, *The Road Less Travelled*, Touchstone Book, Simon and Schuster (NY 1979).
    U. S. Anderson, *Three Magic Words*, Wilshire Book Co. (N. Hollywood, Calif. 1978).
    Shakti Gawain, *Creative Visualization*, Whatever Publishing (Mill Valley, Calif. 1982).
    The Findhorn Community, *The Findhorn Garden*, Harper & Row (NY 1975).

D. W. Olsen, *Knowing Your Intuitive Mind*, Crystalline Publications (Eugene, Oregon 1990).

Barbara Hand Clow, *Heart of the Christos*, Bear & Company (Santa Fe, New Mexico 1989).

Donald Holmes, *The Illuminati Conspiracy*, New Falcon Publications (Phoenix, Arizona 1993).

Charles A. Silva, *Date with the Gods*, Living Waters Publishing (Pontiac, Michigan 1986).

Peter Rengel, *Seeds of Light*, H J Kramer Inc. (Tiburon, Calif. 1987).

CHAPTER 2

1. C. G. Jung, *On Synchronicity*, Bollingen, Princeton University Press (1960).
2. Werner Erhard, *Erhard Seminar Training, Inc. (EST)*, Intensive experiential seminars conducted in 1980s, sometimes referred to as Self-Help Psychotherapy or Primal Scream Therapy.
3. Stewart Emery, *The Owner's Manual of Your Life*, Doubleday & Co. (Garden City, NY 1982). Author of Actualizations, book and psychotherapy workshops conducted in 1980s.
4. *Kant, Gesammelte Schriften*, Prussian Academy of Sciences, Critical Edition, 22 Volumes (Berlin 1902-1944). See specifically the metaphysical ideas expressed in Kant's *Kritik der reinen Vernunft* (*Critique of Pure Reason*), published first in 1781.
5. Andrija Puharich, *Uri*, Lab Nine Ltd. (1974).
6. Phyllis Schlemmer, *The Only Planet of Choice*, Gateway Books (1994).

CHAPTER 3

CHAPTER 4

1. Fritjof Capra, *The Turning Point*, Simon & Schuster (NY 1982), also Bantam Books (1984).

2.   Fritjof Capra, *The Web of Life*, Doubleday (NY 1996).
3.   *Mindwalk*, Motion picture with Liv Ullmann, Sam Waterston and John Heard, produced by Bernt Capra, Mindwalk Productions, The Atlas Production Company (1990); Paramount Pictures (1992).
4.   James Redfield, *The Celestine Prophecy*, Warner Books, Inc. (NY 1994).
5.   *Prosperity: Your Divine Right*, Seminar hosted by Terry Cole-Whittaker Ministries (San Diego, Calif., 1982).
6.   Frederick Eikerenkoetter, *Rev. Ike's Secrets for Health, Happiness and Prosperity - for You!*, Science of Living Publications, Science of Living Institute (Brookline, Mass. 1982).
7.   Eduard «Billy» Meier, *Private Communications* (1997); also, E. A. Meier, *Leben und Tod*; also, *OM*; also, *Aus den Tiefen des Weltenraumes...*, Wassermannszeit-Verlag, FIGU (Zürich, Switzerland, ca. 1980-1997).
8.   Theodore Roszak, *The Cult of Information*, Pantheon (1986).
9.   Carl G. Jung, *Memories, Dreams, Reflections*, Ed. Aniela Jaffé, Random House (NY 1965).
10.   Barbara Marciniak, *Bringers of the Dawn, Teachings from the Pleiadians*, Bear & Company (Santa Fe, New Mexico, 1992).
11.   Dolores Cannon, *Conversations with Nostradamus*, Vols. II and III, Ozark Mountain Publishers, (Huntsville, Arkansas, 1992, 1994).
12.   Randolph Winters, *The Pleiadian Mission; a Time of Awareness*, The Pleiades Project, Yorba Linda, Calif., printed by Gilliland Printing (Arkansas City, Kansas, 1995).

CHAPTER 5

1.   R. M. Littauer, H. F. Schopper, R. R. Wilson, Phys. Rev. Letters 7 (1961) 144.
2.   M. J. Duff, Plenary Lecture, International Conference on High Energy Physics, Bari, Italy (July 1985).
3.   A. A. Michelson, E. W. Morley, Amer. J. Science 34 (1887) 333; also Phil. Mag. 24 (1887) 449.

4. Experiments performed by G. Sagnac in 1913 and by Michelson and Gale in 1925; referenced on pages 65-67 by D. W. Sciama, The Physical Foundations of General Relativity, Heinemann Educational Books Ltd. (London).

5. James H. Smith, *Introduction to Special Relativity*, W. A. Benjamin, Inc. (NY 1965) Ch. 6.

6. James Clerk Maxwell, *Treatise on Electricity and Magnetism*, 3rd edition, Oxford University Press (1904); first published in 1873.

7. P. A. M. Dirac, Proc. Roy. Soc. London 117 (1928) 610; Proc. Roy. Soc. London 118 (1928) 351.

8. Menahem Simhony, *The Electron-Positron Lattice Space; Cause of Relativity and Quantum Effects*, Physics Section, The Hebrew University, Jerusalem (1988), self-published.

9. R. D. Pearson, *Origin of Mind* (1992) and *Key to Consciousness: Quantum Gravitation* (1994), distributed by M. Roll, 28 Westerleigh Rd., Downend, Bristol BS16 6AH.

10. Rodolfo Benavides, *En la Noche de los Tiempos* (Mexico), referenced in: Charles A. Silva, *Date with the Gods*, Living Waters Publishing (Pontiac, Mich. 1986).

11. Eduard «Billy» Meier, *Semjase Reports*, Wassermannszeit-Verlag, FIGU (Zürich, Switzerland, ca. 1980 - 1997).

12. D. Walsh et al., Nature 279 (1979) 381; R. J. Weymann et al., Nature 285 (1980)641; D. W. Weedman et al, Astrophys. J. (Letters) 255 (1982) L5; C. R. Lawrence et al., Science 223 (1984) 46; J. Huchra et al., Astron. J. 90 (1985) 691; J. Surdej et al., Nature 329 (1987) 695.

13. P. Schneider, J. Ehlers, E. E. Falco, *Gravitational Lenses*, Springer Verlag (Berlin, Heidelberg, NY 1992) Chapter 7: Wave Optics in Gravitational Lensing, P. 217.

14. see, for example: F. A. Jenkins, H. E. White, *Fundamentals of Optics*, McGraw-Hill Book Co. (NY 1957) 618.

15. S. Chandrasekhar, *The Maximum Mass of Ideal White Dwarfs*, Astrophys. Journal 74 (1931) 81.

16. Karl Schwarzschild, *On the Gravitational Field of a Point Mass in Einstein's Theory*, Sitzungsberichte Deutsch. Akadem. Wissenschaften, Kl. Math. Phys. Tech. (Berlin 1916) 189.

17. Dietmar E. Rothe, Calculations performed during the last decade. A scientific paper entitled: *Are Black Holes out of Sight?* is in preparation for publication.

18. Bertram Schwarzschild, *Hubble Finds Surprisingly Dense Galactic Core*, Physics Today 43 (November 1990) 21.

19. Arthur I. Berman, *The Physical Principles of Astronautics; Fundamentals of Dynamical Astronomy and Space Flight*, John Wiley & Sons (NY 1961).

20. see e.g. the beautiful collection of color photos by Timothy Ferris, *Galaxies*, Harrison House (NY 1987).

21. Alexander A. Friedmann, Zeitschrift der Physik 10 (1922) 377.

22. Abbé Georges E. Lemaître, Annales de la Société Scientifique de Bruxelles 47A (1927) 49; Nature 127 (1931) 706.

23. Willem de Sitter, Bulletin of the Astronomical Institutes of the Netherlands 5 (1930) No. 193.

24. George Gamow, Phys. Rev. 74 (1948) 505; Nature 162 (1948) 680.

25. George Gamow, *Creation of the Universe*, Viking Press (NY 1952).

26. Physics Today 45 (June 1992) 17.

27. H. C. Ferguson, R. E. Williams, L. L. Cowie, *Probing the Faintest Galaxies*, Physics Today 50 (April 1997) 24.

28. Thomas A. Weil, *Looking Back Cosmologically*, Sky and Telescope 94 (Sep. 1997) 61.

29. Bertram Schwarzschild, *Very Distant Supernovae Suggest that the Cosmic Expansion is Speeding up*, Physics Today 51 (June 1998) 17.

30. Richard H. Price, Kip S. Thorne, *The Membrane Paradigm for Black Holes*, Scientific American 258 (April 1988) 69.

CHAPTER 6

1. Friedrich Nietzsche, *Also sprach Zarathustra; Ein Buch für Alle und Keinen*, Ernst Schmeitzner, (Chemnitz 1884); for an English translation see e.g. Nietzsche, *Thus Spoke Zarathustra; A Book for None and All*, Transl. by Walter Kaufmann, Viking Penguin, Inc. (NY 1966).

2. Erich von Däniken, *Chariots of the Gods*, G. P. Putnam's Sons (NY 1970), Bantam Books (NY 1971).
3. Erich von Däniken, *Gods from Outer Space*, G. P. Putnam's Sons (NY 1971), Bantam Books (NY 1972).
4. Erich von Däniken, *The Gold of the Gods*, G. P. Putnam's Sons (NY 1973), Bantam Books (NY 1974).
5. John B. Noss, *Man's Religions*, The Macmillan Co. (NY 1956).
6. E. P. Sanders, *Jesus and Judaism*, Fortress Press (1985); also Michael D. Goulder, Midrash and Lection in Matthews, SPCK (London 1974).
7. Joseph C. Pearce, *Magical Child*, Bantam Books (NY 1981) and, *Magical Child Matures*, Bantam Books (NY 1986).
8. Alan Watts, *UFO Visitation*, Blandford (London 1996), US Distributor: Sterling Publishing Co., N.Y.
9. Barbara Marciniak, *Bringers of the Dawn; Teachings from the Pleiadians*, Bear & Company (Santa Fe, NM 1992).
10. Cotti Burland, Werner Forman, *The Aztecs, Gods and Fate in Ancient Mexico*, Galahad Books (NY 1980).
11. Adrian G. Gilbert, Maurice M. Cottrell, *The Mayan Prophesies*, Element Books, Ltd. (Rockport, Mass. 1995).

CHAPTER 7

1. Thomas Byrom, *The Dhammapada; The Sayings of the Buddha*, Vintage Books, Div. Random House (NY 1976).
2. James W. Deardorff, *Celestial Teachings; The Emergence of the True Testament of Jmmanuel*, Wild Flower Press (Tigard, Oregon 1990).
3. *Talmud Jmmanuel; Die Lehren Jmmanuels*, transl. into German by Isa Rashid, Wild Flower Press; *The Talmud of Jmmanuel*, transl. into English by Julie H. Ziegler and B. L. Greene, Wild Flower Press (Newberg, Oregon 1992).
4. Elizabeth Clare Prophet, *The Lost Teachings of Jesus 1*, Summit University Press (Livingston, Montana 1988).
5. Hyam Maccoby, *The Mythmaker; Paul and the Invention of Christianity*, Barnes & Noble Books (NY 1998).

6. Origen, *On First Principles 1.5.3*, trans. G.W. Butterworth, Peter Smith (Gloucester, Mass. 1973) p 47.
7. Genesis 25:21-28; Malachi 1:2; Romans 9:13.
8. Doris Agee, *Edgar Cayce on ESP*, Aquarian Press (1989).
9. Ian Stevenson, *Twenty Cases Suggestive of Reincarnation*, American Society for Psychical Research, New York (1966) 17, 306.
Ian Stevenson, *American Children who Claim to Remember Previous Lives*, J. Nervous and Mental Diseases 171 (1983) 742.
Ian Stevenson, *Three New Cases of the Reincarnation Type in Sri Lanka with Written Records Made Before Verification*, J. Scientific Exploration 2 (1988) 217.
10. Ernest Hemingway, *A Farewell to Arms*, Charles Scribner's Sons (NY 1929).
11. Elisabeth Kübler-Ross, *To Live until We Say Goodbye*, Prentice-Hall (Englewood Cliffs, NJ 1978).
12. Raymond A. Moody, Jr., *Life after Life*, Stackpole Books (Harrisburg, Penn. 1975).
13. Kenneth Ring, *Heading towards Omega*, William Morrow (NY 1984).
14. Eduard Billy Meier, A whole library of spiritual wisdom is available from: Freie Interessengemeinschaft für Grenz- und Geisteswissenschaften (FIGU), Semjase Silver Star Center, CH-8499 Hinterschmidrüti, ZH, Switzerland.
15. Association for Research and Enlightenment, P.O. Box 595, Virginia Beach, VA 23451.
16. C. G. Jung, *On Synchronicity*, Bollingen, Princeton University Press (1960).
17. James Redfield, *The Celestine Prophecy*, Warner Books, Inc. (NY 1994).

CHAPTER 8

1. *The Talmud of Jmmanuel*, transl. into English by Julie H. Ziegler and B. L. Greene, Wild Flower Press (Newberg, Oregon 1992).

2. James W. Deardorff, *Celestial Teachings; The Emergence of the True Testament of Jmmanuel*, Wild Flower Press (Tigard, Oregon 1990).
3. Holger Kersten, *Jesus Lived in India*, Element Books (Longmead, England 1986).
4. Fida M. Hassnain, *Search for the Historical Jesus; from Apocryphal, Buddhist, Islamic and Sanskrit Sources*, Gateways Books (1994).
5. Stan Deyo, *The Cosmic Conspiracy*, Adventures Unlimited Press (Kempton, Illinois 1992).
6. Donald Holmes, *The Illuminati Conspiracy*, New Falcon Publications (Phoenix, Ariz. 1993).
7. *Semjase-Berichte (Contact Notes)*, Wassermannzeit Verlag, F.I.G.U., (Schmidrüti ZH, Switzerland 1975-1998).

CHAPTER 9

1. Richard Bach, *Running from Safety, an Adventure of the Spirit*, Delta Publishing (NY 1995).

CHAPTER 10

1. James Redfield, *The Celestine Prophecy*, Warner Books, Inc. (NY 1994).
2. Thomas Byrom, *The Dhammapada; The Sayings of the Buddha*, Vintage Books, Div. Random House (NY 1976).

CHAPTER 11

1. 1 Timothy 6:10.
2. Reverend Ike (Frederick Eikerenkoetter), Prosperity Seminars given in Los Angeles and San Diego (1982).

CHAPTER 12

1. James Redfield, *The Celestine Prophecy*, Warner Books, Inc. (NY 1994).
2. *The Talmud of Jmmanuel*, transl. into English by Julie H. Ziegler and B. L. Greene, Wild Flower Press (Newberg, Oregon 1992).

Isaiah 181
Islam 146, 150, 158, 177

J

jealousy 146, 209, 218
Jefferson, Thomas 3
Jehovah 47, 146-149, 160
Jeremiah 181
Jesus — see Jmmanuel
Jewish holocaust 27-28
Jewish mythology 167
Jews, persecution of 17, 27, 182,
    228-229
Jmmanuel 5, 149, 158-159, 171-
    186, 228, 235
John, the apostle 4, 55, 67, 147,
    179
John, the baptist 159, 175, 182
Jones, Jim 151
Jouret, Luc 151
joy 4, 166, 200-201, 205, 207-
    208, 222, 224, 226-227,
    237, 241, 244-245
Juda Ihariot 173, 176, 180
Judaism 150, 158, 172, 177, 210
Judas Iscariot 173, 176, 180
Jung, Carl 5, 43, 75
justice 20, 216, 220

K

Kant, Immanuel 5, 51, 64
karma 157-159, 175
Kashmir 177
Keller, Helen 54
Kersten, Holger 177
kinetic theory 187-188
knowledge 58-59, 65, 77, 171,
    178, 195, 213, 215, 226,
    232

L

Lao-Tzu 5
laser technology 38, 144, 234
laziness 204-205, 209, 211, 219,
    224, 228
Leibniz, Gottfried W. 23
Lemaitre, Georges 131
liberty 3, 199, 238-239
life 3, 46, 54, 61-77, 91, 99-100,
    165, 193-194, 205, 213-
    214, 236-238, 241-243
life, meaning of xv, 61-77, 79-
    80, 206
life sciences 24
life, web of 63-64
light 84, 92-93
light orbits 120-125
light, speed of 89, 91-93, 134
Lindbergh, Charles 162
logarithmic scales 81
logic 82-83
Lorentz, H. A. 93
love 1, 26, 41, 166, 207-208,
    211, 213, 224-228, 231,
    233, 236-237, 241
Luftwaffe 10, 13, 28
Luke 185, 228

M

Magdeburg 12, 15
magnetic monopoles 83, 137
magnetism 234
Marciniak, Barbara 156
Mark, the apostle 179
marriage 31, 36
Mary 176-177
mass 84
mass, reduced 106
mathematics 7, 23, 82, 89, 92

SHIPPING RATES (HANDLING AND POSTAGE):

USPS Book rate $4.00 first book, $0.50 each addl. up to 5
USPS Priority $5.20 first book, $0.75 each addl. up to 5

UPS Ground $6.00 first book, $0.50 each addl. up to 5

Foreign Surface $4.00 first book, $0.50 each addl. up to 3
Foreign Air $25.00 one or two books

For larger quantities call toll free number.

In Search of
Truth
and
Freedom

A Path from
Ignorance to Awareness

DIETMAR ROTHE

ORDER BLANK
ISBN 0-9677453-2-2, Avila Books

If not available at your local bookstore, additional copies of this book can be ordered online at **avilabooks.com** or from the publisher's distribution center. Copy this page, complete the form and mail with your check, money order, or credit card information to:

The Twiggs Company
P.O. Box 2875
Rapid City, SD 57709-2875

Or place your order toll free at:
800-898-0284 (US/Can)
Or fax order with credit card info to
605-341-0020

Charge to:
Name: ....
Street: ....
City: .... State: .... Zip: ....
Telephone: ....
Card No.: .... Exp.: ....
VISA ❏   MC ❏   DISCOVER ❏   AMEX ❏

Ship to (if different):
....
....
....
....

ORDER:
Qty.: ....   Copies of "In Search of Truth and Freedom"
@ US $ 26.95 per book ....

Shipping and Handling (see rates on adjacent page) ....

South Dakota Residents: Add 6 % Sales Tax _____

TOTAL $ _____

Check/Money Order enclosed ❏